THE SIRDAR
AND
THE KHALIFA

THE SIRDAR AND THE KHALIFA

KITCHENER'S RECONQUEST OF SUDAN, 1896-98

MARK SIMNER

FONTHILL

For Lisa

Fonthill Media Language Policy

Fonthill Media publishes in the international English language market. One language edition is published worldwide. As there are minor differences in spelling and presentation, especially with regard to American English and British English, a policy is necessary to define which form of English to use. The Fonthill Policy is to use the form of English native to the author. Mark Simner was born and educated in England; therefore British English has been adopted in this publication.

Fonthill Media Limited
Fonthill Media LLC
www.fonthillmedia.com
office@fonthillmedia.com

First published in the United Kingdom and the United States of America 2017

British Library Cataloguing in Publication Data:
A catalogue record for this book is available from the British Library

Copyright © Mark Simner 2017

ISBN 978-1-78155-588-0

The right of Mark Simner to be identified as the author of this work has been asserted by him in accordance with the Copyright, Designs and Patents Act 1988.

All rights reserved. No part of this publication may be reproduced, stored in a retrieval system or transmitted in any form or by any means, electronic, mechanical, photocopying, recording or otherwise, without prior permission in writing from Fonthill Media Limited

Typeset in 10.5pt on 13pt MinionPro
Printed and bound in England

CONTENTS

Maps   7
Glossary   13
Chronology   15
Introduction   17

1. The Rise of the *Mahdi*   21
2. The Death of General Gordon   37
3. The Long Road to War   53
4. The *Sirdar* and the Anglo-Egyptian Army   69
5. The *Khalifa* and the *Ansar*   83
6. The Dongola Campaign   93
7. The Campaign Extended   109
8. The Battle of Atbara   123
9. The March to Omdurman   133
10. The Battle of Omdurman: The First Attack   138
11. The Battle of Omdurman: Charge of the 21st Lancers   152
12. The Battle of Omdurman: MacDonald's Saving Action   165
13. The Fall of Omdurman   178
14. The Fashoda Incident   192
15. The Pursuit and Death of the Khalifa   203
16. Aftermath and Legacy   213

Appendix A: Anglo-Egyptian Orders of Battle   220
Appendix B: Ansar Orders of Battle   225
Appendix C: Casualty Statistics   228
Appendix D: Victoria Cross Citations   232
Bibliography   234
Index   237

Maps

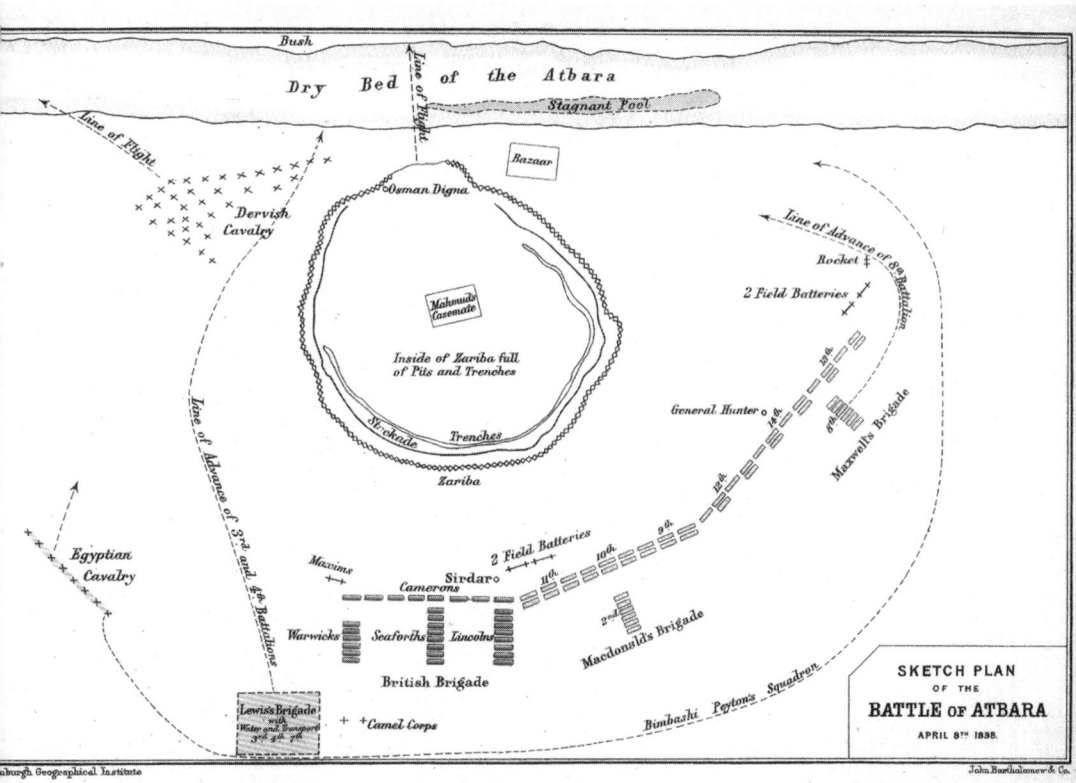

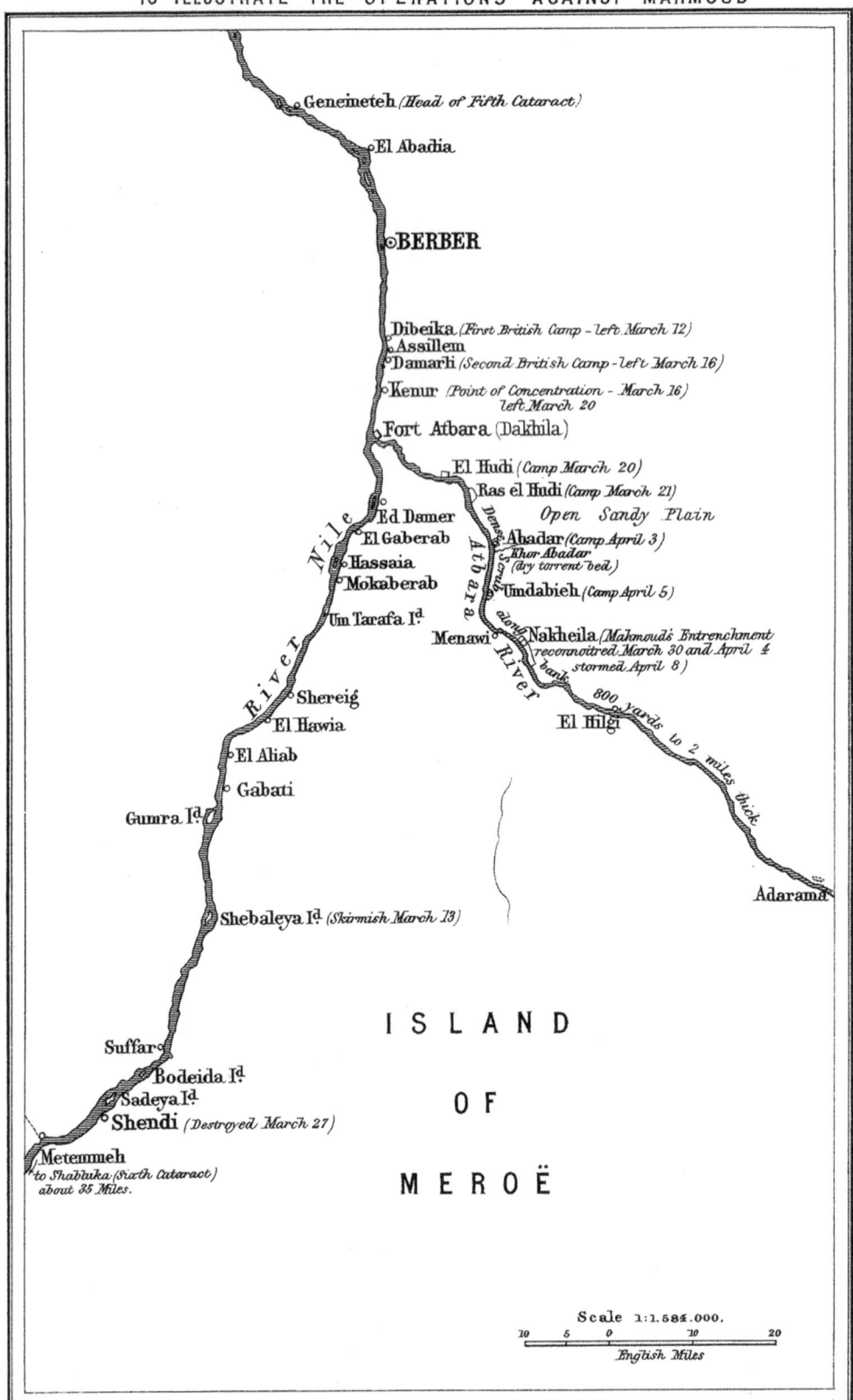

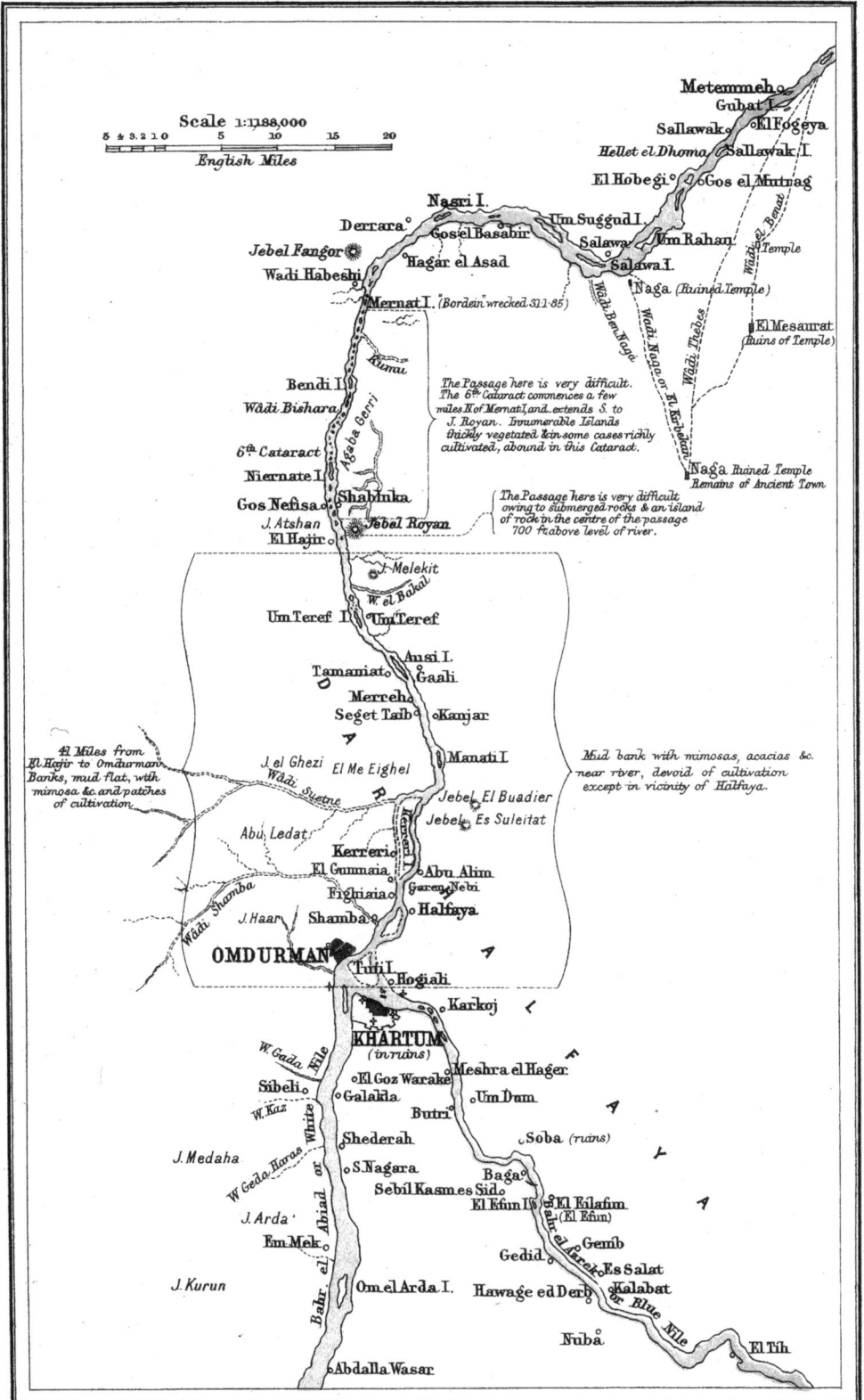

KHARTUM AND OMDURMAN

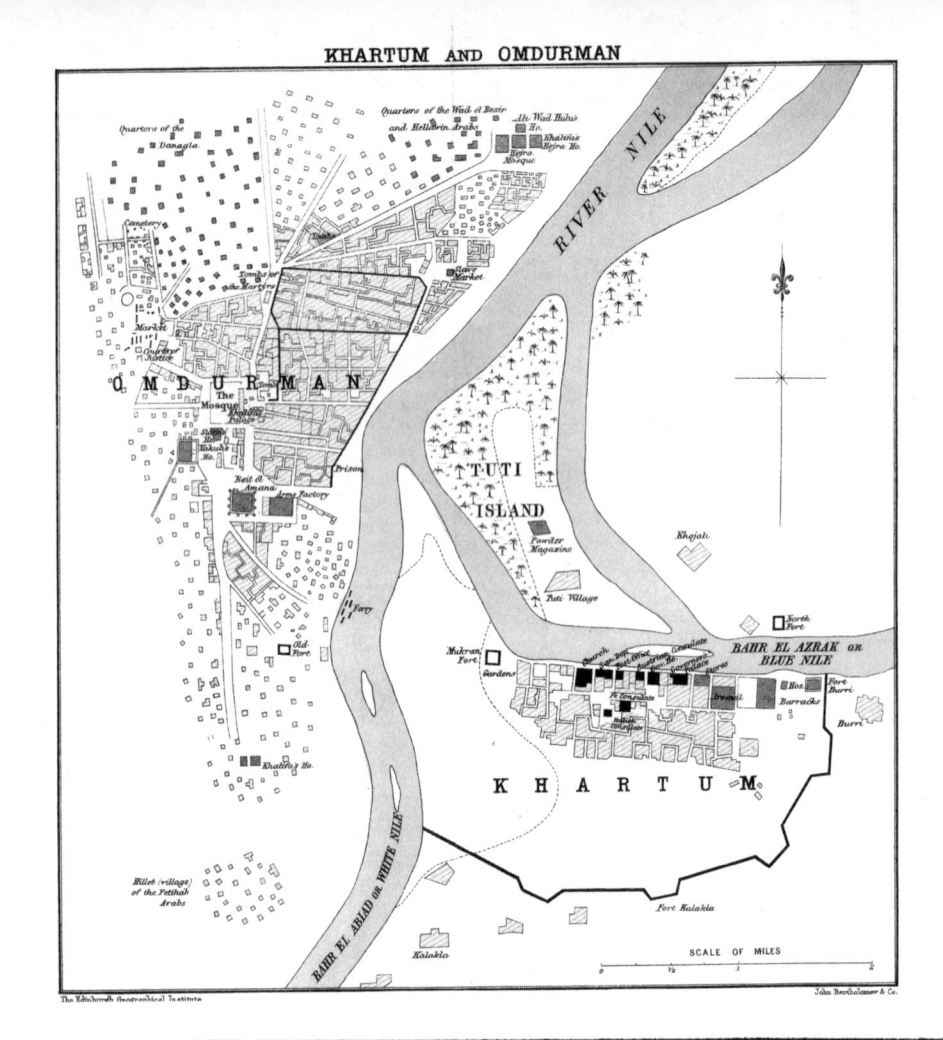

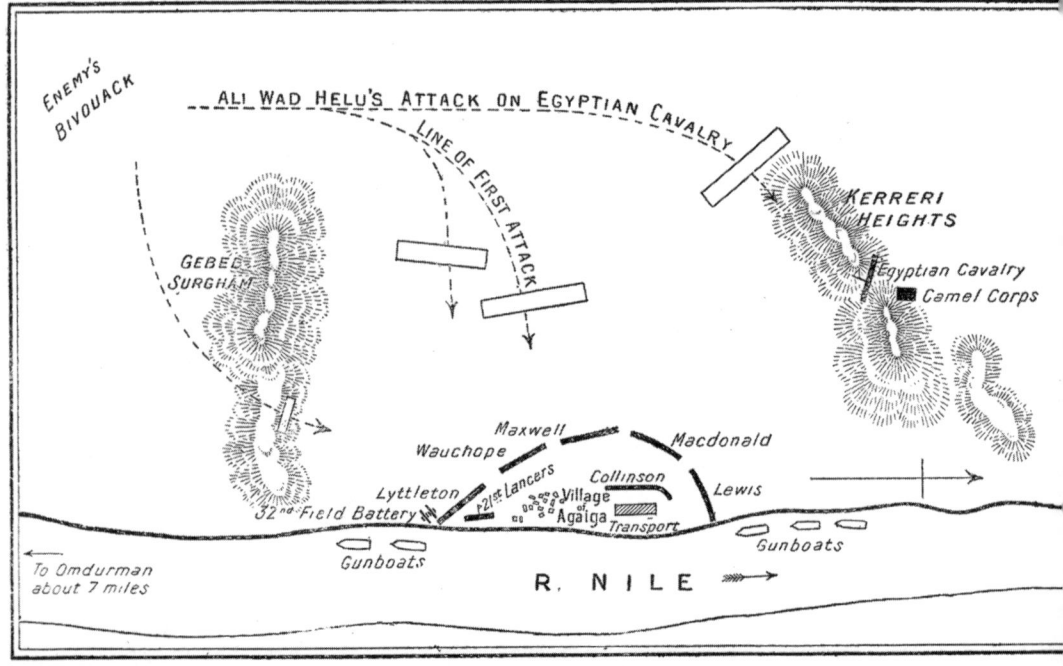

BATTLE OF OMDURMAN, PHASE ONE, 7 A.M.

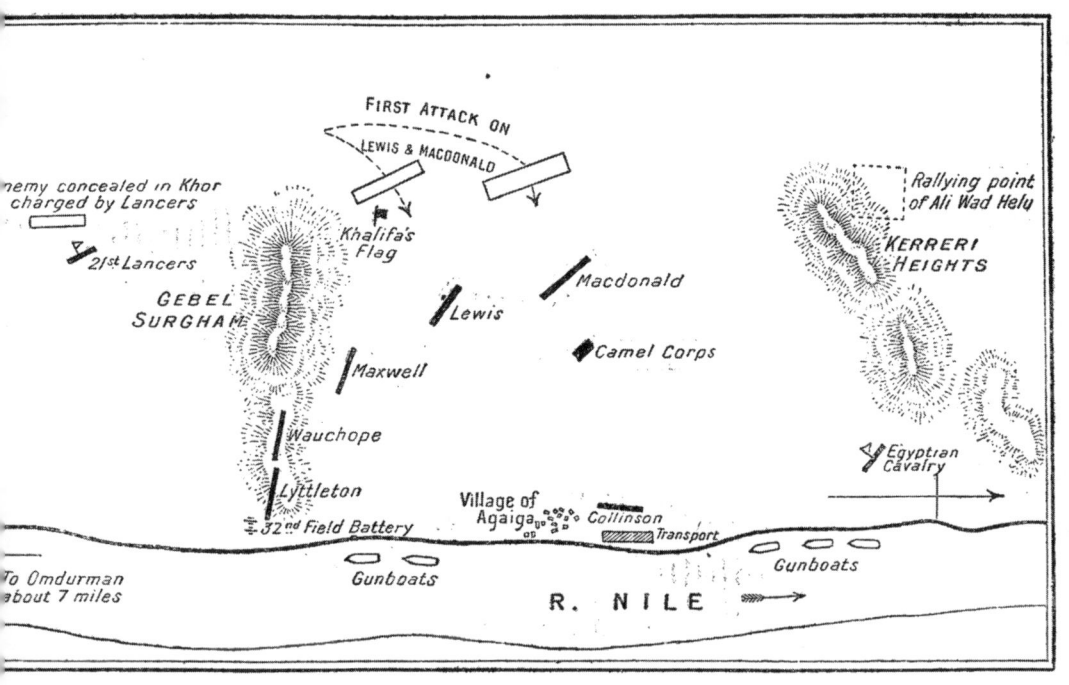

BATTLE OF OMDURMAN, Phase Two, 9.40 a.m.

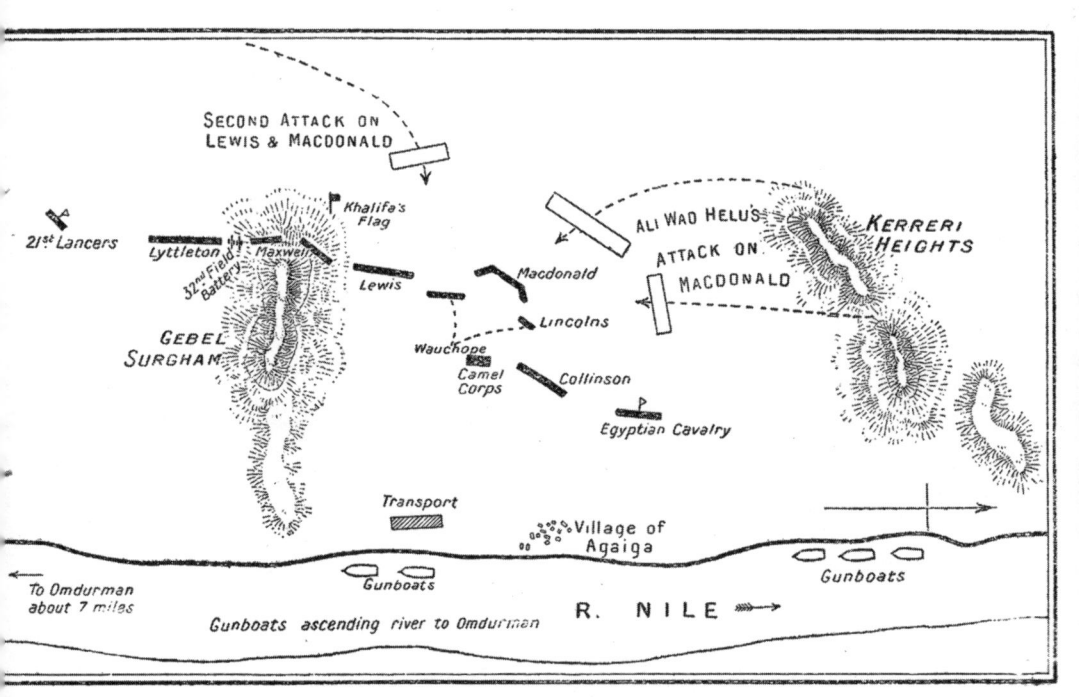

BATTLE OF OMDURMAN, Phase Three, 10.10 a.m.

Glossary

Amir	Islamic military commander or chief
Ansar	followers of the *Mahdi*
Bayt al-mal	treasury
Bey	Ottoman title recognising high political or military status
Bimbashi	Egyptian military rank equivalent to major
Cataract	shallow length or white water rapid of the Nile
Effendi	title of respect
Faqi	Islamic holy man
Farik	Egyptian military rank equivalent to lieutenant-general
Fellahin	Egyptian peasantry
Fez	felt headdress
Firman	royal mandate or decree
Gendarmerie	military force charged with police duties
Hadith	collection of traditions of the sayings of the Prophet Muhammad
Hafiz	a person who has memorised the *Quran*
Hajj	Islamic pilgrimage to Mecca
Hijra	Prophet Muhammad's flight from Mecca to Medina
Imala	administrative district of Mahdist Sudan
Jebel	a mountain or hill
Jibba	Mahdist dress
Jihad	Islamic war or struggle against unbelievers
Jihadiya	Mahdist riflemen
Kaimakam	Egyptian military rank equivalent to lieutenant-colonel
Kaskara	type of double-edged sword
Khalifa	leader of a Caliphate/successor to the *Mahdi*
Khedive	ruler of Egypt
Khor	a dry watercourse or ravine
Kroomen	ex-slaves from West Africa recruited by the Royal Navy
Lewa	Egyptian military rank equivalent to major-general

Mahdi	prophesised redeemer of Islam
Mahdiyya	religious movement of Muhammad Ahmed
Miralai	Egyptian military rank equivalent to colonel
Mulazim awal	Egyptian military rank equivalent to lieutenant
Mulazim tani	Egyptian military rank equivalent to second-lieutenant
Muluazimayya	elite warriors of the Mahdist army
Muqaddam	commander of a quarter of a hundred in the Mahdist army
Noggara	a type of drum
Pasha	Ottoman title recognising high political or military status
Picquet	small detachment of soldiers
Quran	central religious text of Islam
Rasmiya	commander of a hundred in the Mahdist army
Rub	basic military unit of the Mahdist army
Saghkolaghasi	Egyptian military rank equivalent to adjutant-major
Sheikh	chief or head of an Arab tribe
Sirdar	commander-in-Chief of the Egyptian Army
Sultan	Islamic sovereign
Tirailleur	African soldier in French colonial army
Tricolore	French national flag
Trombash	throwing stick
Vedette	a mounted sentry
Wadi	a dry ravine or valley
Yuzbashi	Egyptian military rank equivalent to captain
Zariba	thorn fence fortifying a camp or village

Chronology

1881
29 June: Muhammad Ahmed declares himself to be the *Mahdi*.
12 August: Muhammad Ahmed proclaims *jihad* against Egyptian rule in Sudan.

1882
11 July: The British Royal Navy commences a bombardment of Alexandria.
13 September: Wolseley defeats the Egyptians at the Battle of Tel el-Kebir.

1883
5 November: Hicks *Pasha*'s force is annihilated by the *Ansar*.

1885
26 January: Khartoum falls and General Gordon is killed.
10 February: British troops defeat a Mahdist force at the Battle of Kirbekan.
22 June: Muhammad Ahmed dies; he is succeeded by Abdullahi al-Taishi as *Khalifa*.

1888
3 August: The Mahdist invasion of Egypt is defeated at the Battle of Toski.
20 December: Grenfell defeats Osman Digna at the Battle of Gemaizah.

1891
19 February: Egyptian forces defeat the Mahdists at Tokar.

1892
13 April: Kitchener is appointed *Sirdar* of the Egyptian Army.

1896
1 March: The Italians are defeated by the Abyssinians at the Battle of Adwa.
12 March: Britain agrees to limited operations in Dongola at the request of the Italians.
1 May: Egyptian cavalry clash with a Mahdist force near Akasha.

7 June: Egyptian forces defeat the Mahdists at the Battle of Firket.
19 September: Kitchener's gunboats clash with Mahdist forces at Hafir.
23 September: Anglo-Egyptian troops enter Dongola.

1897
7 August: Egyptian forces defeat the Mahdists at the Action of Abu Hamed.
21 August: The Mahdists abandon Berber.
31 August: Kitchener occupies Berber.
25 December: Kassala is transferred from Italian to Egyptian control.

1898
1 January: Kitchener formally requests British troop reinforcements.
16 February: Anglo-Egyptian forces begin concentrating.
27 March: Shendi is captured and destroyed.
30 March: Hunter conducts a reconnaissance of Mahmud's *zariba*.
4 April: Broadwood's cavalry clash with Baggara horsemen near Mahmud's *zariba*.
8 April: Kitchener defeats Mahmud at the Battle of Atbara.
28 August: Anglo-Egyptian forces concentrate for final advance to Omdurman.
1 September: Kitchener and Abdullahi al-Taishi make preparations for battle.
2 September: Kitchener defeats Abdullahi al-Taishi at the Battle of Omdurman, after which Anglo-Egyptian troops enter the city.
4 September: A memorial service is held for Gordon at Khartoum.
9 September: Kitchener leaves for Fashoda following reports of Europeans occupying the village.
19 September: Kitchener and Marchand meet and the Fashoda Incident begins.
22 September: Egyptian forces under Parsons capture Gedarif.
26 December: Egyptian forces under Lewis defeat those under Ahmed Fedil at Dakhila (Roseires Cataract).

1899
22 November: Wingate defeats Abdullahi al-Taishi at the Battle of Umm Diwaykarat, during which the *Khalifa* is killed.

Introduction

In 1882, the British took the fateful decision to invade Egypt. Little did they know, it would be the first step towards a largely—at least initially—unwilling involvement in neighbouring Sudan. On 26 January 1885, one of Britain's most beloved generals, Charles 'Chinese' Gordon, was killed by warriors of the *Mahdi* at his palace in Khartoum. His death caused public outrage in Britain, but the newly elected Conservative government, led by Lord Salisbury, showed little desire in avenging the killing. Indeed, it would not be until over a decade later, in 1896, that a limited campaign in Sudan against the Mahdists was authorised, ironically by a re-elected Salisbury. Military operations were later extended into a fully-blown reconquest of Egypt's lost territory, which would culminate in the epic Battle of Omdurman (known as the Battle of Karari to the Sudanese), on 2 September 1898.

The Sudanese campaign of 1896 to 1898, on which this book focuses, was a contest between two men: Major-General Horatio Herbert Kitchener, the *Sirdar* of the Egyptian Army, and Abdullahi al-Taishi, the *Khalifa* of Sudan and successor to the *Mahdi*. There are, of course, a whole host of other characters in our story, including: Lord Cromer, the consul-general of Egypt; Francis Reginald Wingate, Kitchener's intelligence officer and successor as *Sirdar*; Édouard Percy Cranwill Girouard, the Canadian railway builder, who was responsible for the construction of the all-important Sudan Military Railway; and Winston Churchill, then a young subaltern, who took part in the famous charge of the 21st Lancers. On the side of the Mahdists, there is: Ya'qub Muhammad Turshain, the commander of the Black Flag; Osman al-Din, the *Khalifa*'s eldest son, who commanded the *muluazimayya*; Osman Azrak, who fought the Egyptians at the Battle of Firket; and Osman Digna, chief of the Hadendowa, who was a thorn in the side of the British for over a decade. There are, of course, many others who we will meet in the following chapters.

Although the subject of this book is Kitchener's reconquest of Sudan, I understand the reader may not necessarily be familiar with events that led to military operations that began in 1896. As such, I have attempted to provide a brief yet reasonably detailed account of the history of Egypt and Sudan—both political and military—from the rise of the *Mahdi* in 1881 to the eve of war in the mid-1890s. These include the British invasion of Egypt in 1882, the siege of Khartoum—during which Gordon was killed—in 1884-85, and Wolseley's failed expedition to save him, as well as some of the numerous minor actions involving British and Egyptian troops against the Mahdists prior to the Dongola campaign. Likewise, I have included details of key events following the Battle of Omdurman; these are important aspects of the history of Sudan in the aftermath of the Mahdist defeat, yet many previous authors provide scant or even no details at all about them.

For those who wish to learn more about Egypt and Sudan of the early to mid-1880s, I would like to wholeheartedly suggest the following titles. For the rise of the *Mahdi*, *The Mahdi of Sudan and the Death of General Gordon* by Fergus Nicoll is perhaps one of the most detailed accounts of how Muhammad Ahmed rose to prominence and initiated Mahdism, which would endure, to varying degrees of success, in Sudan from 1881 through to 1899, and even *bey*ond. Two other important works in recent years are those written by Dr Mike Snook, including *Go Strong into the Desert: The Mahdist Uprising in Sudan, 1881-85* and *Beyond the Reach of Empire: Wolseley's Failed Campaign to Save Gordon and Khartoum*. The former offers the reader an excellent overview of the *Mahdi*'s rebellion until his death in 1885, while the latter is by far the most comprehensive study of the Nile campaign of 1884-85 yet written. Finally, in terms of recent publications, Michael Asher's *Khartoum: The Ultimate Imperial Adventure* presents a thoroughly enjoyable single-volume overview of the conflict in Sudan over its lengthy eighteen-year course.

Books published at the time of the 1896-98 campaigns, or just afterwards, are more numerous. While every history book should be read with a critical eye, particular care should be taken when referring to early works, since new information often comes to light in the years following a war, and the author, writing at a time when many had nationalistic tendencies, may be more inclined to bias. That said, there are, of course, a number of late Victorian eyewitness accounts that are of much value and interest to our study of Sudan. One such title is *With Kitchener to Khartum* by George Warrington Steevens, published in 1898, who was a war correspondent travelling with Kitchener's force. Another is *The Downfall of the Dervishes: Being a Sketch of the Final Sudan Campaign of 1898*, by Ernest Nathaniel Bennett, also published in 1898, who was an academic and special correspondent for *The Westminster Gazette* and likewise present during the campaign. Perhaps a more famous author writing at the time was Winston Churchill, who took an active part in the Battle of Omdurman, and who later published, in 1899, *The River War: An Historical Account of the Reconquest of the Soudan*.

While not directly relevant to Kitchener's prosecution of his reconquest, there are several other first-hand accounts of great importance to any study of Mahdist Sudan. Firstly, there is *Ten Years' Captivity in the Mahdi's Camp, 1882-1892* by

Father Joseph Ohrwalder, an Austrian priest who became witness to much of what was taking place among the Mahdists during his time as their prisoner; his account in English was compiled from original manuscripts by Major Wingate. Secondly, there is *Fire and Sword in the Sudan: A Personal Narrative of Fighting and Serving the Dervishes, 1879-1895* by Rudolf Carl von Slatin. Slatin was an Anglo-Austrian serving as a colonel in the Egyptian Army intelligence department, who, like Ohrwalder, became a prisoner of the Mahdists; again the English version of his book was compiled and translated by Wingate. Following their escape from captivity, their personal accounts of the *Mahdi* and his followers did much to swing British public opinion towards the desire for further military intervention in Sudan. We will meet both Ohrwalder and Slatin, along with other unfortunate prisoners, again later in this book.

As with most Victorian campaigns fought by the British against their colonial adversaries, there is often only relatively little available from the non-British point of view. There are, however, two useful and interesting books that help partially fill this void as regards to Sudan. The first is *The Memoirs of Babikr Bedri*, translated by Yousef Bedri and George Scott, published in 1969. Babikr Bedri was a Mahdist warrior, who was present at the Battle of Omdurman. The second is *Karari: The Sudanese Account of the Battle of Omdurman* by 'Ismat Hasan Zulfo, translated from the original Arabic by Peter Clark. Zulfo was an officer in the Sudanese Army, who first published his study in 1973, with the English version becoming available in 1980. Both titles are invaluable to the study of the Mahdists and Kitchener's reconquest, offering the reader an insight into how the Sudanese viewed the campaign.

Before proceeding to examine Kitchener's Sudanese campaigns, I have also provided several chapters that consider the two key protagonists and their respective armies in some detail. In terms of Anglo-Egyptian forces, the reader should be aware that there were two armies in Egypt during the time of the British occupation. Firstly, there was what could be described as the British Army of Occupation, which was made up of British troops who were commanded by British officers. Secondly, there was the Egyptian Army, consisting of Egyptian troops—and, later, Sudanese troops—who were commanded by both British and Egyptian officers. Kitchener's army during the 1896-98 campaigns consisted of regiments from both armies, although the burden of the fighting would often fall on the Egyptian and Sudanese units. I have, therefore, employed the term 'Anglo-Egyptian' when referring to Kitchener's forces.

A final note should be made about the spelling of names used in this book. As with my previous works, I have leaned towards that in use at the time in order to assist the reader who wishes to learn more by consulting period and first-hand accounts, although even then different spellings are sometimes encountered. Thus, I have used 'Osman Digna' rather than ''Uthman Diqna' and 'Osman Azrak' rather than ''Uthman Azraq', and so on. Also as regards to names, I have tended, with only the odd exception, to write them out in full when referring to the Mahdists—the reason being that names like Muhammad and Osman etc. are common, and so sometimes making it confusing to the reader if the full name is not given. Similarly, I have also opted for the period spelling of place names. Thus, I have used '*Jebel* Surgham' rather than 'Jabal Surkab' and 'Egeiga' instead of 'al-'Ijayja' etc. The latter will help the reader when consulting period maps, which are often more accurate than those more recently drawn, since names of places change and landmarks move or even disappear altogether. The maps used in this book are all from the period.

I hope in the following pages I have been able to produce one of the most detailed accounts of the reconquest in terms of a military history of the campaigns. Although I have spent years reading about the subject, I have also learned much during my more recent research for this work. May this book help keep alive the memories of all, regardless of nationality, who fell during the conflict.

Mark Simner
Staffordshire
October 2016

1

The Rise of the *Mahdi*

Muhammad Ahmed Ibn Al-Sayyid Abdullah, better remembered today simply as the '*Mahdi*', was born on 12 August 1844 on the small Nile River island of Lebab, ten miles south of Dongola in northern Sudan. He was the third of four sons of Abdullah Fahl, a boat builder who constructed vessels and waterwheels of various descriptions to satisfy the needs of local fishermen and farmers, as well as merchants who traded throughout the region. Abdullah Fahl had adopted the term *al-Sayyid* (an Arabic honorific title) based on the belief that his ancestry stretched back to Ali bin Abi Talib, who was the son-in-law of the Prophet Muhammad; just how credible this claim is remains unclear, but it was firmly believed by the family.

At this time, much of Sudan was under the rule of Egypt, following Muhammad Ali *Pasha*'s invasion of twenty years earlier. Muhammad Ali, the governor of Egypt, was a puppet of the Turkish *sultan*ate (known as the Porte), yet he remained fiercely ambitious and viewed his country as effectively an independent state, and one that he sought to grow into an empire of his own. He was also ruthless, having massacred many Mamluk chiefs gathered in the citadel at Cairo in 1811, while forcing others to flee Egypt for their lives, thus ending their centuries-old mastership of the country. Muhammad Ali's rule of Sudan would be one of oppression and riddled throughout with corruption; it is against this background that the future Islamic leader, who would go on to shock the world's most powerful empire, would experience his formative years.

Dongola itself, which was known as al-Urdi during Muhammad Ahmed's early years, was in fact a military settlement founded by refugees from Egypt, who, further down-river, had built a fortress called Urdi al-Manfukh. The town, which consisted of mostly basic mud-brick, single-storey buildings, developed haphazardly as it grew to serve the needs of the fortress, before becoming a proper settlement in its own right. To the few Europeans who visited, usually *en route* to elsewhere, Dongola was nothing more than a filthy and unhealthy little feature on the map that was best left long behind.

When Muhammad Ahmed was only five years of age, he relocated with his *ménage*, including his father, pregnant mother, and two older brothers (Muhammad and Hamid), to Omdurman in search of more plentiful supplies for their business following the award of a sizeable government contract. If there was a resentment towards Egyptian rule in Dongola, there was an even greater hatred towards Muhammad Ali among the residents of Omdurman. Indeed, the town was a hotbed of political opposition to the Egyptian governor and his Ottoman boss, feelings that no doubt would rub-off on Muhammad Ahmed as he grew up. Unfortunately for the family, disaster struck during their journey, as Abdullah Fahl fell desperately ill and subsequently died. The two older brothers took over the running of the business and were quick to ensure it became firmly established at its new location.

It is likely that Muhammad Ahmed was brought up at home in a devoutly religious atmosphere, which almost certainly influenced his own particularly strong beliefs in later life. The family business had little need for his presence, and so he was allowed, by his older brothers, to attend one of the religious schools where he was taught mathematics, astronomy, and theology by strict holy men, known as *faqis*; they included: Sharaf al-Din Abu-al-Sadiq, Mahbub al-Habashi, and *Sheikh* Mahmud al-Mubarak. During his time in class, Muhammad Ahmed was noted for his high levels of concentration and devotion to his studies, particularly when learning the Qu*fbey*ran, becoming a *hafiz*—someone who has learned the entire religious text off by heart. In addition, his teachers were struck by his incredible self-discipline, drive, and the ability to deprive himself in the name of his religion; he would be rewarded for these abilities with highly-regarded responsibilities usually only given to those of more mature years.

Later, as a young adult, Muhammad Ahmed took the decision to live his life on the Nile island of Aba, where, for a time, he led a solitary existence. It is unclear why he chose to live in such a self-inflicted virtual exile, but, on his return to civilization, he claimed to have heard voices and experienced premonitions. It is, perhaps, these voices and visions that sparked his personal belief of being the *Mahdi* (meaning the 'guided one'), which he would later claim to be at the age of thirty-seven. Today, many would view such a self-proclamation as nothing more than the delusions of a religious nutcase, but it should be remembered that at the time, many certainly believed him and were willing to follow him anywhere, even to their deaths, as thousands eventually did.

In 1861, Muhammad Ahmed joined the Summaniya Dervish, a particularly strict Islamic religious sect, but he was soon at odds with the leader of his local branch on account of a celebration held by the latter, which included the spectacle of dancing girls and unlimited opportunities for sex. For a devoutly religious man who firmly believed in asceticism, it was nothing short of outrageous, and Muhammad Ahmed was quick to protest. Unfortunately for the young man, his complaints merely angered the sect leader, who responded by banishing him from the group. The future

Mahdi was prone to arrogance, often believing himself to be superior to others, and had little hesitation to express sharp disapproval or criticism towards others, even highly-respected elders. His own conceit had backfired, but Muhammad Ahmed would view it as little more than a minor setback.

Travelling to Mesellamiya, Muhammad Ahmed was admitted to the local branch of the Summaniya Dervish, where he met Abdullahi al-Taishi, a highly practical man who was a Baggara. Baggara was the name given to a collection of Arabic nomadic tribes that inhabited Africa's Sahel, and whose people would later form the backbone of the Mahdist army in Sudan. Although very different in personality, the two men were quick to become friends, a friendship that would prove to be of much importance to Muhammad Ahmed's later actions as the *Mahdi*.

Over time, Muhammad Ahmed attracted increasing numbers of followers, and, as a result, the level of influence he came to enjoy also sharply increased. In particular, his words proved popular with the poor, since he encouraged— even demanded—those who would listen to his preaches to abandon all worldly pleasures and instead embrace God. For many, this was—perhaps unsurprisingly—appealing, since they had little hope of enjoying the former but could certainly devote to the latter. However, this simple message was accompanied by a more sinister one: to condemn those who disagreed, and, if necessary, even use violence against them. These teachings would slowly create a feeling of unrest among his followers towards their Egyptian masters and, years later, the British.

One reason Muhammad Ahmed was so successful in spreading his message was due to the fact he travelled widely, visiting villages and other homesteads that would otherwise never hear his name, let alone consciously decide to support him. If the poor people of the larger settlements were willing to embrace his teachings, then those in these tiny communities, who were even poorer and had next to no education, were the perfect audience. Thus, the future self-proclaimed *Mahdi* wandered from community to community, persuading more and more to follow his religious—and political—ideology.

By 1880, Muhammad Ahmed had become well-known throughout northern Sudan, and, it is said, once met no one ever forgot him. His holiness was seen as *bey*ond question, and his charismatic personality appealed to most who met him. Despite this, he remained a mysterious figure and often aloof. However, when he publically announced himself to be the *Mahdi* on 29 June 1881, the news spread like wildfire across the region; most were happy to believe the claim, with few feeling surprised that he was indeed the 'guided one' who guides others. Those who had listened so intently to his preaches received the news with much joy and enthusiasm; the redeemer of Islam had finally come and he would soon lead a rebellion against the hated Egyptian and Sudanese authorities.

The notion of the *Mahdi* cannot be found in the *Quran*; it is not mentioned at all in the religious text, although references to it can be found in the *Hadith*, but rather it was an honorific term given to the Prophet Muhammad and his four deputies, known as *Khulafá al-rashídún*, by their followers. In addition, it should be understood that both the Sunni and Shia branches of Islam have differing views on the concept of the *Mahdi*; the former viewed the *Mahdi* as the successor to Muhammad, who is still awaited, while for the latter, he has already been born, but will remain hidden until such a time he is ready to dispense justice to the world. For many centuries, the meaning and legitimacy of the *Mahdi* have also been subject to intense debate within the Islamic world, and some today believe he would never actually claim the title for himself while he was alive, but rather would be recognised as such after his death. As at the time of Kitchener's reconquest of Sudan in 1896-98, there remains little real consensus regarding the *Mahdi* within Islam.

Muhammad Ahmed was not the first—nor the last—to make the claim to be the *Mahdi*. A number of other claimants over the centuries have made similar self-proclamations, largely to give credence to their political activities. Two such claimants, contemporary to Muhammad Ahmed, include: Siyyid Ali Muḥammad Shirazi, a merchant from Persia and founder of Babism, who made his claim in 1847, and Mirza Ghulam Ahmed, founder of the Ahmediyya Movement in India in 1889, who announced his belief in being the *Mahdi* in the likeness of Jesus. The latter strongly believed in spreading Islam peacefully and discouraged the idea of violent *jihad* among his followers. Muhammad Ahmed, therefore, was just another claimant willing to use the title of *Mahdi* in order achieve his political goals, but, unlike Mirza Ghulam Ahmed, he had little fear of calling for the use of violence to get what he wanted.

While the oppressed of Sudan rejoiced, the Egyptian and Turkish rulers grew increasingly concerned about developing events. Sudan had been subjected to repression for many years, and the current resentment of the people towards their foreign masters was not lost on the authorities. This powder-keg now had a potential means of ignition, and, to the more astute, it was only a matter of time until the region exploded into large scale open revolt of extreme violence. In this assumption, they would be proved horrifically correct.

Naturally, despite Muhammad Ahmed's popularity and large following, he was by no means universally loved or seen as the true *Mahdi*. One principal group that opposed him was the Ulama, the orthodox and highly-respected religious local authorities, who openly expressed their distaste for the self-proclamation. The Ulama did not criticise the concept of the *Mahdi* itself, since they themselves believed that he would one day come, but argued that Muhammad Ahmed's claim did not match that laid out in the *Hadith*, and in particular that he was not a descendant of Fatimah, the daughter of the Prophet Muhammad. They also argued that he did not bear the physical characteristics that the true *Mahdi* was said to possess, including a V-shaped gap between his front teeth (although others would later describe him as having such) and a birthmark on his right cheek.

Later, Muhammad Ahmed would go on and attempt to make important and controversial changes to Islam, such as the revision of the five pillars—and the adding of a sixth, the belief in the *Mahdiyya*—which would further alienate the Ulama and others. However, his supporters remained numerous; this popularity enabled him to exert much influence and flex his religious and political power.

No known photograph of Muhammad Ahmed exists, although a number of contemporary engravings were published at the time. However, Father Joseph Ohrwalder described him as follows:

> His outward appearance was strangely fascinating; he was a man of strong constitution, very dark complexion, and his face always wore a pleasant smile, to which he had by long practice accustomed himself. Under this smile gleamed a set of singularly white teeth, and between the two upper middle ones was a V-shaped space, which in the Sudan is considered a sign that the owner will be lucky. His mode of conversation too had by training become exceptionally pleasant and sweet. As a messenger of God, he pretended to be in direct communication with the Deity. All orders which he gave were supposed to have come to him by inspiration, and it became therefore a sin to refuse to *obey* them; disobedience to the *Mahdi*'s orders was tantamount to resistance to the will of God, and was therefore punishable by death.

At about the same time as Muhammad Ahmed was making his announcement of being the true *Mahdi*, the latest leader of the local government in Khartoum was also settling down to his new job. The man given this responsibility was an Egyptian Army general by the name of Muhammad Rauf *Pasha*, an officer with much—somewhat undistinguished—service in Sudan. He was little regarded by the British, having being removed from both the governorships of the Equatoria and Harar provinces by General Gordon, during the latter's tenure as governor-general of Sudan. However, such was the level of corruption in the Egyptian authorities at the time that Rauf would be given this undeserved and high-profile position following Gordon's resignation.

Sudan was crippling the Egyptian economy, costing Cairo more money than the local taxes were bringing in. This in turn exacerbated the huge national debts Egypt had already acquired as a result of the extensive building of railways, hospitals and schools in an attempt to modernise the country. Despite the immensely important and lucrative Suez Canal, which had been opened in 1869, Egypt's spiralling debts were getting out of control and the Egyptian Government was forced to turn to the banks in London and Paris for loans, which both the British and French eagerly lent, adding loan on top of loan. When the Egyptians, somewhat predictably, then struggled to pay the money back, both countries saw the situation as an excuse to interfere with Egypt, both financially and politically.

Due to the ever worsening state of the Egyptian economy, the *Khedive* of Egypt, Ismail *Pasha*, who had ruled the country since 1863, was forced to resign on 26 June 1879 after the British and French governments put pressure on the *Sultan* to remove him from office. Ismail then went into exile, but the now-former Egyptian ruler had had the foresight to ensure, by bribing corrupt Ottoman officials, that he would be succeeded by his son, Tewfik. It would be Tewfik *Pasha*, who had reluctantly accepted Gordon's resignation—itself forced due to his current state of exhaustion from his relentless attempts to supress the slave trade in Bahr al-Ghazal and Darfur—and appointed the inefficient Rauf as his replacement. Curiously, Gordon had asked for his predecessor as governor, Ismail Ayub, to be re-appointed as his replacement, which was duly done; within days, the decision was reversed and Rauf given the post instead, much to the British officer's disgust. The consequences of this ill-informed appointment would be great, since it would now be the inadequate Rauf who would have to deal with the troublesome Muhammad Ahmed.

After taking up his post in Khartoum, Rauf was approached by Muhammad al-Sharif Nur al-Daim, a mentor of the *Mahdi* who had seemingly fallen out with his former student, accusing Muhammad Ahmed of proclaiming himself as the *Mahdi* by the 'Satan of arrogance'. Yet despite this, Rauf decided to reach out to Muhammad Ahmed and inform him that he would be welcomed by the Egyptian and Sudanese authorities if he affirmed his position as a Sudanese loyalist. Unsurprisingly, the newly appointed governor of Khartoum received, in the form of a telegram sent at the beginning of the holy month of Ramadan, a somewhat negative reply. Muhammad Ahmed reasserted his belief that he was the true *Mahdi*, and that anyone who refused to believe in him would be put to the sword. An incensed Rauf responded by summoning Muhammad Ahmed to Khartoum, where he intended to place him before the Ulama, who, he believed, would promptly discredit him and prove to others that he was not the real *Mahdi*. Failing this, he would have Muhammad Ahmed arrested, and, in a single stroke, cut off the head of the movement he rightly believed now threatened peace in Sudan.

Subsequently, on 7 August 1881, a meeting took place between Muhammad Ahmed and Muhammad Abu Suud—Rauf's representative and childhood friend—at a place called Jazira Aba. The meeting, or rather heated argument, was said to have been intense after Muhammad Ahmed refused the summons to Khartoum, stating there was no higher authority than the *Mahdi*, thus rendering the summons invalid. The response from Rauf's envoy was one of fury, demanding why Muhammad Ahmed thought he could take on the might of the government with his poor following. Muhammad Ahmed merely responded that he would fight with what he had, and that he, and his followers, were willing to die for their cause. Unable to make any headway, the irritated envoy left and returned to Khartoum.

Carl Giegler, a German gentleman who was employed as the deputy governor-general of Sudan, was quietly watching events unfold. Giegler, however, dismissed Muhammad Ahmed as nothing more than an irritation who would have little chance of defeating the armies of Egypt and Sudan. The deputy governor-general's attitude towards the *Mahdi* was not unique, since many at this time did not believe any serious threat of large-scale unrest was on the cards. This attitude would be shaken, when, on 12 August, the first battle of what some today refer to as the Mahdist War took place, an action which ended in victory for Muhammad Ahmed.

Following his failure on the 7th, Abu Suud had boarded the Nile steamer *Ismailia* at Khartoum on the 11th, and, with 200 armed men, set off once again for Jazira Aba; his intention this time was to force a solution to the problem. Disembarking his troops at a place quarter of a mile away from Jazira Aba, the small force formed up and marched through torrential rain towards the small settlement. Unfortunately for Abu Suud, the *Mahdi* had sent instructions for men from the settlements at Dighaim, Husunat, and Fallata to come to his aid, having wisely suspected the coming attack. Muhammad Ahmed's followers faithfully responded, and, with just over 300 men, the *Mahdi* waited quietly for Abu Suud and his troops.

As night fell, the Egyptian troops could be seen in a square formation before dividing into two separate groups for their final advance on Jazira Aba. As the soldiers moved forward, the *Mahdi* gave orders for his men to attack, and what followed was a panicked response from the Egyptians in the form of a poorly aimed volley of fire, which did little or no damage to their attackers. Undeterred, Muhammad Ahmed's men lunged forward and soon overwhelmed Abu Suud's small army, forcing them to scramble back towards the bank and where they had landed earlier. The men on the steamer opened fire in support of their comrades on the banks, but this, too, had little adverse effect on the *Mahdi*'s warriors, who simply retuned fire at the *Ismailia*. The battle ended in the deaths of 120 Egyptian troops; their bodies were left behind as the few panicked survivors fled for their lives. Abu Suud was one of the lucky survivors, and it was later learned that Muhammad Ahmed had been lightly wounded during the skirmish, although only twelve of his followers had been killed; all of them were later regarded as martyrs by the Mahdists. News of the defeat of the Egyptians failed to make much of an impression on the world outside of Sudan, but it was a significant victory for the *Mahdi*, since, although the battle was small and insignificant in itself, it sent a clear signal to the authorities in both Cairo and Khartoum that he was not some minor irritation that could be easily defeated.

Muhammad Ahmed, however, knew his victory had in fact been a lucky one and that larger numbers of Egyptian troops would now likely be sent against him in revenge. He also knew that, despite his own growing following, he could not yet count on a big enough army with which to take on the might of the government. He was, therefore, left with little alternative but to flee to the relative safety of the hills in Kordofan, where—due to the local communities feeling sympathetic towards the *Mahdi* and his cause—he could rely on much needed supplies; although he did, in fact, meet some resistance at *Jebel* al-Jarada, where he had to fight his way through. Also, due to the difficulties of the terrain, any pursuing army would be seriously handicapped and unable to operate and supply itself for any meaningful period of time. Within hours of triumphantly watching battered Egyptian troops sailing off down the Nile aboard the *Ismailia*, Muhammad Ahmed and his small band of followers were already on their journey towards the Nuba Mountains.

This journey became known as the *Mahdi*'s *hijra*—after either the Prophet Muhammad's migration from Mecca to Yathrib (later known as Medina) or his earlier flight to Abyssinia to escape persecution at Mecca—which would take seventy-nine days to complete and end at a place called *Jebel* Gadír, although Muhammad Ahmed would later rename it *Jebel* Massa. It would be here that the *Mahdi* decided those who had followed him to this place, as well as his followers more generally, would from now on be known as the *Ansar* (meaning 'helpers'). This, it should be understood, was a clever move on the part of Muhammad Ahmed, since those who followed him came from many different tribes that were often at odds with one another and sometimes refused to cooperate. However, by honouring them in this way, he had offered them a unified title under which they could work—and fight—together under the banner of the *Mahdi* himself. He next set about spreading his teachings and calling for more men.

Back in Khartoum, while Muhammad Ahmed was embarking on his *hijra*, Rauf was steaming with fury about the defeat of Abu Suud at Jazira Aba. Again, the governor of Khartoum sought to play-down the event, possibly to placate his superiors in the Egyptian Government, and possibly because he still viewed the self-proclaimed *Mahdi* as nothing more than a temporary problem that would yet be swiftly dealt with. In order to deflect blame, Rauf laid responsibility for the disaster on the officers who had commanded the expedition. With blame firmly shifted away from him, the governor next set about planning to take on the *Mahdi* and deal him a knock-out blow. The Nile fleet of steamers were increased and instructions were issued to Muhammad Said, the governor and senior officer in command of Egyptian forces in Kordofan, to begin concentrating his forces in readiness to attack the *Mahdi*.

When his forces were ready, Said marched on Jazira Aba, news of which reached Muhammad Ahmed while he was roughly half-way through his *hijra*. While at the settlement, Said completely destroyed it and the surrounding farms, after which he continued his pursuit. Ultimately, however, the *Mahdi* and his followers were able to escape the Egyptian general, who later returned to his base without even setting eyes on his prize.

It would not be until 8 December that a force of 200 Egyptian troops, under the command of Rashid Ayman, the governor of Fashoda, caught up with the *Mahdi* at *Jebel* Gadír, albeit acting without orders from his superior in Khartoum. Again, the force sent against Muhammad Ahmed was simply not strong enough, and the ensuing battle ended in another victory for the *Mahdi*. Egyptian casualties included Rashid himself killed, while over 100 were taken prisoner. Around thirty of the *Mahdi*'s men were also killed, all of which were buried and again treated as martyrs to the cause. Emboldened by another victory, the *Ansar* gathered up the supplies abandoned by the Egyptians, while Muhammad Ahmed used his latest triumph to win over yet more followers; in particular, many of the Baggara tribe now flocked in numbers to the Mahdist banner.

To further unite the fractious tribes under his command, Muhammad Ahmed next introduced a new style of dress known as the *jibba*, the design of which the *Mahdi* claimed came from the Prophet Muhammad himself. Members of the *Ansar* were also expected to take part in communal prayers, while any form of disobedience was severely punished. Sharia law was rigidly and ruthlessly enforced by Ahmed Jubara, one of the *Mahdi*'s earliest followers. Muhammad Ahmed now had his own legal system; next, he needed an organised and substantial army with which to defeat the Egyptians once again, since, no doubt, they would be plotting to send even more powerful forces against him.

Command of the *Mahdi*'s growing army was given to his older brother, Muhammad, under the title *Amír juyúsh al-Mahdía*, who was presented with a White flag or banner. The *Ansar* army was then sub-divided into three divisions, each of which would be commanded by a *khalifa*, who would also have his own unique banner or flag. These included the Baggara under a Black flag, the Kinana and Dighaim under a Green flag, and those from Jazira under a Red flag. Weapons were always eagerly sought to equip the men of the *Ansar*, yet, curiously, Muhammad Ahmed forbade the use of firearms captured from defeated Egyptian troops, since he declared the use of weapons used by the infidel would contaminate the purity of his men. It may seem to the modern reader that such a move would only serve to hinder the fighting potential of the *Ansar*, but it demonstrates how strict—even fanatical—the *Mahdi* was regarding his personal mission.

When news reached Rauf of the defeat of Rashid, the governor was quick to again avoid blame by pointing out that the latter had acted without orders. Realising that the *Mahdi* was a much harder nut to crack than first thought, Rauf sent a request to Cairo for additional troops, but none would be forthcoming. Instead, the governor was removed from his post and recalled by Tewfik to the Egyptian capital on 4 March, after which he was replaced by Abd-al-Qadir Hilmi, a major-general who had served both in Sudan and Abyssinia. However, the new governor would not be able to reach Khartoum for several weeks, and so Giegler was made acting-governor in the interim. The German at once ordered the Egyptian troops in Sudan to concentrate on the White Nile, and as soon as they were in sufficient numbers they were to make for the Nuba Mountains to engage the *Mahdi* and his *Ansar*.

The first clash of arms during this renewed offensive against Muhammad Ahmed came in Jazira, where the *Mahdi* had ordered some of his followers to lay siege to the town of Sennar. Hearing of the desperate plight of the town's ill-equipped and tiny garrison, Giegler promptly ordered 200 men to be despatched in an attempt to lift the siege. This time the operation proved to be a success for the Egyptian troops, who relieved the settlement on 13 April 1882.

Elsewhere, Giegler was making preparations to lead a force against *Sheikh* al-Sharif Ahmed Taha, a well-known proponent of the *Mahdi* in Jazira. The Egyptian troops boarded the steamer *Abbas*, but a strange rumour began to circulate among them that the *Mahdi* was able to turn Egyptian bullets into water, and that cannons had been sent by air to aid the *sheikh*. However, before such rumours could be proved false, the expedition was called back by Abd-al-Qadir Hilmi, who had by now arrived in Sudan. Giegler, who was technically a civilian, was replaced by a senior army officer who was then ordered to carry out the attack on the *sheikh* at Massallamia. Unfortunately for the new governor-general of Khartoum, the ensuing action, fought on 3 May, was a disaster for his men and yet another victory for the *Mahdi*.

Giegler, angry at being countermanded, had assembled a force of 2,500 Shukria tribesmen (fighters known to be loyal to the government at Khartoum) and marched against *Sheikh* Taha, engaging him in battle near Abu-Haraz on 5 May. Finally, the forces of the *Mahdi* suffered their first defeat, much to the fury of Muhammad Ahmed who now viewed the Shukria as traitors.

Later, on the 15th, the main force of 2,000 men assembled by Giegler, now under the command of an experienced Sudanese general by the name of Yusuf Hassan al-Shallali, marched out of Khartoum; he was subsequently forced to pause at Kawa in order to wait for additional men *en route* from El Obeid. This delay was to prove disastrous, since substantial numbers of troops, possibly believing the rumours about the powerful *Mahdi*, began to desert their units, whittling down the number of men available for the coming operations. Eventually, however, the force set off again towards Fashoda and the Nuba Mountains. During the advance, four Mahdist spies were captured and brought before Shallali, who had each of them tortured before ordering their limbs cut off in front of his own soldiers. Such was the barbaric nature of the war to come.

By the 29th, Shallali's army was seen by the *Mahdi* encamped within a *zariba*. Muhammad Ahmed now determined to attack the following day immediately after morning prayers. The ensuing assault came as a major shock to the Egyptian general's troops, who were rudely awakened by the war cries of thousands of *Ansar* warriors rushing the *zariba*, which was soon penetrated and fierce hand-to-hand fighting erupted across the camp. Many of Shallali's soldiers simply ran for their lives but were hunted down and put to death by frenzied warriors, sensing yet another victory was easily theirs for the taking. The Battle of Massa, as Muhammad Ahmed would later call it, was added to his list of triumphs over the

Khartoum Government. Thousands of Egyptian soldiers were killed, compared to around a mere 200 *Ansar* martyrs, which included Muhammad Ahmed's older brother, Hamid.

Emboldened again by their latest victory, the *Ansar*, now around 50,000 strong, left their base in southern Kordofan and began an advance on El Obeid. The *Mahdi* himself was among them, riding on his camel, Debelan. The town of El Obeid was wealthy, benefiting from numerous strong commercial links, but also of strategic importance to Muhammad Ahmed, since he knew it would act as an ideal base of operations for his army. However, the town was defended by some 6,000 well-armed Egyptian troops, and seizing it would be no easy undertaking, even with the large numbers of fighters now available to the *Mahdi*.

Muhammad Ahmed was by now posing a very significant threat to Egyptian rule in Sudan, a fact not lost on many of the tribes who resided close to El Obeid. Indeed, many tribesmen now openly supported the *Mahdi's jihad* and rallied to his banner, while others, far lower in number, either threw in their lot with the local authorities by seeking shelter in the town or otherwise made off towards Khartoum.

With the town now virtually under siege by the greatly swelled ranks of the *Ansar*, which Ohrwalder estimated to number an incredible 100,000 men, the *Mahdi* sent several messengers to inform the population that they had the opportunity to either join him or perish. The reply by the garrison, however, was equally as blunt, since Muhammad Said had both messengers hanged. El Obeid was not going to surrender without a fight.

At first glance, it might seem impossible for a garrison of 6,000 Egyptian troops, many of whom were understandably suffering from low morale, to stand even the slightest chance against the sheer number of warriors now arrayed against them. However, this belief almost lost Muhammad Ahmed the coming battle, since he was unprepared for the determined resistance of the well-armed defenders, who not only strengthened their defences while their adversary pondered his next move, but also benefited from the presence of an able commander. Unlike those Muhammad Ahmed had defeated earlier, Muhammad Said knew what he was doing.

The battle for El Obeid began on 8 September, when the *Mahdi's* forces attempted to rush the town in a somewhat ill-calculated, all-out frontal assault. As the mass of *Ansar* warriors charged forward, Muhammad Said's men opened a heavy and murderous fire into their ranks. Muhammad Ahmed's remaining older brother, Muhammad, managed to lead a group of *Ansar* forward and break into a *zariba*, but as he did so, a number of hidden defenders suddenly appeared as if from nowhere and delivered devastating volleys into the attackers. The first attack on El Obeid would prove to be a disaster for the *Mahdi*, with an estimated 10,000 *Ansar* warriors either killed or wounded, as opposed to less than 290 lost by the garrison.

Fortune, however, would eventually smile on the *Mahdi*, because Muhammad Said failed to go on the offensive in pursuit of his stunned and wounded enemy. This lack of action allowed Muhammad Ahmed to reorganise and return to continue the siege. In addition, a 2,500 strong relief force sent to El Obeid from Khartoum by Abd-al-Qadir Hilmi, and led by Ali *Bey* Lutfi, was destroyed by the *Ansar* near Bara, itself now also under siege.

The siege of El Obeid would drag on for months, during which a comet was seen in the sky; the garrison took this event for a bad omen, while those who supported the *Mahdi* viewed it as proof of the righteousness of their leader. As the weeks turned to months, food supplies within the city slowly began to dwindle and morale among the defenders dropped further. Many within the town began to fall ill, while others became victim of the *Mahdi*'s snipers who constantly watched the outer defences for movement and the chance of a kill. To exacerbate falling morale even further, news of the fall of Barra reached the El Obeid garrison and its civilian residents in early January 1883. It seemed the same fate now almost certainly awaited the hungry defenders of El Obeid.

Eventually, Muhammad Said decided to do what had previously been unthinkable—surrender to Muhammad Ahmed. On 19 January, the town of El Obeid accepted surrender terms laid down to them by the *Mahdi*, and yet another victory was handed to the fanatical Islamic religious leader. By this time, only around 3,500 of the original garrison were still alive, many of which, fearing being put to death, were left with little choice but to swear allegiance to the *Mahdi* and agree to fight for him. The surrender of the garrison also saw over 6,000 rifles fall into the hands of the *Ansar*, along with sizeable stocks of ammunition. Reversing his decision not to use captured Egyptian weapons, these were now gathered up and distributed among the *Ansar* warriors on the *Mahdi*'s instructions. Artillery, too, was now available from the spoils of the town, and those who once operated the guns on the orders of Muhammad Said were now forced to do so on the orders of Muhammad Ahmed.

El Obeid was also plundered for anything of value, and, being a relatively wealthy town, the plunderers found much in the way of money, gold, silver, and other precious items. Many notable figures within the town were executed, and Muhammad Said, along with his deputy, Ali Sharif, would not survive; the former was beheaded on the orders of *Sheikh* Ismail at Alloba, while the latter suffered a botched execution—the blow of a sword failing to properly cut off his head, after which he was thrown alive down a well where he died an agonising death. The *Mahdi*, now basing himself at El Obeid, next looked towards Khartoum itself.

While events were becoming increasingly desperate in Sudan, the financial crisis in Egypt—and the inevitable growing discontent among the Egyptian people as a result—was about to come to a head. The Egyptian Army was also beginning to feel the strain, with huge cuts made to its budget, which resulted in the sacking of thousands of troops and reduced prospects for promotion for its officers. There were even acts of discrimination against certain officers; their only crime was being born Arabic speakers. After years of strain, the army had finally had enough and rebelled against their *Khedive*, the young Tewfik.

The army expressed its discontent through one of its own officers, a colonel by the name of Ahmed Arabi, who was an ardent nationalist. Previously, in 1881, he had presented the *Khedive* with a petition that outlined the grievances of the Egyptian Army, which the seemingly interested Tewfik promised to address. The move was seen as a victory for Arabi, which in turn made him increasingly popular among nationalist supporters. The following year, both the British and the French publically announced their support of the *Khedive*, which merely rendered the Egyptian ruler, in the eyes of the Egyptian people, as nothing more than the puppet of the two European powers, who were increasingly exerting political influence over the country through the huge debts owing. Resentment of this interference from London and Paris grew, and so did support for the nationalists. Before long, Arabi was appointed war minister, a post in which he learned of the Egyptian defeats in Sudan; due to the inaction of the *Khedive*, he was unable to send the troops he would have liked to reinforce the forces based at Khartoum.

By early 1882, serious civil unrest in Egypt was threatening, and Arabi found himself receiving encouraging messages of support from Constantinople, the *Sultan* had had enough of the weak Tewfik. On 14 March, Arabi was promoted to brigadier-general—not by the *Khedive* but by the *Sultan*—and granted the title 'Pasha'. Arabi *Pasha* was also awarded the Order of the Medjidieh First Class on 24 June. He had become popular with Constantinople and many of the Egyptian people, and, perhaps most importantly, had the full support of the army.

Public disorder, however, continued to get worse, and the port city of Alexandria was fast becoming a centre for the nationalists. On 11 June, riots broke out which resulted in the killing of fifty non-Egyptian nationals, as resentment towards foreigners reached fever pitch. Naturally, many foreigners now began to flee Egypt, concerned a similar fate may await them and their property. The situation was deteriorating rapidly.

William Ewart Gladstone, the British prime minister, began to grow concerned for the security of the Suez Canal, the all-important artery to British India. In response, with international support, particularly from Paris, he ordered Royal Navy warships in the Mediterranean to sail for Alexandria and take up station off the coast. This use of gunboat diplomacy, a regular feature of Victorian international politics, did not sway the nationalists; thus, on 12 July, the guns of the mighty Royal Navy opened a bombardment of the city. The shells devastated sections of Alexandria, after which British troops were put ashore in order to show support for the now useless Tewfik, and put an end to what was seen as Arabi *Pasha*'s rebellion.

A month later, on 13 August, Lieutenant-General Sir Garnet Wolseley arrived to take command of a substantial British expedition to Egypt. The ensuing campaign would last a mere thirty-days, with the British defeating Arabi *Pasha*'s army at the Battle of Tel el-Kebir on 13 September. The Egyptian general fled the battle scene but was later captured and put on trial, and, after being found guilty of armed revolt, was sentenced to death. Tewfik, however, commuted the death sentence, since the British felt it would merely make Arabi a martyr in the eyes of many ordinary Egyptians; instead, he was sent into exile to Ceylon. The *Khedive*, however, remained weak, and so the British had no realistic option but to retain its forces in Egypt until such a point the Egyptian ruler was deemed in a more secure position.

As part of this strengthening of the *Khedive*'s authority, the Egyptian Army needed to be rebuilt, a not inconsiderable task that would be given to Major-General Sir Evelyn Wood. A civilian consul-general was also appointed, in the form Evelyn Baring, while Lord Dufferin was moved from his post as ambassador at Constantinople to Cairo to carry out a similar rebuilding of the Egyptian civil service. As the newly installed authorities set about their work, it would not be long until the ongoing crisis in Sudan became a British problem. Ideally for London, the *Khedive* would agree to abandon Sudan, thus allowing the former to concentrate on reconstructing Egypt. Tewfik bluntly and resolutely refused to let go of his territories south of the Egyptian border. In turn, the British refused to get involved, thus leaving Abd-al-Qadir Hilmi at Khartoum to resolve his problems on his own. They did, however, despatch Lieutenant-Colonel Donald Stewart, an officer of the 11th Hussars, to conduct a secret reconnaissance of Sudan in order to acquire intelligence.

In early 1883, with no prospect of help from the British, the *Khedive* took it upon himself to attempt to deal with the Mahdist uprising. To do this, he selected Colonel William Hicks, a retired British Army officer who had seen active service during the Indian Mutiny and the British expedition to Abyssinia. He did not, however, have any experience of Sudan, but no serving British officers would be permitted to lead the relief expedition being proposed by the Egyptian ruler. Unfortunately for the *Khedive*, he had chosen a man of somewhat weak character, who was seen by his fellow British officers as honest but indecisive, and arguably ill-suited to the position now offered him.

Arriving in Cairo, the fifty-three-year-old Hicks was made a major-general in the Egyptian Army and given command of a sizeable force. His new army, however, was not of particularly good quality, since many were unenthusiastic conscripts, while others were rejects from the newly reconstructed Egyptian Army or otherwise disgraced soldiers of Arabi *Pasha*'s rebellion. These men were treated little better than prisoners, given harsh punishments for the slightest of crimes, and routinely abused by their own non-commissioned officers. Desertion, as a result, was a persistent problem; it was with these low grade and reluctant troops that Hicks was being asked to take on a fanatical enemy who were willing to lay down their lives in the name of the *Mahdi*.

The general plan was to go on the offensive against Muhammad Ahmed and retake both El Obeid and Bara, after which he was to destroy the *Mahdi* and his army. Stewart, from his observations in Sudan, held the view that Hicks' intended operations in Kordofan were doomed from the start; when the two men met face-to-face in Khartoum in March, he told the major-general so. Hicks, however, ignored the colonel and pushed on with his plans regardless. The following month, the major-general led some four and a half battalions of infantry, supported by a number of Sudanese Bashi Bazouk mounted mercenaries, four Nordenfelt machine guns and some artillery out of Khartoum. His first confrontation with the *Ansar* came on the 29th at *Jebel* Ain, where he gave orders to his troops to form defensive squares. Pouring intense rifle and machine gun fire into the ranks of the attacking Mahdists, as well as using his artillery, the British commander inflicted a heavy defeat on his enemy. Over 500 *Ansar* warriors were claimed to have been killed for only seven casualties among the Egyptian force; Hicks felt vindicated in ignoring Stewart's advice.

On 9 September, Hicks *Pasha*, as he had become known, marched out again with the intention of retaking El Obeid, a campaign that would last for over two months and end on 5 November in total disaster. Encountering substantial numbers of Muhammad Ahmed's warriors on the 3rd, the British officer ordered his troops to again form square. This time, after two days of attacks, the *Ansar* were able to break into the square, after which Hicks' entire force was all-but destroyed, the major-general himself also being killed. In all, some 7,000 of Hicks' men lost their lives, while several thousand *Ansar* were also believed to have perished. Rudolf Carl von Slatin, then a colonel in the Egyptian Army, stated:

> With the exception of two or three hundred who had escaped death by hiding themselves under heaps of dead bodies, the entire force had been annihilated. Little mercy was shown; a few of the survivors were pardoned, but the majority of them were subsequently executed. Ahmed ed Dalia, the *Mahdi*'s executioner, told me that he and Yakub, *Khalifa* Abdullahi's brother, with a few hundred horsemen, came across a party of about one hundred Egyptians who showed fight.... Yakub sent them a message that their lives would be spared if they gave up their arms; but no sooner had they done so than he and his men, calling them unfaithful dogs, charged, and killed every one.

With the battle over, the *Mahdi*'s men set about gathering up the substantial number of Egyptian weapons now lying on the battlefield; these included thousands of modern Remington rifles, Krupp field guns, and Nordenfelt machine guns, not to mention substantial stocks of ammunition.

This latest victory for the *Mahdi* encouraged yet further tribesmen to flock to his banner, and the ongoing *jihad* against the Egyptian and Sudanese authorities was becoming increasingly powerful. One particularly influential local Sudanese leader, who had by now joined the Mahdist cause, was Osman Digna, adding his own Hadendowa followers of the Beja tribe to the *Ansar*. Interestingly, it would be these very men that Kipling would later refer to in some of his poems as the 'fuzzy-wuzzies'. Osman Digna, as will be seen, would play an important role in Muhammad Ahmed's later operations and *bey*ond.

Despite their reluctance in getting involved in Sudan, the British would quickly be sucked into the rebellion. Indeed, Khartoum would soon see a familiar face return to the city, in the form of one of the most famous British military men in history, General Charles George Gordon.

2

The Death of General Gordon

The destruction of Hicks *Pasha*'s expedition merely reinforced the British view, particularly the opinion of the Liberal Prime Minister Gladstone, that the ongoing problems in Sudan—which was increasingly falling under the control of the *Mahdi*—were not worth getting involved in. Indeed, the British Government at this time had no appetite whatsoever for sending British troops, who would no doubt suffer substantial casualties in combat against the *Ansar*, to bail out Tewfik's beleaguered garrisons. The official line was to continue to attempt to persuade the *Khedive* to abandon the territory altogether, allowing the Egyptians to concentrate on issues within their own borders. Hicks had acted without the official sanction of the British Government, and London now sought to distance itself from his spectacular failure.

However, there were those, including Sir Evelyn Baring, who were of the opinion that the fall of Khartoum, which was surely Muhammad Ahmed's chief goal, would ultimately put Egypt at increased risk. This in turn would potentially result in the retaining of British forces in the country for far longer than was desirable. It was also recognised by the British Government that it could not itself take the decision to sever Egypt's relationship with Sudan, since both countries were technically part of the Ottoman Empire and the *Sultan* may not be willing to lose one of his territories. That said, the Ottoman ruler was not in a position to send military forces himself to wrestle control of Sudan away from the rebellious *Mahdi*, due to financial reasons. Tewfik also continued to be reluctant to abandon what he saw as part of his own personal empire. Even for the British, Sudan had already become a highly complicated matter, and one they had probably not foreseen when they invaded Egypt in 1882.

Despite their hesitation in getting involved, serious consideration by the British, however, had to be given to the question of how best to extricate Egyptian troops from Khartoum without having to deploy substantial numbers of British soldiers in order to do it. To answer this, the British Government turned to the one man who had vast experience of Sudan, General Gordon. Although he admired the general, Gladstone also knew Gordon might openly oppose his policy of abandoning the country, and so the entire matter would have to be handled with the greatest of care and political expertise. No one else was seen as suitably qualified for the difficult and unenviable task ahead, and so, in January 1884, the decision was made—Gordon would go back to Khartoum.

Charles Gordon was born on 28 January 1833 in Woolwich, near London, being the son of a senior army officer in the artillery. Following in his father's footsteps, Gordon joined the British Army in 1852 and was commissioned a second-lieutenant in the Royal Engineers. Active service soon followed when he was sent to Crimea, where he would distinguish himself by showing reckless bravery in the trenches during the siege of Sebastopol. By 1859, he had been promoted to captain, and, the following year, volunteered to join British forces heading for China during the Second Anglo-Chinese War, after which he was present in the subsequent occupation of Beijing. Several years later, he would take command of the so-called 'Ever Victorious Army', which had been raised to defend the city of Shanghai when it was threatened during the Taiping Rebellion. Upon his return to England, the public dubbed him 'Chinese Gordon' and he took up an appointment as commander of Royal Engineers at Gravesend in Kent for the next five years. However, it would be in 1873 that Gordon first went to Sudan, after Ismail *Pasha* offered him the position of governor of Equatoria, before becoming governor-general of all Sudan several years later. As has been previously mentioned, he exerted much energy in the destruction of the slave trade in Sudan, resulting in him suffering poor health, which eventually forced him to return to England in order to recuperate. Gordon was also noted for being a somewhat unorthodox Christian who believed in reincarnation.

With hindsight, it seems as though the British Government was asking for trouble appointing Gordon to undertake this important mission. The general certainly made no secret about his desire to defeat the *Ansar* and retake Mahdist controlled territory for the *Khedive*. Additionally, it is arguable that, despite his previous, considerable experience of Sudan, Gordon had no knowledge of the phenomenon that was now spreading like wildfire in the country—the fast growing support of Mahdism—since it had begun after his return to England. Nor was he popular with many of the ordinary people in Sudan, owing to his crackdown on the slave trade, putting many Sudanese out of business—a business that was both long-established and lucrative.

Regardless of these issues, an enthusiastic Gordon departed England and arrived in Cairo in late January, where, on instructions from Lord Granville, the British foreign-secretary, he was to report to Baring. The latter, however, was opposed to the general's re-appointment as governor-general of Khartoum; after all, he was very much aware of Gordon's feelings regarding Sudan and its capital. Similarly, the British general had no love for Tewfik, who he viewed as weak and ineffective, but the Egyptian ruler nevertheless agreed to Gordon's appointment and issued the necessary *firman*. With the formalities over, the general boarded a train on the 26th, and set off for Khartoum.

Joining Gordon at Khartoum were Colonel Stewart, as *aide-de-camp*, who himself had by now gained an in-depth knowledge of Sudan and its people, and Ibrahim Fawzi *Pasha*, who had once served as governor of Equatoria but had fallen from grace following charges of misconduct. Narrowly escaping a death sentence, Fawzi had been serving a term in prison when the British general arrived, who was willing to give him a second chance.

As he journeyed south, Gordon issued what seems today an extraordinary offer to the *Mahdi*, promising to recognise him as the '*Sultan* of Kordofan' and asking him to meet for talks. Muhammad Ahmed was somewhat bemused by this offer, since he already controlled the territory—and much more besides—that the British general was now promising him. Father Ohrwalder recalled the reaction when Gordon's letter arrived:

> A few days later he [the *Mahdi*] received a letter from Gordon, and the anxiety to know what it contained was enormous. Nothing else was talked about, and when the *Mahdi* ordered the letter to be read in public the disappointment was very great.
>
> In this letter Gordon offered the *Mahdi* the whole of the Western Sudan, of which he said he should be considered the *Sultan*. He authorised the continuance of the slave trade, and free transit to all pilgrims going to Mecca; and, in conclusion, he asked for the release of the prisoners. The *Mahdi* laughed at Gordon's proposals, and thought him a very cunning unbeliever, who was attempting to delude him with vain promises merely to gain time. He could not understand how it was Gordon came to offer him what he already possessed some time ago; and he remarked that the very ground on which Gordon was standing was practically in his hands. The fact that Gordon had brought no troops with him served to further increase his pride, and his reply was couched in the following terms:—He said that when he was at Abba Island he had warned the Government officials that if they refused to recognise him as the *Mahdi*, they would undoubtedly perish. He had repeated the same warning to Yusef *Pasha* Esh Shellali, and to Hicks *Pasha*. He informed him of the surrender of Darfur, and concluded by saying that he had no desire for worldly benefits. His object was to reform the people, and he invited Gordon to come and join him. With the letter the *Mahdi* sent him a complete set of Dervish garments, viz., a jibbeh, takia, turban, girth, and pair of sandals.

It was around this time that Muhammad Ahmed abandoned El Obeid as his base of operations, a decision forced on him due to the fact his *Ansar* was now so numerous and fast growing that the town could no longer provide the supplies—particularly water—that was required to sustain the army. Instead, the

Mahdi installed himself at Rahad to the south-east, where he began planning his capture of Khartoum. However, before he could begin his move on the Sudanese capital, he first had to deal with several other issues that were preventing his final advance, such as gaining total dominance of the Nuba Mountains, which would take a number of months to complete.

Meanwhile, Gordon finally arrived in Khartoum aboard the steamer *Ismailia*, on 18 February; to his relief no siege had yet been started by Muhammad Ahmed. The welcome he received was a warm one, including an artillery salute from the Omdurman fort and joyous scenes from the ordinary people of the city. Addressing the people, he made two proclamations, the first aimed at the 'Notables of the Soudan':

> In accordance with an agreement between Great Britain and the *Khedive*, I have been named *Vali* of the Soudan. In consequence thereof, this country has become independent and *autonome*, and I have given orders in this sense to all the Mudirs and employés of the Government. I am decided to give you back the happiness and prosperity which you enjoyed formerly under His Highness Saïd *Pasha*. Know also that His Majesty the *Sultan*, Emir of believers and Khalife of God, had the intention to send, in order to restore order, a powerful *corps d'armée* composed of Turkish soldiers famed for their courage and valor. But I have preserved, from four years passed in the Soudan as Governor-General, a great affection for you. I have had pity of your situation, and I have contributed with all my force to prevent the sending of these Turkish troops. I have come myself, hoping to put an end to the effusion of blood, which is against the will of God, of his prophet, and of his saints. You have heard that for your good, and to obviate all complaints, I have formed a council composed of *Moulouks* of the Soudan, and it is they who will govern in the future. This council will assemble twice a week, and oftener if it is judged necessary.
>
> I abandon to you all the unpaid taxes and imposts up to the end of 1883, also the half of that which you ought to pay now. That which I do by this present, is to show you my desire to give you back your happiness and prosperity, and to establish among you that justice which constitutes the progress of a country.
>
> Believe that which I say, for I call God to witness that it is the truth.

His second—and much shorter—proclamation, which was in direct contradiction to his previous efforts to supress the slave trade, was addressed to the ordinary 'People of the Soudan':

> My desire is very great to give you peace and tranquillity. I know that the hardship which opposition to the slave traffic had caused you is very great. To-day I desire you recommence with perfect freedom the traffic in slaves, and I have given orders that public criers shall make this known to all, that they may

dispose of their domestics as they may see proper, and no one in the future shall interfere with the commerce.

Neither proclomation mentioned the intended abandonment of Sudan, nor the planned evacuation of Egyptian forces from the city. His reversal of policy regarding the slave trade appeared welcomed, which was no doubt aimed at winning over many in his audience, but it would be less well-received back in Britain and elsewhere. After all, Britain had prided itself as being the leader in anti-slavery for many years.

Gordon's next task was to organise the defences of Khartoum in readiness for the expected attack by the *Mahdi*. The city itself was surrounded on the southern and eastern sides by almost fifteen miles of fortifications, most of which consisteed of ditches and roughly constructed ramparts with a number of bastions or forts at certain points. To the north and west were the Blue and White Niles respectively, which presented a formidable barrier to any attacker. To man the defences, the general had around 7,500 men, of which 1,500 were regular soldiers of the Egyptian Army and 5,000 were militiamen, the balance being made up by various other volunteers. Such numbers proved too few to effectively hold the line, but constructing a new, shorter line was impossible in the limited time available. Instead, orders were issued to make what improvements were possible to the existing defences, including the use of artillery shells as makeshift landmines, sharpened iron stakes, wire entanglements, and wooden boxes filled with explosives and packed with nails or broken glass, the latter of which could be remotely detonated via fuzes.

The fort at Omdurman was only lightly defended, so Gordon sent some of his troops to reinforce the defenders, while all available provisions were audited. Thankfully for the garrison, a substantial number of modern firearms and large stocks of ammunition were found, although some of the latter were for older weapons and thus of little use. In addition, two Krupp 20-pounder guns were found, as well as eleven older 7-pounder brass mountain-guns, ten smaller guns of varying type and quality, and several Nordenfelt and Gardner machine guns. Finally, orders were given for all Europeans found in the city to be evacuated and sent to Egypt, since their likely fate at the hands of the *Ansar* would be a grim one at best. Not all would, however, be willing to leave.

The siege of Khartoum began on 13 March 1884, when 30,000 *Ansar* warriors advanced on the city under the command of one of Muhammad Ahmed's brothers-in-law. Leading elements of this force clashed with members of Gordon's garrison who were holding Halfaya, a position located a few miles from Khartoum on the eastern-bank of the Nile. This brutal skirmish would last for about five hours and end in the retreat of part of the garrison back towards the city, while others were left behind, cut-off and with no choice but to surrender. Thus, the first action of the long siege ahead resulted in defeat for Gordon and another, albeit minor, victory for the *Mahdi*.

A few days later, on the 16th, Gordon decided to retake Halfaya, sending out a sizeable force that managed to push back a number of warriors of the *Ansar* left holding the position. However, the sortie ended in disaster when two high-ranking Egyptian Army officers betrayed Gordon by ordering the supporting artillery to cease fire. This sudden lifting of the artillery barrage allowed the *Mahdi*'s men to fight back and drive off the garrison once again. As a result, a quantity of guns, ammunition, transports, and other supplies fell into the hands of the Mahdists. Later, both officers were put on trial, convicted, and executed by firing squad for treason.

News of Gordon's plight of becoming besieged at Khartoum soon reached the attention of the British public, who, increasingly fuelled by a critical media, were turning against Gladstone's apparent lack of action and support for their beloved general. Even Queen Victoria expressed her personal disgust of the fact that one of her generals was seemingly being abandoned by his fellow countrymen. Eventually, after Lord Hartington, the secretary of state for war, threatened to resign over the issue, the prime minister reluctantly agreed to authorise a relief force to be sent to Sudan in order to extricate Gordon. Funding for the expedition was voted for by Parliament on 5 August, and Sir Garnet Wolseley, who arrived in Cairo on 9 September, was appointed to overall command of the expeditionary force.

Wolseley, who was the same age as Gordon, had been born in 1833 in Golden Bridge, County Dublin in Ireland, being the son of an army major. He joined the British Army in 1852 and saw active service in the Second Anglo-Burmese War, the Crimean War, and the Indian Mutiny. During these campaigns, he would be wounded a number of times, including the loss of sight in one of his eyes. However, at the age of only twenty-five, he would become the youngest lieutenant-colonel in the army following a series of rapid promotions. As well as later serving in the Second Anglo-Chinese War, Wolseley was sent to Canada in 1863 in order to increase its defences in response to fears of possible invasion by the Americans, who, at that time, were in the middle of a civil war. While in Canada, he commanded the Red River Expedition sent against the rebellious Louis Riel in 1870. After leaving North America, more active service would follow, this time leading a punitive expedition against the Ashanti in 1873, before moving to South Africa to supersede Lord Chelmsford during the Anglo-Zulu War of 1879—although the latter finally defeated the Zulus at Ulundi before Wolseley arrived. He headed back to England in 1880 to take up the position of quartermaster general at the War Office, after which he became adjutant-general several years later, the latter post he held when he received orders to leave for Cairo to put down Arabi *Pasha*'s nationalist revolt.

It would, however, take time for Wolseley to assemble his troops, many of which had to sail from Portsmouth in England and disembark at Alexandria. Others came from Gibraltar and Malta, while some would have to travel from as far away as India. Once in Egypt, a number of men were trained to ride camels—which proved to be an interesting experience for many of them—forming the now much-lauded camel regiments. A camp was established at Korti, under the command of Brigadier-General Sir Herbert Stewart (not to be confused with Lieutenant-Colonel John Stewart, who was with Gordon at Khartoum), which became the concentration point for many of the units arriving to form the expedition. Wolseley himself arrived at Korti on 16 December, but it would not be until the end of the month before the general was ready to begin his advance.

The expedition would be split into two, including a Desert Column under the command of Brigadier-General Stewart and a River Column under the command of Major-General William Earle. The former, mounted on camels, would advance across the Bayuda Desert towards Metammeh, securing the oases at Gakdul and Abu Klea as it did so. Meanwhile, the latter would sail up the Nile with the aim of linking up with the Desert Column at Metammeh, capturing Abu Hamed and flushing out the *Mahdi*'s men who were occupying Berber. To make the advance up the Nile possible, orders had been placed for the construction of 800 whaling gigs, each capable of carrying ten soldiers with their kit plus two crew. These little wooden boats were to be operated by sailors and voyageurs, with over 380 of the latter river men recruited from Canada. Initially, they would be towed up the river to *Wadi* Halfa by paddle steamers provided by the Thomas Cook travel agency, after which they would be powered by sail, the use of oars or otherwise carried by *kroomen*.

On 30 December, a messenger came in from Gordon with a note for Wolseley explaining the current military situation at Khartoum:

> We are besieged on three sides, Omdurman, Halfiyeh and Khojali. Fighting goes on day and night. Enemy cannot take us, except by starving us out. Do not scatter your troops. Enemy are numerous. Bring plenty of troops if you can. We still hold Omdurman on the left bank and the fort on the right bank. The *Mahdi*'s people have thrown up earthworks within rifle-shot of Omdurman. The *Mahdi* lives out of gun-shot. About four weeks ago the *Mahdi*'s people attacked Omdurman and disabled one steamer. We disabled one of the *Mahdi*'s guns. Three days after fighting was renewed on the south and the rebels were again driven back.

He then went on to describe how desperate the situation—mainly due to the lack of supplies—was becoming in the Sudanese capital:

> Our troops in Khartoum are suffering from lack of provisions. Food we still have is little; some grain and biscuit. We want you to come quickly. You should come by Metammeh or Berber. Make by these two roads. Do not leave Berber in your rear. Keep enemy in your front and when you have taken Berber send me word

from Berber. Do this without letting rumours of your approach spread abroad. In Khartoum there are no butter nor dates, and little meat. All food is very dear.

On the same day as the note was received, Stewart's Desert Column left Korti, arriving at Gakdul on the 2 January 1885, where he ordered the Royal Engineers and some of the camel regiments to hold the position while he marched back to Korti in order to bring up further supplies. He again left Korti on the 8th and arrived back at Gakdul four days later. Earle's River Column left Korti on the 3rd, when it began to board the steamers and whaling gigs for the advance up the Nile. Stewart would move out of Gakdul on the 14th for his advance on Abu Klea, and, two days later, when he was within three miles of the oasis, he gave orders for his force of 1,800 military men and 350 non-European personnel to halt. Scouts had been sent on ahead to reconnoitre and a message was received from Lieutenant-Colonel Percy Barrow of the 19th Hussars, who reported seeing about fifty of the enemy on hills four miles to the north-east of Abu Klea. It later became apparent that the *Ansar* was present in the area in force; their number was later estimated by Colonel Sir Charles Wilson, the intelligence officer attached to the column, to be between 9,000 and 11,000 men, while Stewart himself thought the total number later engaged was around 10,000. Since it was already 2 p.m., the brigadier-general decided he would attack the following morning and ordered his force to bivouac for the night.

Stewart's men now set about building a *zariba* for their protection. Their presence was known to the *Mahdi*'s forces, who, during the night, kept up long-range harassing fire into the British camp, although little damage was done. Water supplies were beginning to run low, and the brigadier-general knew it was imperative to quickly drive off the *Ansar* in order to secure the vital wells at Abu Klea. As the morning daylight broke, orders were issued to the men to 'stand-to' and clean their rifles for the coming battle. Stewart had hoped his enemy would commence their own attack while his force was within the *zariba*, but they appeared to hesitate and no such assault was forthcoming.

At 10 a.m., Stewart marched out of the *zariba* with the majority of his men, leaving a small force behind to guard the camp and the baggage. The advance was made in square formation, with the Guards Camel Regiment, along with three 7-pounder guns, forming the front-face. As the formation moved slowly forward, *Ansar* rifle fire was aimed at the square from the front and from both flanks, wounding a number of men. A flutter of banners could be seen in the distance; as the square paused to re-dress, a large number of Mahdist warriors suddenly appeared and began shouting before making their own advance on Stewart's force. The British troops responded with a withering fire, which became increasingly heavy as their enemy drew nearer. Despite suffering many casualties to this fire, Muhammad Ahmed's warriors charged on regardless.

A near-disaster then struck the British force when, according to Stewart:

> The rear portion of this face [the more advanced left-front portion of the square] taking a moment or two to close up, was not in such a favourable position to receive the enemy's attack, and I regret to say that the square was penetrated at this point by the sheer weight of the enemy's numbers.

However, the *Ansar* warriors who managed to get inside the square were quickly dealt with at the point of the bayonet. Stewart went on:

> The steadiness of the troops enabled the hand to hand conflict to be maintained, whilst severe punishment was still being meted out to those of the enemy continuing to advance, with the result that a general retreat of the enemy under a heavy artillery and rifle fire soon took place.

Having neutralised this threat, the square was reformed, and the 19th Hussars, who had been attempting to cover the left-flank, now made a dash for the wells at Abu Klea. By 5 p.m., these were finally secured and the battle was effectively over. British casualties amounted to nine officers killed and another nine wounded, while sixty-six other ranks were also killed and a further eighty-three wounded. Estimates of *Ansar* casualties were, as often was the case, more difficult to determine, although Stewart believed that no less than 800 were left dead on the field and that the number of their wounded was 'exceptional'. Although he would have liked to have immediately recommenced his advance on Metammeh, the brigadier-general had to halt at Abu Klea in order to replenish his much-needed water supplies. The wounded would also have to be left behind at Abu Klea, under the guard of a detachment of the Royal Sussex Regiment.

On the 18th, Stewart's force resumed its advance with the 19th Hussars leading. It would be early the following morning that cavalry scouts brought in information that a body of *Ansar* warriors were waiting about a mile and a half ahead. More scouts were sent out, who found what appeared to be a substantial body of the enemy, who were themselves marching out of Metammeh and heading towards the Desert Column. Upon receiving this news, Stewart ordered his men to make a *zariba* near a place called Abu Kru.

As the warriors grew closer to the British column, an erratic fire was directed at the *zariba*. This fire resulted in a sizeable number of casualties among the British, including Stewart himself. Wilson, perhaps realising the brigadier-general's wounds were mortal, assumed command of the column. Leaving 300 men in the *zariba* to guard the guns and baggage, the colonel ordered his men to form square and advance to the Nile River, the banks of which were some four miles away. However, Wilson's square was under constant harassment from the *Ansar*, slowing the advance so much that, after two painful hours, only one and a half miles had been covered before the *Mahdi*'s men launched the first of two major assaults of the action. However, despite the fanatical courage of the *Ansar* warriors, both attacks were repulsed by rifle fire from the disciplined British soldiers. The action of Abu Kru then came to an abrupt end after the Mahdists simply gave up and left the field. Two officers (one of which actually died of his wounds after the battle), two war correspondents, and twenty-four enlisted men were killed, while a further eighty-five to ninety were wounded.

With a force of about 1,000 men, Wilson marched on Metammeh on the 21st. In his later dispatch of 14 March 1885, he described what happened next:

> … a garrison having been left in camp to protect the wounded, the force marched towards Matammeh, which was found to be a long village of mud houses with loop-holed walls and two or three mountain guns. Whilst the reconnaisance was in progress, four Egyptian steamers, under Nushi *Pasha*, appeared and landed a contingent under Khashm el Mus *Bey*, which took part in the operations. Whilst the guns were attempting to form a breach in the wall, Khashm el Mus informed me that he had seen the force under Feki Mustapha marching down the left bank, and that it would reach Matammeh before sunset, or very early next morning. It was, therefore, probable that the force would have to fight an unbeaten portion of the enemy within the next twenty-four hours, and as it had already lost one-tenth of its effective strength, and there were over 100 wounded in hospital, I hesitated to press an attack, which could not have been carried to a successful issue without further heavy losses. I also considered that the town was too large for the force to hold after the losses it had sustained, and the return of the convoy and escort to Jakdul. Under these circumstances I determined to withdraw without pressing the attack, and at the same time made arrangements for bringing in Major Davison and the stores which-had-been-left at the zeribah.

Throughout the months of May and June 1884, the Mahdists had progressively put pressure on the city of Khartoum and its defenders. Food stocks became dangerously low and many began to feel the effects of starvation, which was coupled with ever decreasing morale. During August, Gordon gave instructions to Colonel Muhammad Ali Hussein—who has been described as one of the British general's best officers, and was known as 'The Fighting *Pasha*'—to conduct a number of sorties outside the city against Muhammad Ahmed's besieging forces.

On 27 July, Gordon gave orders for an attack to be made on the *Ansar* from the fort at Burri, which included the use of 800 Egyptian soldiers and militiamen, as well as four armoured stamers under the command of Muhammad Ali. As the troops advanced in squares along the river, the steamers opened a heavy fire on the *Mahdi*'s men using their guns and the rifles of other troops posted onboard. The attack was a success and it was quickly followed by another towards Halfaya, which enjoyed similar success when it drove off *Ansar* warriors holding the post.

However, despite these successes, Muhammad Ahmed remained undeterred, especially since many thousands of additional followers were still arriving near Khartoum to join in the besieging of the city.

In September, Muhammad Ali led a steamer expedition to al-Alayfun, located about twenty miles south of Khartoum on the Blue Nile, which ended in disaster for the Fighting *Pasha*. After capturing the town, Muhammad Ali became overly confident and gave orders to his men to pursue some fleeing warriors into nearby woods. Unfortunately, the guides leading the way turned against their fellow soldiers and led them directly into a waiting trap. The expedition ended with the death of Muhammad Ali and a thousand of his men. Additionally, a thousand modern Remington rifles—and another substantial quantity of ammunition—fell into the hands of the Mahdists.

Gordon was by now growing very concerned for the defence of Khartoum, and so he instructed Colonel Stewart and Frank Power, a correspondent for *The Times* newspaper, to board the steamer *Abbas* and leave the city in the hope of getting word of the dire circumstances within the city to the outside world; this, in turn, he hoped would result in greater efforts to relieve the siege. Unfortunately for the British general, the steamer was captured between Abu Hamed and Merowi, with both Stewart and Power being taken prisoner and later put to death.

Food stocks became so low that many of the inhabitants of Khartoum resorted to eating donkeys and dogs, although famine would finally prevail. Many began to suffer from diarrhoea, and death became commonplace, with corpses seen lying abandoned on the streets, since no one had enough energy to dispose of them. Soldiers, too, became so weak that they could not adequately man the defences. The Mahdists kept up their harassment of the defenders, picking some off with long range rifle fire, while also keeping up night attacks on the outer defences.

On 6 January 1885, Gordon, fearing the fast-depleting stocks of food were about to run out completely, issued a proclamation to the effect that any of the civilian population who wanted to leave the city and go over to the *Mahdi* would be allowed to do so. As many as 20,000 seized the opportunity to escape what they felt was now a lost cause and decided to take their chances with the enemy. In an attempt to ensure these people enjoyed a safe passage, Gordon wrote a letter to Muhammad Ahmed asking him to feed and look after them, after all they were 'poor Moslem people', who the British general had himself fed and looked after for months.

Gordon did his best to reassure the remaining people of Khartoum that a British relief expedition was on its way and that it would not be long before it would finally arrive. Every day, Gordon would go up onto the roof of his palace in the hope of spotting Wolseley's approaching army, yet each day brought only bitter disappointment. Some of the inhabitants of the city had lost so much faith in the British officer that they began to conduct secret communications with the *Mahdi,* in the vain hope of switching their allegiance to him to save their lives in the event of the city being captured.

It should perhaps be noted that the feeling of anxiety and worry of defeat was not unique to Gordon and the citizens of Khartoum. Within forty-eight hours of the end of the Battle of Abu Klea, news of the British victory had reached the *Mahdi*'s camp where it caused much consternation. It is said that Muhammad Ahmed considered lifting the siege and returning to El Obeid. However, he was persuaded by Muhammad ibn Abd al-Kermin, one of the *Mahdi*'s relatives, to continue the siege and take the city by force, after which, he argued, there would still be time to retire to El Obeid or elsewhere. This argument was accepted and the siege continued, but it does show that Muhammad Ahmed's nerves were beginning to fail him.

News of the recent British victory also reached Gordon, who called for a council to be held at his palace. In attendance were Farag *Pasha*, the military commandant, a number of chief government officials, the Greek consul, and leading members of the Greek colony. Once assembled, Gordon informed his audience of the good news about Abu Klea, and that he strongly believed the relief force would arrive within only two or three days. Elated, the members of the meeting left feeling a renewed confidence that they would in fact finally prevail against the besiegers; but, as a number of days passed, it soon became apparent that the British force was not as close as had been hoped or had otherwise been held up by the Mahdists.

The strain was beginning to show on Gordon, when, on the 23rd, he had a heated argument with Farag. The encounter allegedly took place after the commandant had left a fort improperly defended, an error for which the British general had reproached him. To make matters worse, Farag informed Gordon that it was his opinion that it was now time to consider surrendering Khartoum to the *Mahdi*. Tempers became frayed and the general is said to have struck his commandant; perhaps, Farag was acting out of the knowledge that numbers of his own men had deserted the garrison and defected to the *Mahdi*, and more were likely to follow. Indeed, it has been argued that the commandant himself had been in contact with Muhammad Ahmed, and it is almost certain a number of notable civilians were sending out feelers to the besiegers in a desperate attempt to save their skins when *Ansar* warriors inevitably poured into the city.

All knew the end was now in sight, and Gordon took the decision to move the remaining stocks of ammunition and gunpowder from the city's arsenal to the Catholic Church located not far from his palace. His intention was to blow the lot up if the *Mahdi*'s men entered the city, a task made easier by the church being near to his headquarters. He also ordered the steamer *Ismailia* to be moored near the palace, in which he would instruct the remaining Europeans in the city to board and make best possible speed out of Khartoum in the event of its fall. Despite his best efforts to secure their escape, a disagreement with the Greek consul prevented the plan ever being put into action.

On the 25th, although now feeling ill, Gordon made one last appeal to all the men of Khartoum to man the fortifications in the hope that the relief force would finally arrive within the next twenty-four hours, just in the nick of time. However, as the day wore on, no sign of the British force was seen; by the time night fell, many of the soldiers manning the ramparts abandoned their positions in an attempt to find something to eat, while others failed to turn up to their posts due to being too weak to do so. Although all knew the city was living on borrowed time, none were aware that the *Mahdi* was now about to make his final bid to take Khartoum, his ultimate prize in Sudan.

It would be around 2 a.m. on the 26th that Muhammad Ahmed began his move, when some 40,000 to 50,000 men of the *Ansar* made their advance to attack. The Mahdist force was split into two divisions, the first with orders to attack Khartoum from the west between the Messalamieh Gate and the White Nile, while the second was to make its assault from the east towards Burri. The second division, however, was also instructed to reinforce the first if the attack on the White Nile was successful and it became possible to enter the city at this point. The entire advance was to be conducted as quietly as possible until the moment of the initial attack.

The *Mahdi*'s men were so silent that they were able to get right up to the ditches outside the city largely undetected under the cover of darkness. Eventually, however, they were spotted and a small number of the defenders opened fire, which the Mahdists returned with a fire of their own. Upon reaching the ditches, it became apparent that some of them were already partially filled with mud and parts of the ramparts that had fallen down into the trenches, a fact that greatly assisted the *Mahdi*'s assault. The *Ansar* warriors, who had carried with them pre-prepared bundles of brushwood to fill in the ditches to form crossing points, were quickly able to get into the outer-defence works. As the mass of warriors poured through the broken fortifications, a few of the defenders attempted to repel the attack, but they were too few to offer any meaningful resistance; in any case, much of the garrison was simply too weak from lack of food to be able to put up a fight. Muhammad Ahmed's men now managed to enter Khartoum and began attacking members of the garrison manning positions along other parts of the defences from the rear.

There were, however, some examples of more resolute resistance, including Muhammad Ibrahim, who ordered several companies of his men to form square on open ground situated between the outer-lines and the city itself. These men put up a determined fight, but eventually they were over-powered and most, including Ibrahim, were killed. Another act of courage of the garrison was demonstrated by Colonel Bakhit Betraki, who commanded the defenders positioned within the Burri Fort. Betraki and his party held their ground against overwhelming numbers of Mahdists until they were all killed. Other defenders simply made off in the hope of escaping death, including many of the troops manning the armed vessels on the White Nile. Other soldiers on Tuti Island, who had largely escaped much of the fighting throughout the assault, offered little more than a few *ad hoc* long-range rifle shots, after which they finally surrendered when the city seemed all but lost.

Once inside the city, Muhammad Ahmed's warriors almost immediately turned their attention to looting and killing anyone who got in their way. Thoughts, however, soon turned to the palace where Gordon was known to have his headquarters, possibly more in the hope of finding treasure than the British general himself. After being woken by the initial attack, Gordon had gone up onto the roof of his palace, from where he could see the mass of *Ansar* warriors pouring into the city. He had directed the fire of a gun positioned on the roof, but his enemy got so close that it could no longer be depressed low enough to fire upon them. It is said that, realising further resistance was now futile, Gordon came down from the roof and put on his white uniform, fastened his sword belt and, with revolver firmly in hand, stood near the top of a stairway in the north-eastern part of the palace to await his fate. A number of Mahdists quickly appeared and began to scramble up the stairs, at which time Gordon allegedly asked them who their leader was, only to be hit by a spear and killed in reply.

It has often been alleged that the killing of General Gordon was carried out against the orders of Muhammad Ahmed, who wanted his adversary alive in order to trade him for Arabi *Pasha*. Those who killed the general had set about hacking his body, including the severing of his head, which was then wrapped in a cloth and taken to the *Mahdi* as a prize. Upon seeing the battered head, Muhammad Ahmed was allegedly filled with rage that his instructions had not been carried out. However, Rudolf von Slatin—by now a prisoner of the *Mahdi*—was not convinced of this claim:

> When Gordon's head was brought to the *Mahdi*, [he] remarked he would have been better pleased had they taken him alive; for it was his intention to convert him [to Islam], and then hand him over to the English Government in exchange for Ahmed Arabi *Pasha*, as he hoped that the latter would have been of assistance to him in helping him to conquer Egypt. My own opinion, however, is that this regret on the part of the *Mahdi* was merely assumed; for had he expressed any wish that Gordon's life should be spared, no one would have dared diso*bey* his orders.

Whatever the truth, Gordon was dead and Khartoum was finally and firmly in the hands of Muhammad Ahmed and his thousands of fanatical followers.

While Gordon was still alive and clinging on to the hope of being rescued by Wolseley's relief force, four river steamers, which had previously been sent out from Khartoum, arrived at Wilson's position, carrying news of the increasingly desperate situation in the city. After some consideration, the colonel made the decision to use two of the vessels to make a dash for Khartoum up the river in an equally desperate hope of saving the general. However, to render the steamers suitable for the difficult task ahead, three critical days were spent installing additional armour and selecting crewmembers and soldiers to carry out the operation.

On 24 January, the steamers *Bordein* and *Telahwiya* were finally ready to set off. On board were a total of 240 Egyptian troops along with twenty red coated British soldiers of the Royal Sussex Regiment; the latter it was hoped would strike fear into the Mahdists who were well aware of the effectiveness of British firepower following Tel el-Kebir. Wilson would also travel with the little force aboard the *Bordein*, while the *Telahwiya* would tow a barge carrying grain supplies. The journey would be fraught with problems, the steamers sometimes running aground in the shallow water and the soldiers frequently engaging in firefights with Mahdist forces lined along the banks of the river.

By the 28th, Khartoum came within sight, but the large number of enemy that could be seen betrayed the fact that the city had already fallen. Wilson, saddened by his failure to rescue Gordon, had no choice but to order the vessels to head back at full speed in an attempt to escape a similar fate. The following day, the *Telahwiya* hit a rock and began to sink, with the crew and troops on board managing to transfer to the *Bordein* before it did so. However, on the 31st, the *Bordein* ran aground near Mirat Island, forcing Wilson and his men to abandon the steamer for the safety of the island. The little force would be rescued several days later by Captain Lord Charles Beresford aboard the steamer *Safieh,* after frantically fighting its way up the river to offer assistance. Fortunately for the two officers and their men, the return journey was largely uneventful.

Wolseley's bid to save Gordon had been a miserable failure, but the British would yet fight a successful action against the Mahdists. The River Column under Earle had left Korti on 28 December, heading towards Abu Hamed. When it reached Berti, on 4 February, the major-general learned of the fall of Khartoum, but, after a temporary halt, he resumed his advance four days later. Earle then ordered his men to disembark from their whale gigs and other vessels, and marched across the desert for Abu Hamed. On the 10th, he came into contact with a large body of the *Ansar*.

Before Earle's eyes were around 2,000 of the *Mahdi*'s followers, positioned on a ridge at a place known as Kirbekan. The British force consisted of approximately 1,150 men, the majority of which were infantrymen of the South Staffordshire Regiment and the Black Watch. Also present was a detachment of the 19th Hussars, as well as elements of an Egyptian camel company and several artillery pieces. Earle's plan was to conduct a feint attack to the front of the *Ansar*, while a number of companies from both British infantry regiments and the cavalry worked around the left-flank of their enemy in order to attack them in the rear.

The attack was a success, and the *Ansar* were defeated with minimal loss to the British force. However, Earle had accompanied the infantry and, while conducting a sweep of the crest of the ridge looking for any of the enemy still hiding in holes and among rocks, an *Ansar* warrior shot the major-general dead from the cover of a stone built hut. Meanwhile, having played no real part in the attack, the 19th Hussars rode off in order to find and take the enemy's camp, which was eventually located near the Shukool Pass. The day ended in victory for the British, but it cost them the commanding officers of the River Column and both the South Staffordshire Regiment and the Black Watch. Mahdist casualties were believed to have numbered in the hundreds.

Operations would continue for a short time, but, on 22 March, final orders were given for the Nile Expedition to return to Cairo, which was reached by mid-July. The Nile campaign was now officially over, but British troops would yet see further action in Sudan against the triumphant Mahdists.

3

The Long Road to War

In February 1884, British forces were also engaged in operations against the Mahdists elsewhere, in what would be Lieutenant-General Sir Gerald Graham's first expedition to Suakin, a port city in north-eastern Sudan. At about the same time as Hicks *Pasha* was facing defeat, Osman Digna's Hadendowa tribesmen, in support of Muhammad Ahmed's rising, laid siege to the Egyptian garrisons at Tokar and Sinkat. In an attempt to relieve Tokar, Major-General Valentine Baker had led out a force of *gendarmerie* from Trinkatat in January. Baker, once a British cavalry officer, had previously disgraced himself when he indecently assaulted a young woman on a train, which resulted in him being sentenced to a prison term and cashiered from the British Army. Following his release, he fought for Turkey during its war with Russia, after which he was invited to Egypt, arriving in Cairo in 1882, where he was given command of the *gendarmerie*. Unfortunately for the general, his relieving force was virtually annihilated by Osman Digna's men, on 4 February, at the First Battle of El Teb, with Baker narrowly escaping death himself. Tokar subsequently fell weeks later.

Back in London, news of yet another disaster in Sudan began to make some in government realise—rather reluctantly—that British troops would have to be deployed to restore order. Off the coast of Suakin were several naval vessels under the command of Admiral Sir William Hewitt of the Royal Navy, who was instructed to land a force at Suakin. This force consisted of both sailors and marines, supported by two Gatling guns. Orders were also issued to Graham to assemble another force—drawn from troops from Egypt, Aden and India—and sail for Suakin, where he was to disembark and attempt to relieve Tokar, which, at this point in time, had not yet fallen. Graham's force would be split into two infantry brigades under the command of Major-Generals Redvers Buller and John Davis, and a cavalry brigade under Brigadier-General Sir Herbert Stewart. By the time Graham's forces had concentrated at Suakin, the news of the fall of Tokar reached the lieutenant-general; he would no longer lead a relief force, but rather go on the offensive.

It would be on 29 February that Graham began his advance from Trinkatat with the intention of defeating Osman Digna and his tribesmen. For the advance, the infantry formed square, with mounted infantry and a detachment of the 10th Hussars advancing on ahead, while the remaining cavalry brought up the rear. The Sudanese chief soon learned of Graham's moves and concentrated a force of around 6,000 warriors near El Teb, supported by four captured Krupp guns, two Gatling guns and several other artillery pieces. Seeing the waiting Mahdists as he grew near, Graham manoeuvred his force towards his right in the hope of turning Osman Digna's left. The Mahdists then opened fire with their artillery—manned by gunners captured at Tokar, who were forced into serving the *Mahdi*—to which Graham, at a distance of about 900 yards, replied with artillery fire of his own, while the infantry were ordered to lie down to protect themselves from the *Ansar* shells.

Eventually, Osman Digna's guns were put out of action after his reluctant gunners fled the effects of the British artillery fire. Graham now ordered his infantry to get back on their feet and resume their advance, firing volleys of rifle fire as they did so. The Mahdists then conducted a mass charge at the square, forcing the men of The York and Lancaster Regiment to give ground, which resulted in the opening of a gap in the square through which a number of tribesmen rushed in. These warriors, however, were quickly dealt with by the men of the Royal Marines. Undeterred, Osman Digna's fighters carried out a second massed rush on the square from all sides, but again many were simply gunned down by the disciplined fire of the British soldiers or bayonetted at close-quarters. The battered Hadendowa tribesmen then began to withdraw. Stewart next ordered his cavalry to pursue, but as they did so, the Mahdists fought back, including the use of mounted warriors of their own. Graham later wrote of the bitter nature of the clash between the British cavalry and the Hadendowa warriors:

> The enemy, as reported by Brigadier-General Stewart, fought simply with fanaticism and spared no wounded or dismounted men, although, in most cases, instantly paying their penalty with their own lives; and it is to the desperate character of the struggle that the large proportion of deaths in the Cavalry Brigade is to be attributed.

The Second Battle of El Teb would come to an end at around 2 p.m., after Osman Digna's warriors simply gave up and left the field, leaving behind an estimated 1,500 dead, with a similar number thought to have also been wounded. British casualties were comparatively light, at around thirty to thirty-five killed and 140 to 155 wounded. Graham then resumed his march to Tokar, which he reached on 3 March.

Intelligence came in that another large body of the *Ansar* were gathering near a village called Tamai, which was located about sixteen miles to the south-west of Suakin. In response, on 10 March, Graham gave orders for The Black Watch to march out of Suakin as an advanced force and take possession of a *zariba* situated eight and a half miles away along the Sinkat Road. Twenty-four hours later, the remainder of Graham's men also marched out along the same route. On 12 March, the reunited force began an advance towards Tamai in several large squares, although the actual planned attack on the tribesmen would not be carried out until the following day.

On the day of the Battle of Tamai, Graham again ordered his men to form two squares, which were made up of Buller's 1st Brigade and Davis' 2nd Brigade, the latter leading the advance with the former following in echelon to the right-rear. The cavalry also followed in echelon to the left-rear, with detachments pushed out to the front of the advancing formations.

As Graham continued his advance, a large number of enemy tribesmen suddenly appeared and charged at his squares, the warriors being met with intense rifle volleys from the infantry. Ahead was a ravine which contained the majority of Osman Digna's army—although the tribesmen were probably under the command Mahsud Musa, a cousin of the Sudanese leader, on the day of the battle. The task of attacking this ravine was given to the men of The Black Watch, who were—against orders—followed by a number of men of the York and Lancaster Regiment. Unfortunately for Graham, the latter had left a gap in one face of Davis' square and also exposed several Gatling and Gardner machine guns, which soon became threatened by tribesmen who had commenced an attack of The Black Watch. Seeing that the guns would soon be overrun, the men of the Naval Brigade locked and secured them—to prevent the weapons being used by the enemy—before they themselves had to withdraw. Other tribesmen were, by now, putting pressure on the Royal Marines in the square, forcing it to slowly fall back until their enemy's thrust was eventually checked.

Meanwhile, Buller's square was also under attack, but 1st Brigade was enjoying more success in repelling the tribesmen, with their intense and accurate rifle fire cutting through the ranks of the warriors. Their fire was so effective that Buller, now under lessening pressure, was soon able to order some of his men to fire upon the tribesmen assaulting Davis' square. Also now supporting 2nd Brigade was the cavalry, the troopers having dismounted in order to fire upon the tribesmen with their carbines. It would not be long before the combination of fire from both squares and the cavalry forced the warriors to break off their assault and begin a retirement.

The battle entered its final stage when 2nd Brigade re-established its broken square formation, and, after a short pause of about fifteen minutes, Graham ordered his entire force to recommence its advance. Davis' brigade then opened a heavy fire on the Mahdists in the ravine, forcing them to give ground and eventually abandon their position completely. Continuing its advance, 2nd Brigade next seized the ridge above Tamai, after which the action began to die down and gradually come to an end, in what was now a clear victory for the

British. Casualties for Graham's force were somewhat heavier than at El Teb, with over 100 killed and a similar number wounded; *Ansar* losses were estimated at around 4,000, of which about half were fatal.

In his despatch of 15 March 1884, Graham felt sufficiently moved to comment on his losses at Tamai:

> Our loss was very grievous, many brave men of the Royal Highlanders and York and Lancaster devoting themselves to certain death in noble efforts to maintain the honour of their regiments.
>
> The Naval Brigade, too, fought desperately for their guns, three Officers and seven men being killed beside them; but they did not abandon them till they were locked, so that the enemy could not turn them against us.

Despite the victories at El Teb and Tamai, the British had achieved little against the Mahdists, since they still had a large and effective fighting force in the area. The *Mahdi* also still had possession of Sinkat and Tokar, as well as control of the road from Suakin to Berber. Graham, however, received orders on the 28th to conclude operations and embark his troops—except for several battalions to garrison Suakin—for their return to Egypt, which was commenced on 3 April. Graham's first expedition to Suakin was over.

Just over a year later, following news of Gordon's death at Khartoum, Graham would again receive orders to return to Suakin and lead a second expedition against Osman Digna. The need for a second campaign was due to the fact that the British were building a railway line from Suakin to Berber, which was being constructed to assist in the deployment of troops but which was under threat from the Hadendowa. The aim of the new expedition, therefore, was to provide protection for the workers on the railway, and to seek out and eliminate the Mahdists in the surrounding area. Thus, in early March 1885, Graham landed back at Suakin, this time in command of a much larger British force of almost 10,500 men.

Graham soon learned that the Mahdists were occupying a line stretching from Tamai through Hasheen and on to Handoub, although the main concentration of Osman Digna's army—numbering around 7,000 warriors—appeared to be at Tamai. Handoub, however, would subsequently be evacuated by the Sudanese, and so the British turned their attention to the tribal forces holding Hasheen, since it formed an obstacle to the intended line of advance to Tamai. The advance began on 20 March, but, as Graham marched, the Hadendowa fighters would persistently attack sentries and stragglers at night.

For the coming operations, the British force was divided into four brigades, which were supported by artillery and engineers. The brigades included: the Guards Brigade under Major-General Lyon Fremantle; 2nd Infantry Brigade under Major-General Sir John McNeill; the Indian Brigade under Brigadier-General J. Hudson; and the Cavalry Brigade under Major-General Sir Henry Ewart.

The Battle of Hasheen was also fought on the 20th, and commenced when the British advanced on their enemy in their usual square formation, while the cavalry provided cover for the front and flanks. As Graham's force manoeuvred forward, the tribesmen fell back towards Dhillbat Hill, from where they decided to make their stand. Orders were issued for the men of the Royal Berkshire Regiment, supported by four companies of Royal Marines, to advance up the slopes of the hill. A heavy fire was then directed at the Mahdists, who soon began to show signs of giving way. Meanwhile, the Guards Brigade—consisting of the Grenadier, Coldstream and Scots Guards—occupied a gorge located between Dhillbat Hill and another smaller nearby hill along with the artillery.

The movement of the infantry was made difficult by the bush terrain, and the tribesmen carried out a number of stinging attacks on Graham's force as it struggled forward. An assault was also made on the 9th Bengal Cavalry, which had been attempting to pursue some of Osman Digna's warriors, during which one of the squadrons had dismounted in order to open a fire with their carbines. However, the Indian sowars were driven back by overwhelming numbers of warriors towards the Guards, having lost nine men in the desperate clash. The Mahdists also attempted to turn the British right-flank, but they were counter-charged by the 5th Lancers and two other squadrons of the 9th Bengal Cavalry, the effects of which stopped the Mahdists dead in their tracks. Eventually, the British were able to completely drive off their enemy and took possession of Dhillbat Hill.

After nine and a half hours, the battle came to an end with the loss of twenty-two British officers and men killed and a further forty-three wounded. Mahdist casualties are harder to determine, with various estimates ranging from 250 to over 1,000. Although a successful action for the Suakin Field Force, the Battle of Hasheen was not a decisive one.

The next action, fought at Tofrek, took place only two days later. Following Hasheen, Major-General McNeill led out a force in order to construct a number of *zaribas* at several locations between Hasheen and Tamai, to act as supply depots. This advance was again conducted in two squares, which reached Tofrek, located about six miles from Suakin, at midday. It would be here that McNeill decided to build three square *zaribas*, which were placed in a diagonal formation. While the work was conducted, the 5th Lancers were sent out to form a protective screen around the site.

At 2 p.m., the infantrymen and the Royal Marines temporarily ceased work on the fortifications so they could have something to eat. As they prepared their food, a trooper came galloping in, informing the men that a large body of the enemy had been seen marching towards the unfinished depot. However, there was little or no time to prepare before the remaining cavalry suddenly appeared being pursued by Osman Digna's warriors. The infantrymen and marines desperately ran to grab their rifles, which had been piled earlier while they worked. The sepoys of the 17th

Bengal Infantry, however, had managed to fire off an equally desperate volley at the attackers before they turned and ran for the central *zariba* in order to seek a degree of protection.

Meanwhile, some soldiers of the Royal Berkshire Regiment had quickly formed a square just outside the central *zariba*; they began delivering deadly volleys into the ranks of their rushing enemy, killing and wounding many of them. Most men of the regiment were now in the southern *zariba*, fending off what proved to be the main thrust of the Mahdist attack. With the warriors checked, the men of this small formation slowly worked their way into the northern *zariba*, which was being manned by the Royal Marines. The marines were also frantically fending off an attack, during which a few Mahdists managed to break their way into the position, only to be swiftly dealt with at the point of the bayonet.

As the action wore on, a large number of tribesmen suddenly crashed their way into the central *zariba* where the baggage animals and camp followers were located, causing many of them, including a number of Indian sepoys, to flee for their lives. The men of the Berkshires and Royal Marines then turned their guns on the *zariba* and opened fire on the warriors, killing many camels and donkeys along with their enemy. Elsewhere, Indian infantrymen of the 15th Sikhs and 28th Bombay Infantry held their ground and fought off other repeated attacks. Eventually, however, the combined fire of the infantry and marines proved too much for the tribesmen, who now began to make off, bringing the battle to an end.

Casualties for the Battle of Tofrek were quite severe, costing the British and Indian troops over 100 dead and 140 wounded. In addition, some 900 camels had been lost, while an estimated 1,000 to 2,000 Mahdists were said to have perished.

The British had now fought a number of actions against the *Mahdi*'s followers, and they were proving to be a courageous and fanatical enemy. However, on 5 May, Graham received orders from Wolseley to abandon the building of the railway and return all his men to Suakin, from where they would be again withdrawn back to Egypt. The Suakin campaign had achieved little, but thousands of men from both sides now lay dead in the sands of Sudan.

Following the fall of Khartoum, Muhammad Ahmed was able to effectively rule Sudan as an Islamic state. He introduced the *Mahdiyya*, his new regime, and imposed a modified version of Sharia law on the people, which was enforced through courts presided over by imams. *Jihad* became one of the five pillars of Islam, effectively replacing *hajj*, and he ordered the systematic removal of many things associated with the old regime. Despite finally achieving his ultimate triumph at a relatively young age, the *Mahdi* would not get to enjoy the fruits of his endeavours for long. Within six months of the death of General Gordon, Muhammad Ahmed would also be dead, having succumbed to typhus, although others believe he was poisoned. His body was laid to rest in a tomb built within the ruins of Omdurman. Joseph Ohrwalder, still a prisoner of the Mahdists, wrote of the *Mahdi*'s passing:

It is, indeed, terrible to think of the awful misery and distress brought upon his own country by this one man. His disease grew rapidly worse; he complained of pain in the heart, and died, on the 22nd of June, 1885, of fatty degeneration of the heart. Some say that he was a victim to the vengeance of a woman who had lost husband and children in the fall of Khartum, and who repaid the *Mahdi*'s outrage on her own person by giving him poison in his food. This may be so; and it is true, poison is generally used in the Sudan to put people out of the way; but I am rather inclined to think that it was outraged nature that took vengeance on its victim; and that it was the *Mahdi*'s debauched and dissolute mode of life which caused his early death.

Interestingly, despite his earlier strict avoidance of worldly pleasures, Ohrwalder claimed that Muhammad Ahmed took many wives, some as young as eight years, dressed in the finest clothes available in Khartoum, and grew 'enormously fat', living 'a life of pleasure and debauchery'; this would ultimately have profound negative effects on his health and contribute to his demise. The Austrian went on to say:

Thus ended the *Mahdi*—a man who left behind him a hundred thousand murdered men, women, and children, hundreds of devastated towns and villages, poverty, and famine. Upon his devoted head lies the curse of his people whom he had forced into a wild and fanatical war, which brought indescribable ruin upon the country, and which exposed his countrymen to the rule of a cruel tyrant, from whom it was impossible to free themselves.

Although the *Mahdi* was no more, his vision and work would—after overcoming strong opposition posed by several other caliphs—be carried on by Abdullahi al-Taishi, who assumed the title Khalifat al-*Mahdi* (meaning successor to the *Mahdi*), or, as he is perhaps better remembered today, simply as the *Khalifa*.

With the withdrawal of Graham's Suakin Field Force, the British Government had all but abandoned its limited interest in Sudan. From late 1885 through to the beginning of Kitchener's campaign eleven years later, the Mahdists, under the ruthless *Khalifa*, were left to rule the country as they wished. However, there would be one more major European expedition into southern Sudan, albeit a non-military and private venture. Today it is referred to by some as the Emin *Pasha* Relief Expedition.

Emin *Pasha*, who was born Eduard Schnitzer, was a German naturalist who had been born in Oppein in 1840. He was a well-educated man, having attended universities in Breslau, Berlin, and Konigsberg; he had strong interests in zoology and ornithology. In 1864, he travelled to Turkey, where he practiced medicine and became the quarantine medical officer at Antivari the following year. In 1875, he went to Cairo in Egypt, after which he continued his travels southwards, ending up in Khartoum, from where he hoped to visit the interior of Africa. It would be in 1876 that, while in Equatoria, he met Charles Gordon, who was then governor of the province. By this time, Eduard Schnitzer had become known as Emin Effendi and would serve the British officer as his medical officer. However, as time went by, the future British general began to entrust his German friend with an increasing number of political issues. When Gordon left his post as governor, to take up the governor-general post at Khartoum, the governorship of Equatoria passed to Ibrahim Fawzi *Pasha*; as mentioned in the previous chapter, he was removed from his post following charges of misconduct. The position of governor was then offered to Emin Effendi, who was also given the title '*Bey*'.

Over the next few years, Emin Effendi would take to his work with much enthusiasm, beginning numerous projects in the hope of improving the infrastructure of Equatoria. However, on a visit to Khartoum in 1882, he learned of the *Mahdi*'s uprising against the Egyptian and Sudanese authorities in Kordofan. The territories under his control then began to fall to the advancing *Ansar*, and, by 1884, the German governor was becoming increasingly isolated, and especially more so after the fall of the Sudanese capital early the following year. During this time, Emin Effendi was forced to abandon Lado as his administrative centre and moved to Wadelai, the former having been taken by the Mahdists. News then reached him that the Egyptian government in Cairo was refusing to send troops to assist in the southern province; Emin Effendi was on his own, with only the options of either staying put or risking a retirement to the coast in a bid to escape by sea. The governor, now known as Emin *Pasha* following another promotion, considered a move to Zanzibar, but ultimately decided to stay put.

In a desperate attempt to seek help, Emin *Pasha* turned to the British with the proposal that they annex the province as part of their empire. The government in London, who had worked so hard to persuade the *Khedive* to abandon Sudan, had no interest in the idea and flatly refused to even consider it. However, the British public, upon hearing of his plight, held much sympathy for Emin *Pasha*, since he was now in a similar position as Gordon had been less than two years earlier. Despite this, neither the British nor the Egyptian authorities in Cairo or elsewhere had any appetite to risk the sending of troops so far into Sudan—which was crawling with hostile Mahdists—in an attempt to extract a man who, if truth be known, had little intention of leaving Equatoria anyway.

Faced with this lack of official action, a number of private British citizens now took it upon themselves to conduct a relief expedition of their own. Two businessmen, William Mackinnon and James Frederick Hutton, set up the Emin *Pasha* Relief Committee, which eventually raised enough money to finance the costly venture. The man chosen to lead the expedition was Sir Henry Morton Stanley, a Welshman who is today perhaps best remembered for his exploits exploring central Africa, his quest for the source of the Nile, and for his search for the explorer David Livingstone. To Mackinnon and Hutton, Stanley seemed the logical choice, and the explorer was certainly more than enthusiastic to accept the challenge.

Stanley left England for Cairo in late January 1887, where he stayed for a short time before moving on to Zanzibar. Here, he found that his agents had already recruited 600 men for the planned expedition, although the number would rise by another hundred before it set off on the 25 February, aboard steamers that sailed for the mouth of the Congo River. Stanley would have to travel over twelve hundred miles to the Aruwimi River—a tributary of the Congo River—from where his men would march another four hundred miles through unknown territory to reach Emin *Pasha*. This long journey, however, would be greatly hampered due to defective transports.

After leaving for the wilderness of Africa, little was known by the watching outside world as to what was happening. Rumours spread quickly, some claiming Stanley had found Emin *Pasha*, while others suggested the entire expedition had been massacred by African tribesmen. Others still even went as far as to suggest that, along with Emin *Pasha*'s small number of troops, he was marching on Khartoum to avenge the murder of Gordon—such was the interest and thirst for news in Britain and across the world.

In reality, the expedition was having a difficult time of it, being totally unprepared for the arduous journey they were undertaking. Stanley had split his force into two, including an 'advanced' and a 'rear' column. Speed was of the essence for the explorer, and so he ordered the advanced column to push on ahead while the rear column remained encamped at a place called Yambuya, where it would wait for further supplies before following on after Stanley. By early December, however, over half the men of the advanced column had perished, having succumbed to starvation or killed by hostile local tribesmen. Having finally got past the Ituri Rainforest in mid-December, Stanley was disappointed in being unable to locate Emin *Pasha*; but by April 1888, word at last reached him from the governor, after which the two men finally met on the 27th.

It soon became apparent to Stanley that Emin *Pasha* had no intentions of abandoning Equatoria and leaving with him back to safety. Unable to persuade him to leave—after a month of trying—the Welshman gave up and left the governor, heading back in order to find his rear column which he had received no word from since his initial advance from Yambuya. Eventually, in August, Stanley found what was the remains of the column, which, in an attempt to find the explorer, who they themselves had heard nothing of for over 12-months, had suffered many deaths and desertions. To make matters worse, Stanley received news in mid-January 1889 that the Mahdists had continued their advance across Equatoria, and that Emin *Pasha* had been removed from his post as governor by his own military officers who had been worried about their precarious futures after having lost faith in the governor.

Fortunately for Stanley, Emin *Pasha* had already been released from captivity by the time the message was received, and the two men met again in February near Lake Albert. With what was left of his original expedition, plus a handful of soldiers still loyal to the former governor, the men—although Emin *Pasha* was still seemingly reluctant to leave—set off for the coast on 10 April. However, it would not be until early December that Emin *Pasha* finally reached the port city of Bagamoyo and safety, after a long and difficult journey. Meeting them was Hermann Wissmann, the local German administrator, who laid on a dinner to celebrate Emin *Pasha*'s safe return. However, the latter got extremely drunk and somehow fell out of a second story window, injuring himself when he hit the ground.

After almost two years, the expedition had achieved its goal of evacuating Emin *Pasha* from Equatoria, albeit with a considerable loss of life, money, and equipment in the process. Stanley returned home in May 1890, where he was received as a hero by the public and showered with numerous honours, although much criticism of the affair would follow later as the details became public. Emin *Pasha*, meanwhile, took up a new post with the German East Africa Company, only to be murdered in Kinena in Uganda in October 1892. The story of Emin *Pasha*, and the subsequent privately organised efforts to relieve him, did, however, have an effect on the British public, some of whom were increasingly calling for action against the Mahdists.

While Stanley was attempting to save Emin *Pasha* in Equatoria, the Mahdists under the *Khalifa* were continuing their attempt to spread their ideology and the *Mahdiyya*. In 1887, the *Ansar* was sent into Abyssinia where it enjoyed much success, and, at the Battle of Metemma in March 1889, the Mahdists killed the Abyssinian emperor, Yohannes IV. Emboldened by this victory, the *Khalifa* next ordered an invasion of Egypt late during the same year. The *Ansar*, under Abd ar Rahman an Nujumi, clashed with British-led Egyptian troops at the Battle of Toski on 3 August. Learning of the advance into Egyptian territory, the Egyptian Army, under command of Major-General Sir Francis Grenfell, who at that time was *Sirdar*, advanced on Toski, where the Mahdists had made their camp; they attacked, decisively destroying the Mahdist force and killing Abd ar Rahman an Nujumi in the process. The British later estimated their enemy lost over 1,500 killed while a further 8,000 were taken prisoner, compared to less than 200 Anglo-Egyptian casualties. With the end of the battle came the end of the *Khalifa*'s only attempt to seize Egyptian territory.

Earlier, on 20 December 1888, Osman Digna had also clashed with an Anglo-Egyptian force under Grenfell at the Battle of Gemaizah. Again, the action ended in a defeat for the tribesmen, and Osman Digna was wounded in the arm during the fighting. Likewise, the Mahdists lost hundreds of warriors while British casualty numbers were tiny. Further defeat for the *Khalifa* came in June 1890, when his warriors fought an action against Italian troops at the Battle of Agordat. The Italians again defeated the Mahdists at the Battle of Serobeti in June 1892, which, coupled with the Anglo-Egyptian victories of several years earlier, proved that the *Ansar* was not the unbeatable force many feared it was.

Between 1892 and 1895, a media campaign was mounted by Major Francis Reginald Wingate, a British military intelligence officer based in Cairo, in an attempt to further swing public opinion against the Mahdists in Sudan. Wingate had been born in 1861 in Port Glasgow in Renfrewshire, Scotland, although he moved with his family to Jersey following his father's death when he was barely a year old. After completing his education, he joined the British Army in 1880, taking a commission in the Royal Artillery. Three years later, he was serving with the recently reorganised Egyptian Army, in the wake of the British invasion of the country in 1882, in which he would take part in both Wolseley's failed expedition to save Gordon and Graham's operations near Suakin. His service in Egypt and Sudan enabled him to gain considerable knowledge of the two countries and their people, not to mention the fact that he learned to speak Arabic very quickly, which made him particularly suitable for the intelligence work in which he was now engaged. By 1892, he had become the director of the Egyptian Army Intelligence Branch and published a book entitled *Mahdism and the Egyptian Sudan*.

At about the same time Wingate completed his manuscript, Father Joseph Ohrwalder had managed to escape his Mahdist captors after a painful ten years as a prisoner, firstly of the *Mahdi* himself and then the *Khalifa*. Ohrwalder was an Austrian Roman Catholic priest who had been born in 1856, and who had come to Sudan as a missionary. During Muhammad Ahmed's siege of El Obeid, the *Mahdi* had encountered a number of European missionaries, including Ohrwalder, and ordered they be taken prisoner. Shortly after his capture, the priest and his fellow missionaries were taken to see Muhammad Ahmed, who, realising they were religious men, talked to his new prisoners about the virtues of the Islamic religion. Yet, according to Ohrwalder, he never attempted to convert them to becoming Muslims, since he knew they would likely refuse.

The *Mahdi* then sent the Austrian and his colleagues to Abdullahi al-Taishi, who informed them that they—in stark contrast to Muhammad Ahmed's previous conversation with them—must convert to Islam or face execution. Ohrwalder and the others, however, remained resolutely faithful to their own religion and point-blank refused to become Muslims, at which the sentence of death was promptly announced and the meeting terminated. Muhammad Ahmed, for reasons that remain unclear, later commuted the sentence, and the missionaries began their long years as prisoners of the Mahdists.

During the next ten years, Ohrwalder would be witness to much suffering in Sudan while it was under Mahdist rule. He would also be witness—although sometimes from a distance—to the fall of El Obeid, the defeat of Hicks *Pasha*, the fall of Khartoum and the killing of Gordon, the death of the *Mahdi*, and events that took place under the subsequent rule of the *Khalifa*. It is, therefore, unsurprising that Wingate, in his role as director of military intelligence, took a serious interest in Ohrwalder after his escape in 1892. In the same year, both Ohrwalder and Wingate would co-write and publish the book *Ten Years' Captivity in the Mahdi's Camp, 1882–1892*, which was aimed primarily at the British public. Wingate, it has been argued by historians, effectively wrote the book himself, which he himself almost admits to in the preface:

> It should be borne in mind that the circumstances under which Father Ohrwalder lived in the Sudan precluded him from keeping any written record of his life; it was therefore agreed that I should supervise his work which, I need scarcely add, it has given me great pleasure to do. Father Ohrwalder's manuscript, which was in the first instance written in German, was roughly translated into English by Yusef Effendi Cudzi, a Syrian; this I entirely rewrote in narrative form. The work does not therefore profess to be a literal translation of the original manuscript, but rather an English version, in which I have sought to reproduce accurately Father Ohrwalder's meaning in the language of simple narration.

The book was well-received in Britain and caused much uproar and anger towards the Mahdists—feelings that Wingate had obviously hoped for.

Ohrwalder was not the only European prisoner of the Mahdists who would prove of great service in the political campaign against them. Rudolf Anton Carl Freiherr von Slatin, also known as Slatin *Pasha*, was an Austrian soldier who had been born near Vienna in 1857. In the 1870s, Slatin had travelled to Sudan, where he met Emin *Pasha*, and had intended to gain an audience with Gordon in the hope of acquiring employment with the Sudanese authorities. However, he was recalled to Austria, having received his conscription orders, and left Sudan before he had chance to meet with the British governor. Back home, he joined the Austro-Hungarian Army as an infantry officer. However, in 1878, he received a letter from Gordon—who was by then governor-general of all Sudan at Khartoum—inviting him to return to discuss the possibility of employment. Having been released from the army, Slatin arrived at Khartoum in January 1879, where he was initially given a junior role in the Sudanese civil service before being made governor of Dara. By 1881, he was promoted to governor-general of Darfur.

It would be as governor-general of Darfur that Slatin would first clash with Mahdist forces during their rising throughout Sudan. At first, he would enjoy some success, but, at the Battle of Om Waragat in 1883, he suffered a major defeat that saw the loss of 8,000 of his troops and only narrowly escaped death himself, although he did receive a number of wounds. Curiously, he believed his men had blamed their defeat on him personally because he was a Christian, and so he converted to Islam and took the Islamic name of Abd al-Qadir (not to be confused with Abd-al-Qadir Hilmi) in an attempt to boost morale. This move, however, was in vain due to the success of the Mahdists in capturing El Obeid and defeating Hicks *Pasha*, which effectively isolated Slatin at Darfur. Unable to seek reinforcements and faced with ever-declining morale, the governor-general took the decision to offer a full surrender to Muhammad Ahmed.

Now a prisoner of the *Mahdi*, Slatin was taken to Khartoum in an attempt by Muhammad Ahmed to use him to persuade Gordon to surrender himself and the city. Having failed in this, the Austrian was kept prisoner, and, once the city finally fell, shown the head of Gordon:

> ... three Black soldiers; one named Shatta, formerly belonging to Ahmed *Bey* Dafalla's slave body-guard, carried in his hands a bloody cloth in which something was wrapped up, and behind him followed a crowd of people weeping. The slaves had now approached my tent, and stood before me with insulting gestures; Shatta undid the cloth and showed me the head of General Gordon!
>
> The blood rushed to my head, and my heart seemed to stop beating; but, with a tremendous effort of self-control, I gazed silently at this ghastly spectacle. His blue eyes were half-opened; the mouth was perfectly natural; the hair of his head, and his short whiskers, were almost quite white.

When the *Mahdi* died, the *Khalifa* forced Slatin to serve him as an advisor and interpreter. He would remain in captivity for a total of eleven years.

Escape eventually came in 1895, thanks to the assistance of Wingate, with Slatin finally arriving in Aswan in Egypt in May, having spent three weeks crossing the desert. As with Ohrwadler, the British major began work on co-producing a book, entitled *Fire and Sword in the Sudan: A Personal Narrative of Fighting and Serving the Dervishes, 1879-1895*, about the Austrian's time as a prisoner of the Mahdists; an introductory note was even written by Ohrwalder. Published in 1896, it proved immensely popular, and again caused much public outrage in Britain against the *Khalifa* and his followers. Wingate's campaign appeared to be working.

Despite the death of Gordon and the fall of Khartoum, the defeat of Hicks *Pasha*, Graham's operations near Suakin, the privately financed expedition to relieve Emin *Pasha*, the *Ansar* invasion of Egypt, and the growing resentment of the British public against the Mahdists, the government in London still held little interest in getting further involved in Sudan in the mid-1890s. Indeed, Lord Salisbury, who again had become prime minister of Britain in June 1895, believed that the power of the Mahdists under the leadership of the *Khalifa* was in decline, and that it was only a matter of waiting for the issue to resolve itself. However, it would be events in Abyssinia in early March 1896 that finally, albeit initially in a limited way, encouraged the British Government to take action.

Following the death of Yohannes IV in 1889, Abyssinia, which had been made up of numerous semi-independent kingdoms, entered a period of disorder during which several potential successors began to violently quarrel over who should be the next emperor. The Italians, who like a number of European powers were involved in the scramble for Africa, favoured Sahle Miriam, the king of Shewa. As part of their support for this petty ruler, the Italians had been supplying him with modern weapons and stockpiles of ammunition in an attempt to build up his military power. Using his newly acquired military might, Miriam was able to take over other Abyssinian kingdoms until he became emperor of all of Abyssinia, taking the name Menilek II.

With their preferred candidate now in power, the Italians concluded the Treaty of Wichale, in May 1889, which offered Menilek II a sizeable financial loan on favourable terms in exchange for his recognition of Italy's claim to the coastal territory of Eritrea. Unfortunately, a section of the treaty, known as Article XVII, later led to a serious rupture between the new Abyssinian emperor and the Italian Government. The article, in the eyes of Menilek II, was seen as a promise by the Italians to assist him in dealing with foreign powers, while the Italian authorities interpreted it as meaning Abyssinia was now an Italian protectorate. This misunderstanding caused friction between the two countries; in September 1893, the Abyssinian emperor rejected the treaty outright. In response, the Italian Government ordered its troops in neighbouring Eritrea to make preparations for a military campaign in Abyssinia against their former ally.

The initial confrontations during the campaign went well for the Italians, but Menilek II was able to call on a formidable army of over 100,000 men, many of them armed with modern weapons previously supplied by their adversary. The Italians, however, seemed unaware of exactly just how large the Abyssinian Army was, possibly due to the fact that the Abyssinian emperor had been wise enough to long conceal their true numbers. This possibly led the Italians into a false sense of security.

In early February 1896, the Italian Army under General Oreste Baratieri, ascertained the location of the main Abyssinian force; however, due to supply problems, the Italian commander deemed it prudent to resolve a number of issues before advancing to battle. Likewise, Menilek II did not feel ready to fight a sizeable action, and so both sides simply waited. A furious Italian Government, fed up of the perceived inactivity of its troops, issued orders to Baratieri to take decisive action against the Abyssinians as soon as possible. Although reluctant to do so, the Italian general began his advance towards the town of Adwa. On 1 March, the two armies clashed at the Battle of Adwa in northern Abyssinia.

By noon the same day, the Italian Army was defeated and the survivors in full flight. The outcome was, perhaps, hardly surprising, since the Italian force of around 14,500 men was pitted against over 100,000 Abyssinians, many armed with modern rifles. Casualties were high, with over 6,000 Italian troops (of which about half were Italians and the other half African soldiers under Italian command) were killed, while an additional 3,000 to 4,000 were taken prisoner. Abyssinian casualties were estimated to be around 5,000 killed and 8,000 wounded.

Italy's military forces in Eritrea were now seriously weakened—a fact not lost on the Mahdists, who sent a force to retake Kassala in eastern Sudan, which the Italians had seized from the *Khalifa* in 1894. On 10 March, the Italian ambassador to Britain informed Salisbury that Mahdist forces were advancing towards Eritrea, and formally asked the British prime minister to conduct military operations in Sudan in order to relieve some of the pressure on the remaining Italian forces in the region. In response, Salisbury agreed to make a limited military demonstration in northern Sudan.

Salisbury realised that another major victory against a European power—namely Italy—in Sudan would potentially reverse the decline of Mahdist power and influence in the region. However, the British prime minister did not act out of charity towards the Italians alone; rather, he planned to expand the influence of the Anglo-Egyptian authorities *bey*ond the southern borders of Egypt, and taking action in support of the Italians presented an excellent opportunity to achieve this desire. In particular, the government in London wished to gain control of the Nile Valley right down to Uganda. They also sought to push other European powers involved in the scramble for African colonies out from Sudan; in other words, London wanted the French, a long standing rival of Britain, kept out, and it was feared that Paris was already planning an advance towards the Upper Nile from its territories in West Africa. Sudan itself was of little interest, but control of the Nile promised to be quite profitable. Salisbury's latest moves regarding Sudan, therefore, were firmly rooted in his European politics, and the Battle of Adwa merely determined when to set the wheels in motion.

The prime minister, it has been argued, also sought to further weaken the Ottoman Empire and Islam, the latter of which he viewed as a 'false religion', an opinion he confirmed in a speech made in June 1898. This speech would offend many Muslims within the British Empire, particularly those who served it under arms, and London was forced to quickly follow up with a statement that suggested Salisbury was specifically referring to the *Khalifa* and his followers, who, in the eyes of many orthodox Muslims, continued to adhere to the ideology of Muhammad Ahmed, the false *Mahdi*. This view, of course, betrayed the prime minister's hatred of Islam, and, as a committed Christian who believed in the superiority of his own religion, he was deeply concerned about the recent advances it had made in the east and elsewhere.

Evelyn Baring and Salisbury had previously held little faith in Egyptian troops fighting against the Mahdists—since it pitted Muslims against Muslims—and the former had a poor track record against the latter. However, during the *Khalifa*'s invasion of Egypt in 1889, the Egyptian troops had performed much better than expected, inflicting a decisive defeat on their enemy, which was so complete that the Mahdists never attempted another invasion. Unlike in 1884, perhaps the Egyptian Army could now be better trusted in military operations against the *Ansar*, a tentative belief that, of course, would be later confirmed at the Battle of Omdurman in 1898. Indeed, the Egyptian Army, as we will see in the next chapter, had been extensively rebuilt by the British over the previous decade, and was now in better shape than ever. Both the political and military situations of 1896 were much changed from those of the time of Gordon's siege at Khartoum.

Queen Victoria and the British public wanted to see Khartoum recovered and the murder of Gordon avenged. Salisbury, however, was in no rush to see this happen just yet, although he conceded that it must one day become an objective in his grand plan. Rather, he foresaw a limited military advance towards Dongola, where, once reached, Britain should then resist the temptation to move further south for at least several years. This he impressed upon Baring—now known as Lord Cromer—who had previously held a strong view that Britain should not seek to reconquer Sudan. However, Cromer's stance had begun to change, even before the disastrous Italian action at Adwa; perhaps ironically, it would be him who would later extend the planned limited military demonstration into a full-scale invasion of Sudan and the retaking of Khartoum.

The man chosen to lead the military expedition to Dongola was, of course, Horatio Herbert Kitchener, who had become *Sirdar* of the Egyptian Army in 1892, replacing Francis Grenfell as commander-in-chief at Cairo. It is to Kitchener, and his troops, that we now turn our attention in the next chapter.

4

The *Sirdar* and the Anglo-Egyptian Army

Horatio Herbert Kitchener is perhaps best remembered today for his image on the world famous 'Your Country Needs You' recruitment poster of the First World War, or for his role as commander-in-chief in South Africa, from late 1900, during the Anglo-Boer War. However, it would be his reconquest of Sudan from the grip of the Mahdists that, as *Sirdar* of the Egyptian Army, first shot him to fame as a British general and laid the foundations of his long-lasting reputation as a very able senior military leader.

Born in Ballylongford in Country Kerry, Ireland on 24 June 1850, Kitchener was the son of a lieutenant-colonel in the British Army; he would eventually follow in his father's footsteps. At the age of sixteen, his family moved to Switzerland in an attempt to ease the suffering of Herbert's mother, who had contracted tuberculosis. Unfortunately, the move came too late and she died not long after the family settled into their new home. Herbert stayed on in Switzerland after her death, receiving an informal, private education at the Château du Grand Clos before returning to Britain to attend the Royal Military Academy at Woolwich. He would be commissioned into the British Army as a second-lieutenant in the Royal Engineers on 4 January 1871. Thus began what would prove to be a remarkable, and sometimes controversial, military career.

In 1874, Kitchener was sent to Palestine to survey its western territories as part of the Palestine Exploration Fund, a task he would continue until 1877. The following year, he would travel to Cyprus, after its recent acquisition by the British, to conduct further survey work across the island. On 26 June 1879, he would be appointed vice-consul in Anatolia, although he would return to Cyprus less than a year later. His first experience of Egypt came in 1882, when the Royal Navy conducted the bombardment of Alexandria, after which he landed with the troops in order to gather intelligence.

While in Egypt, Kitchener would be promoted to captain on 4 January 1883, and was posted to the Egyptian cavalry the following month. It was about this time that he is said to have become a Freemason at a lodge in Cairo. Already fluent in French, he soon learned to speak Arabic, which greatly contributed to his appointment as chief intelligence officer to Wolseley's expedition to save Gordon. Although the expedition failed in its objective, Kitchener was able to learn much about the people of both Egypt and Sudan, as well as acquire knowledge of the terrain. During this time, further promotion followed, including brevet major in October 1884 and brevet lieutenant-colonel in June 1885. However, it would be at the time of the latter promotion that he resigned from his service with the Egyptian Army.

Leaving Egypt, Kitchener would take up a position with the Zanzibar Boundary Commission in late 1885, but was subsequently appointed governor-general of the Egyptian provinces in eastern Sudan and the Red Sea Littoral—which included the port city of Suakin—in September the following year. While in this post, he would clash with the Mahdists when he led a military force in the storming of Osman Digna's camp at Handoub in January 1888, during which Kitchener would be wounded in the jaw. He also commanded the Egyptian cavalry at the Battle of Toski on 3 August 1889, when Abd ar Rahman an Nujumi carried out his unsuccessful invasion of Egypt.

Early in 1890, Kitchener was appointed inspector-general of the Egyptian police, spending time reforming it. However, his most significant appointment to-date came on 13 April 1892, when he succeeded Major-General Sir Francis Grenfell as *Sirdar* of the Egyptian Army with the local rank of brigadier-general. The term *Sirdar* originates from the Persian *Sardār*, which was a noble title often used to denote princes or noblemen. In Egypt, under the British, the term was used to describe the commander-in-chief of the Egyptian Army, a post first held by Sir Evelyn Wood between 1883 and 1885, then Grenfell between 1885 and 1892. Kitchener would remain *Sirdar* until 1899, at which point he left Egypt for South Africa to take part in the Anglo-Boer War.

During his reconquest of Sudan, Kitchener was meticulous in his planning of the campaign, paying particular attention to keeping his forces supplied. He made great use of the Nile River for transportation and extended the railways as he advanced. For every operation he embarked upon he would be thorough in his planning, and would always ensure he was totally prepared before commencing operations. The *Sirdar* was remembered by his contemporaries as a physically imposing man, standing well over six feet tall, and was known for being both severe and ruthless in his approach to military command. He was also not known for having much of a sense of humour, always appearing serious; he had a particular dislike of the press and would not allow married officers to serve in his army. It is said that he suffered from a squint in his left eye.

Despite his authoritative attitude, he had, in younger years, displayed a willingness to diso*bey* his superiors. In 1870, he travelled to France without permission to serve in a French field ambulance unit during the Franco-Prussian War, which he had done in eagerness to experience war first-hand; after this, he was severely reprimanded by the Duke of Cambridge. He again acted without official orders in 1882, when he joined British forces headed for Egypt. It is unlikely he would have tolerated the same behaviour from officers under his own command in later life.

As mentioned above, following the reconquest of Sudan, Kitchener would head for South Africa in late 1899. The early stages of the war against the Boers had been going somewhat badly for the British, and large numbers of reinforcements were sent out under the command of Lord Frederick Roberts, to whom Kitchener would act as second-in-command. In November 1900, he would succeed Roberts as commander-in-chief of British forces in South Africa and be promoted to lieutenant-general, eventually defeating the Boers eighteen months later after a long and bitter guerrilla campaign. In 1902, Kitchener would next go to India, where he was tasked with reorganising the Indian Army; by 1911, he was back in Egypt to take up the post of consul-general. Promotion to field marshal came in 1909; in this capacity, he would go on to serve in the early years of the First World War. However, while *en route* to a diplomatic mission in Russia, Kitchener would be killed when the ship he was travelling on, the cruiser HMS *Hampshire*, struck a mine near Orkney on 5 June 1916 with the loss of the majority onboard. He was aged sixty-five.

Throughout the nineteenth-century, the British raised local armies in their colonies to shoulder the burden of military operations, although they would usually be supported by a backbone of British troops. Egypt was no exception, but, in the immediate aftermath of the British invasion of the country in 1882, what remained of the Egyptian Army was in a shocking state. Although it had benefited from the presence of American officers in a training capacity, the Egyptian staff officers had only been taught topographical and exploration work, with the ordinary soldier remaining largely ill-trained in the art of warfare and often too ill-equipped to actually fight effectively. The army needed to be both rebuilt and reorganised, otherwise large numbers of British troops would have to be stationed in the country.

Egyptian soldiers were drawn from the *fellahin*—the local peasantry—who were, more often than not, conscripted into military service against their will. Life in the Egyptian Army before the British came was a harsh one, with pay usually only arriving after long intervals, or not at all; they also dreaded the prospect of being sent to serve in Sudan. The life of the ordinary soldier was so bad that many *fellahs* would cut off their trigger fingers to render them useless when handling a rifle, or otherwise inflict various forms of self-mutilation to make them unfit for military service. Those who were taken away from their villages would be mourned by their family, since the likelihood of their return was very slim. Desertion was common, and those already in uniform would do almost anything to escape, even though they faced severe punishment if caught later. The situation changed dramatically after the British took control of Egypt. Pay improved, both in terms of the rate and the frequency it was given to the troops, and the average soldier could now rest assured that he would be well-fed and clothed. Returning home to his village each year to see his family also became a reality. Life of the ordinary Egyptian soldier was still far from a rosy one, but it was a far cry from life under the previous regime.

It would be on 20 December 1882 that the *Khedive* formally dissolved the old Egyptian Army and announced the establishment of a new one under the command of Sir Evelyn Wood as *Sirdar*. Additionally, other British Army officers would be allowed to enter the new Egyptian Army, to both lead and assist in its rebuilding and reorganisation. Initial discussions on what size and form the army would take were held between Wood and Lord Dufferin; the latter informed the former that it was the opinion of some in Britain that Egypt did not need an army at all. However, an army it would have, with the number of troops being initially set at 6,000. The majority of the men would again come from the Egyptian *fellahin*, although a number of experienced Turkish soldiers from the old army would also be included in order to give it a backbone.

Each of Egypt's fourteen provinces were asked to supply men for the new army, the allocated quota for each being set according to the size of the local population. Due to the requirement for relatively small numbers of troops, the men from these provinces were generally of better physical quality than had been in the past. Originally, men would be expected to serve four years with the colours; this later changed to four years with the colours followed by four years in the police then four years in the first-class reserve. However, it was recognised that the regular army lost too many experienced soldiers under this arrangement, and so, in 1888, the terms of service were again changed, this time to six years with the colours, five with the police and four in reserve. Following their initial recruitment, the men would be sent to a depot at Barrage before moving to barracks at either Toura or Abbassieh near Cairo.

After the first rounds of recruitment, two brigades were established, each consisting of four battalions of infantry. The first brigade, which included the battalions numbered one to four, was placed under the command of British officers, including Grenfell as its first brigade commander, while the second, battalions five to eight, was officered by Egyptians and commanded by El-Lewa Shuhdi *Pasha*. As well as the infantry, there was also artillery and cavalry, the former initially commanded by Lieutenant-Colonel Duncan of the Royal Artillery and the latter by Lieutenant-Colonel Taylor of the 19th Hussars.

Since the British officers were commanding Egyptian troops, they would adopt the use of an Egyptian rank, each of which roughly corresponded to an equivalent rank in the British Army. These included:

BRITISH RANK	EGYPTIAN RANK
Commander-in-chief	*Sirdar*
Lieutenant-General	*Farik*
Major-General	*Lewa*
Colonel	*Miralai*
Lieutenant-Colonel	*Kaimakam*
Major	*Bimbashi*
Adjutant-Major	*Saghkolaghasi*
Captain	*Yuzbashi*
Lieutenant	*Mulazim awal*
Second-Lieutenant	*Mulazim tani*

Those holding the rank of *Sirdar*, *farik* and *lewa* were also granted the title 'Pasha', while those of the rank of *miralai* and *kaimakam* received the title 'Bey'.

Particular attention was paid to recruiting and training Egyptian officers, many of which initially came from the old army, but as time went by, all officers would be graduates of the Military School. Those who displayed the right qualities would steadily rise through the ranks, and, by the time Kitchener began his Dongola campaign of 1896, many Egyptian officers under his command were well-trained in a similar fashion to their British counterparts. In practice, British officers entering Egyptian service were generally granted the next rank up in the Egyptian Army rather than the direct equivalent.

Technically, the *Khedive* remained the commander-in-chief of the army, with the *Sirdar* being the executive commander-in-chief. Next in-line to the *Khedive* was the Egyptian minister for war, who was followed by the under-secretary of state for war, while the *Sirdar* was assisted by his principal staff officers, the adjutant-general and the quartermaster-general. Under these latter two senior staff posts were a series of others with responsibilities for departments involved in recruiting, intelligence, commissariat, ordnance, pay, and engineering, among others.

In May 1884, it was decided to raise a ninth battalion of infantrymen recruited from Sudan, which became known as the 9th Sudanese Battalion. What is interesting about this battalion, aside from the fact it was the first of a number that would later form a Sudanese brigade, was the fact that it was predominately made up of men who had deserted the *Mahdi*. Writing in 1891, Major Wingate said of these Sudanese troops:

> The organisation of a Sudanese battalion differs considerably from that of an Egyptian battalion. The men composing it are for the most part deserters from the enemy … they are almost entirely volunteers, and, having no settled homes, a large percentage of them are permitted to marry and receive an allowance for the maintenance of their wives. They do not pick up their drills and exercises so rapidly as the Egyptians; but, on the other hand, they have greater initiative and

instincts for self-defence. Many of them, especially the Shilluks and Dinkas, are almost savages; and it has been found by experience that in action they require greater control, as their chief desire is to be 'up and at' the enemy. It has therefore been found necessary to organise them into six instead of four companies, with four instead of three English officers per battalion of 759 strong.

Despite these minor issues, the Sudanese troops soon won the respect of their British officers, and, on 2 January 1886, the 10th Sudanese Battalion was also formed. This saw the Egyptian Army increase in size to ten infantry battalions, five batteries of artillery, two squadrons of cavalry, and three companies of the Camel Corps. The 11th Sudanese Battalion was created in 1887, which was followed by the 12th later the same year and the 13th in 1888. During this time, the artillery also gained an extra battery, and the cavalry a further three squadrons.

As can be seen, the rebuilding of the Egyptian Army took place over a long period of time and would be a very different force in 1896 than it had been in the early days after the 1882 invasion. Despite the concerns of Evelyn Baring about pitting Egyptian troops against fellow Muslims of the *Ansar*, they performed increasingly well against the Mahdists. Evidence of this can be seen in the Battle of Toski, in August 1889, when Anglo-Egyptian troops virtually annihilated a large Mahdist force with minimal loss. Although under the command of Grenfell, the only British troops present were a squadron of the 20th Hussars, with the overwhelming majority of the men being of the Egyptian Army.

Acts of personal valour by Egyptian troops were also noted by their British officers. Again, according to Wingate:

> The Egyptian troops behaved well too in the various actions around Suakin, and there were many instances of personal gallantry on the part of Egyptian soldiers ; one may be mentioned in particular, when a private of the Egyptian cavalry, forming one of the reconnaissance party of British and Egyptian troops on February 3rd, 1885, being hard pressed by the enemy, dismounted and picked up a sergeant of the 19th Hussars, who must inevitably have been killed, and brought him out of action; for this signal service Her Majesty the Queen was graciously pleased to bestow on him the medal for distinguished service in the field.

Nevertheless, concerns about the reliability of Egyptian Army troops in battle remained in 1896, and would not be finally laid to rest until after the Battle of Omdurman.

During the lead up to the Omdurman campaign, the Egyptian Army grew further still to include: nineteen battalions of infantry, ten squadrons of cavalry, one horse artillery battery and four field artillery batteries. It also boasted a Camel Corps of eight companies and a number of Maxim machine guns. In total, some

20,000 Egyptian and Sudanese troops were available for service, along with over 140 European officers to command them.

In addition to the Egyptian and Sudanese troops, the British also ensured a number of Queen's soldiers (British troops) were also available if required. These would include men from all arms, such as infantry, cavalry, artillery, engineers, field hospitals, and other supporting services. Unlike Egyptian troops, who were conscripts, all British soldiers were volunteers, who, by the 1890s, enlisted into the army to serve seven years with the colours followed by five years in the reserve. Sometimes, a soldier's service might last eight years with the colours if he was serving overseas, in which case he was only expected to spend four years in the reserve. The men who joined the British Army came from across Britain, and they were widely referred to—albeit unofficially—as 'Tommies' after Tommy Atkins; the origins of this nickname remain debated to this day.

During the reconquest of Sudan, British troops would be brigaded separately from the Egyptian Army; for example, at Omdurman, Kitchener's force was split into two divisions: the British Division, which was sub-divided into two British brigades, and an Egyptian Division, which was subdivided into four brigades. Generally speaking, British infantry regiments were made up of two battalions, each consisting of eight companies of 120 men. Similarly, cavalry regiments usually consisted of four squadrons of 160 men each. This is in contrast to the Egyptian infantry battalions, which had six companies of 150 men each, and cavalry squadrons of 100 men each. The artillery batteries usually consisted of six guns, which were serviced by 113 men (137 in the horse batteries), while the companies of the Camel Corps had 152 men each. However, it should be understood that units were rarely up to strength, and both British and Egyptian battalions often took to the field with substantially lower numbers available for operations.

The *Sirdar* was also able to benefit from the presence of naval forces—since he used the Nile River—which included a number of armoured gunboats under the command of Commander Colin Keppel of the Royal Navy. Each of these vessels were armed with various artillery pieces and Maxim and Nordenfelt machine guns, as well as 6-pounder and 12-pounder quick-firing guns. A total of ten gunboats took part in the campaign. A detailed list of Anglo-Egyptian forces engaged in the actions of the 1896-98 campaigns are listed in Appendix A.

Soldiers in the Egyptian Army wore a khaki-coloured tunic and trousers with a red fez, the latter of which was covered in khaki cloth. He also wore leather boots with blue puttees. However, when deployed on active service, a *fellah* would, in addition, wear a brown jersey and brown leather equipment, which included: a belt, ammunition pouches, braces, waterbottle, and haversack. He would also carry a blanket and an extra ammunition bandolier with him, if required. Sudanese troops were dressed and equipped in a similar fashion, except their jerseys were sometimes dark blue and their fez headdresses were covered in plaited straw.

Egyptian Army troops were armed with the Martini-Henry rifle, a breech-loading single-shot weapon that was loaded by opening the block via the use of a lever situated behind the trigger-guard. A .577/450 cartridge could then be inserted into the breech, which was closed by again using the lever. Once fired, the weapon was re-loaded by repeating the procedure, with the spent cartridge being partially extracted as the breech was opened ready for the next round. The rifle had been introduced into service with the British Army in 1871, and had a reputation for its incredible stopping power, a particularly valuable asset when fighting the fanatical Mahdists in Sudan. Although production of the weapon ended in around 1889, such large numbers were made that it stayed in service for many years afterwards, although British troops would be armed with a more modern replacement by the time of Kitchener's campaign in Sudan. The Egyptian or Sudanese soldier would also be issued with an 18.5-inch triangular socket bayonet, although they were often regarded as being of poor quality.

The British soldier who took to the field in Sudan in the late 1890s wore a khaki tunic and trousers (or kilt for the Highlanders), as well as a khaki covered helmet that had a neck cover to protect the wearer from the sun. He would also wear leather boots with khaki coloured puttees. British equipment was of the Slade Wallace pattern, which was made of a buff-white leather, including: a belt, ammunition pouches, and braces. The soldier would also be issued with a waterbottle and haversack. It should be noted that the boots worn by British soldiers during the reconquest of Sudan often failed to cope with the rigours of campaign, falling apart after only a small number of long marches. Throughout the campaign, these boots would be a major source of complaint among the troops, with the issue even being raised in the House of Commons.

In contrast to his Egyptian and Sudanese comrades, the British infantryman was armed with the modern .303 calibre Lee-Metford bolt-action rifle. The Lee-Metford entered service in the British Army in 1888, replacing the Martini-Henry as the standard infantryman's weapon. The rifle benefited from the use of a detachable eight- or ten-round magazine situated in front of the trigger-guard, and was loaded by opening the bolt by rotating and pulling it backwards. Once opened, a bullet could be loaded either singularly by hand into the breech, or, if the magazine cut-off plate was removed, from the magazine itself by closing the bolt. Once fired the procedure was repeated, a process that allowed the British soldier a far greater rate of fire than previously enjoyed by the Martini-Henry.

The main drawback of the .303 round at the time was its reduced stopping power compared to the .577/450 round of the Martini-Henry, a fact that became a cause of great concern to British troops, who sometimes had to shoot a charging tribesman more than once to bring him down. To get around this, the British arsenal at Woolwich introduced the MK III 'hollow-point' bullet in 1897, which was quickly superseded by the improved MK IV later the same year. This expanding-jacketed projectile, which had an exposed open cavity in the nose, was found to be far more effective in bringing down an enemy, having much greater stopping-power; it also caused the target greater injuries. Sometimes, these rounds are referred to as 'dum-dum' bullets, but they are in fact not the same as those developed in Dum Dum in India and used against the Pathan tribesmen of the North West Frontier during the risings of 1897. The Battle of Omdurman was the first time the MK IV round saw major use in combat, but not all British troops were in possession of the ammunition during the campaign. Others still had the older MK II round, and those with these cartridges filed the nose off in an attempt to render them more effective.

Bennet Burleigh, a war correspondent with the *Daily Telegraph* who was attached to Kitchener's army in 1898, recalled the work to transform the older ammunition into a more effective 'stopper':

> Under superior orders, issued at Dekesh camp, large details from each regiment were engaged daily in filing off the tips of the Lee-Metford bullet. One million rounds had to be so dealt with. They we doing the same thing in Cairo arsenal. It is little short of a scandal that an army in the field has to sit down whilst the men re-make its ammunition. A bullet is put into a rifle to do certain work, and if it does not do so effectually, it is a failure, as the bullet in question is, in the opinion of most men who have seen it fired in warfare. A million is a big number. The tips were filed down till the lead showed through the nickel case. A bullet so treated expands mushroom fashion upon striking any object, and becomes a veritable 'stopper'.

The Lee-Metford rifle only had a relatively short service life, being slowly replaced from 1895 by the Lee-Enfield, itself a very similar weapon. However, Kitchener's men would not receive the new Lee-Enfield before the reconquest of Sudan was complete. The 12-inch bayonet issued to British troops was of the sword-bayonet type; since the Lee-Metford was longer than the Martini-Henry, it was shorter than that used by the Egyptian and Sudanese, not to mention of superior quality.

Artillery in use by the Egyptian Army field batteries at this time included older 6.5-cm Krupp guns, which were transported on mules or camels. From 1897, the Maxim-Nordenfelt 75-mm quick-firing gun was also introduced into service. As such, the Egyptians were using the former during the early part of the reconquest, but had largely switched to the latter by the time of Omdurman. Horse artillery batteries, however, retained their obsolete 7.75-cm Krupp guns, which suffered from a poor rate of fire. Again, in contrast to their Egyptian counter-parts, the British artillery was more modern, including the use of 12- and 15-pounder breech-loading guns for both the field and horse artillery batteries. In addition, the British also had 5.5-inch howitzers, which fired high-explosive lyddite shells.

Machine guns were also used to great effect by the British during the campaign. The Maxim gun was an American designed weapon that could fire up to 650 rounds per minute. These would be mounted on carriages and operated by men from the infantry or cavalry. A Maxim battery was formed by combining Maxim gun sections of the North Staffordshire Regiment and the Connaught Rangers, which resulted in a battery of four guns. The Egyptians also used Maxim guns, including the 'galloping Maxim', which were drawn by teams of six horses. Standard Maxim batteries within the Egyptian Army had four guns, although those of the cavalry had six. The deployment of such weapons on the battlefield had a devastating effect on the enemy, the rapid rate of fire cutting swathes through the densely packed ranks of the *Ansar*.

The British cavalry of the Omdurman campaign—which included only the 21st Lancers—wore the same basic uniform as their infantry counter-parts, but instead of the standard trousers they wore breeches. Their equipment was also slightly different, with a sword belt being worn under the tunic; although, on active service, the 1890 pattern sword was carried in a scabbard secured to the saddle. In addition to the sword, each trooper also carried a carbine (a shorter version of the Lee-Metford) in a brown leather saddle holster at the right-rear, with the ammunition for it being carried in a bandolier worn over the left shoulder. However, the main weapon of the lancers was, of course, the lance, which consisted of a nine-foot long bamboo shaft with a sharp metal point attached to the one end. Egyptian cavalry, however, were armed only with sword and carbine (a shorter version of the Martini-Henry), while other mounted troops included the Camel Corps, who were effectively mounted infantrymen.

Kitchener's tactics will be considered in subsequent chapters, but suffice to say his basic overall plan was to slowly advance towards Omdurman in stages. This way, he could ensure his army was properly supported and supplied by the railway and, where trains were not available, by camel transport. He would also use the Nile to transport men and equipment, but he would have to wait until certain times of the year, when the river would rise, for stretches of it to become passable by his gunboats and other vessels. When the Nile was too low, or a *cataract* presented an insurmountable obstacle, he would order his gunboats to be transported via rail in sections, then reassembled at locations from where they could again set sail.

Once up the Nile, the *Sirdar* intended to bring the Mahdists to battle, where he hoped his vastly superior firepower would defeat his enemy, who had equally vastly superior numbers. Despite the disparity in firepower, Kitchener was acutely aware of how dangerous the *Ansar* could be if they were able to engage his men at close-quarters. He, therefore, needed to engage the warriors at a distance and cause maximum damage before they had chance to close in. While this may sound an easy task for a modern, well-equipped army fighting against tribesmen mostly armed with spears and swords, the *Ansar* commanders equally knew what they must do to achieve victory over such an army, and they already had a string of victories to their credit. The *Sirdar* did not underestimate his enemy.

The Sudan Military Railway (SMR) has been described as the greatest of all weapons employed against the Mahdists during the 1880s and 1890s. Indeed, without it, Kitchener would have had a much more difficult campaign. When the *Sirdar* made his initial advance in 1896, he needed the *Wadi* Haifa to Kerma line in order to transport men, horses, equipment, and supplies; however, following the abandonment of Sudan a decade earlier, the *Khalifa*'s men had broken it up and rendered it totally useless. The line, therefore, had to be rebuilt, and so Kitchener turned to Édouard Percy Cranwell Girouard of the Royal Engineers.

Girouard was a Canadian-born railway builder who had worked for the Canadian Pacific Railway before attending the Military College of Canada; after this, he was commissioned into the Royal Canadian Engineers in 1888. In the same year, he travelled to Britain in order to further his studies before going on to manage the Royal Arsenal Railway. In the few years he had been in Britain, he gained quite a reputation as being a first-class railway designer and builder.

Kitchener had met Girouard in London, after which he had him transferred to the Egyptian Army in 1896 in order to join the expedition to Dongola. The Canadian set about repairing the wrecked railway line, but he was faced with a number of problems that greatly hindered his work—in particular, the poor quality of the Egyptian and Sudanese workers in his employ, many of whom were in fact criminal prisoners. Girouard, however, quickly overcame these issues and was able to complete the line to Dongola, contributing massively to the *Sirdar*'s success in 1896.

When instructions were later given to Kitchener to extend his military operations in an advance to Khartoum, he again turned to Girouard to build further stretches of the line. Many criticised the plan, since no one had attempted to build a railway through the desert where there were no readily available supplies of water, not to mention the large number of roaming hostile tribesmen who were loyal to the *Khalifa*. Yet, he still pushed on with his plans, beginning work on 1 January 1897. To the surprise of many, the pace of work was faster than expected, much to the credit of Girouard, who went to great pains to personally supervise much of the work and to visit his workers with words of praise and encouragement for their efforts.

He did, of course, encounter a number of unforeseen delays, often due to the fact that much of the equipment immediately available for use was old and quickly wearing out. None of this would stop the determined engineer, who managed to complete a remarkable 100 miles of additional track by August. By the time the Battle of Atbara was fought in April 1898, the line was less than fifty miles from the battlefield. These fifty miles would be covered by early July, with the line then totalling around 385 miles from its start point at *Wadi* Haifa.

In constructing the railway, the surveyors, who consisted of several officers of the Royal Engineers, an NCO, and eighteen Egyptian military engineers, would mark out the route ahead with wooden pegs, while a party of friendly Ababda tribesmen scouted the area to keep watch for the enemy. The bankmakers, who built the embankments or made cuttings along the marked route, followed the surveyors. Next came the platelayers, who laid out the wooden sleepers upon which they would place the iron tracks themselves. Finally, the spiking gang would spike the track to hold it in place and ensure it was straight enough for the locomotives and wagons to roll over. There were, of course, many other workers with equally important tasks, but this process highlights the considerable amount of work performed by those who built the railway.

The SMR proved of immense importance to the British reconquest of Sudan, allowing the relatively easy movement of men and supplies, which was in sharp contrast to the painful experience of those who had fought their way up the Nile in the hope of rescuing Gordon over a decade earlier. Yet despite this, the efforts of Girouard and the workers of the SMR have been largely ignored by many historians in the intervening years. Girouard, however, was not ignored at the time, since he would receive the Distinguished Service Order following the defeat of the *Khalifa* and be appointed the president of the Egyptian State Railways; after this, he travelled to South Africa to advise on the railways during the Anglo-Boer War. The SMR was indeed Kitchener's most effective weapon against the Mahdists; for his hard work on it, he earned for himself the nickname the 'Sudan Machine'.

In his book *The River War*, Winston Churchill, who would be present during the campaign in 1898, aptly summed up the importance of the railway and why it is all too often overlooked:

> In a tale of war the reader's mind is filled with the fighting. The battle—with its vivid scenes, its moving incidents, its plain and tremendous results—excites imagination and commands attention. The eye is fixed on the fighting brigades as they move amid the smoke; on the swarming figures of the enemy; on the General, serene and determined, mounted in the middle of his Staff. The long trailing line of communications is unnoticed. The fierce glory that plays on red, triumphant bayonets dazzles the observer; nor does he care to look behind to where, along a thousand miles of rail, road, and river, the convoys are crawling to the front in uninterrupted succession. Victory is the beautiful, bright-coloured flower. Transport is the stem without which it could never have blossomed. Yet even the military student, in his zeal to master the fascinating combinations of the actual conflict, often forgets the far more intricate complications of supply.

Having briefly examined both the *Sirdar* and his Anglo-Egyptian army, it is perhaps useful to end this chapter by taking a look at some of Kitchener's key senior officers who assisted him in his reconquest of Sudan. These include Major-General William Forbes Gatacre, who commanded the British Division at Omdurman, and Major-General Archibald Hunter, who commanded the Egyptian Division. In addition, consideration will also be given to some of the brigade commanders, such as Brigadier-Generals Andrew Gilbert Wauchope, Neville Lyttelton, and Hector

MacDonald. Lastly, there is also Commander Colin Keppel of the Royal Navy, who commanded the naval forces on the Nile in support of Kitchener's land forces.

Major-General Gatacre was born at Herbertshire Castle in Stirlingshire, Scotland in 1843. He joined the British Army in 1862—at a time when commissions and promotions were still obtained by purchase—as an ensign in the 70th Regiment of Foot. His first experience of service overseas was in India, where he was promoted to lieutenant in 1864 and captain in 1870. He returned to Britain and took an instructional role at Sandhurst between 1875 and 1879. The following year, he travelled back to India and was promoted to major in 1881 and lieutenant-colonel the year after. By the early 1890s, Gatacre held the local rank of major-general and would take part in the Chitral Relief Expedition of 1895, for which he would be mentioned in dispatches. He was back in Britain in 1897 in command of a brigade, after which he went to Egypt to take command of the British Division during Kitchener's final advance to Omdurman.

Major-General Hunter, unlike many senior British Army officers of the time, did not come from a military family background; rather, his father was a businessman in whose steps Archibald did not wish to follow. Instead, he joined the Lancashire Regiment as a second-lieutenant in 1875. His first experience of Sudan came during the Nile campaign of 1884-85, and he was later appointed governor for Dongola, after which he was made commandant of the Egyptian Frontier Field Force in 1895; the force was responsible for manning forts and other outposts along the southern Egyptian border and along the Nile. It is, perhaps, his experience of commanding Egyptian troops that prompted Kitchener to choose Hunter to command the Egyptian Division.

Brigadier-General Wauchope had entered the Royal Navy as a cadet in 1859, but he was unhappy with life in the service and so left after less than three years. However, he joined the army in 1865 by purchasing a commission as a second-lieutenant in the 42nd Regiment of Foot. By 1867, he was a full lieutenant, and his first experience of active service came during the Anglo-Ashanti War of 1873-74. After a stint in Cyprus, he returned to Britain as a captain, but he was soon off to South Africa where he took part in the Transvaal Rebellion of 1880-81. The following year, he was in Egypt after the British invasion and would later take part in the Battle of El Teb in 1884, during which he was wounded and mentioned in dispatches. Recovered from his injuries, he was promoted to major in the same year, which was quickly followed by brevet lieutenant-colonel only several months later. His experience of war in Sudan continued; he took part in the Nile expedition and was present at the Battle of Kirbekan in 1885, during which he was again wounded. In 1888, he was promoted to colonel, and in 1894 he became the commanding officer of the 2nd Black Watch. At Omdurman, as a brigadier-general, he would command the 1st Brigade of the British Division.

Brigadier-General Lyttelton was commissioned as a second-lieutenant in the Rifle Brigade in 1865 at the age of nineteen. The following year, he was sent to Canada, where he took part in operations to put down the Fenian Raids. A string of promotions followed, including: lieutenant in 1869, captain in 1877, and major in 1882. He also took part in the campaign in Egypt in 1882, being present at the Battle of Tel el-Kebir, for which he was mentioned in despatches and later promoted to brevet lieutenant-colonel. He next spent time in Gibraltar as assistant military secretary to the governor, and India as military secretary to the governor of Bombay. In 1892, he was a full lieutenant-colonel and spent time commanding the 1st Battalion of the Rifle Brigade, then the 2nd Battalion. During the Omdurman campaign, he was given command of 2nd Brigade of the British Division.

Brigadier-General MacDonald (sometimes written as Macdonald) was a Scottish officer who first experienced military service in the Inverness-shire Highland Rifle Volunteers in 1870, although he enlisted into the 92nd Regiment of Foot as a regular soldier the following year. He rapidly gained promotion through the ranks, and, as a colour-sergeant, fought in the Second Anglo-Afghan War of 1878-80. It would be during this campaign that he distinguished himself in combat, for which he was offered a commission; thus, he was one of only a very few enlisted men to go on to become an officer during the Victorian period. More active service followed in South Africa, taking part in the Battle of Majuba Hill during the Transvaal Rebellion, where he again distinguished himself in action. MacDonald also saw active service in Sudan during the Nile expedition, and was present at the Battle of Toski in 1889 as well as the action at Tokar in 1891, after which he was promoted to major. He would command the 1st Brigade of the Egyptian Division during the Battle of Omdurman.

Commander Keppel of the Royal Navy, who was the son of Admiral Sir Henry Keppel, commanded the naval element of the force sent to re-conquer Sudan. Born in 1862, he had joined the navy as a cadet in 1875 and served on numerous ships in the Mediterranean and elsewhere, rising steadily up the commissioned ranks. In 1897, he was seconded to the Egyptian Government to command a number of armoured gunboats on the Nile River in order to support Kitchener as he advanced towards Khartoum.

Kitchener was, therefore, supported by an experienced number of senior officers during his Sudan campaign, some of which had prior experience of fighting the Mahdists. There are, of course, numerous others, a number of which we will meet later in this book. However, we next turn our attention to the *Khalifa*, the *Ansar*, and its senior commanders.

5

The *Khalifa* and the *Ansar*

Born in 1846, Abdullahi al-Taishi (sometimes referred to in other sources as Abdallahi ibn Muhammad), the *Khalifa* of Sudan, was a Baggara tribesman from Darfur, whose family had lost their home at the hands of the army of Zubair *Pasha* (the then governor of the province of Bahr al-Ghazal, who conquered Darfur in the name of the *Khedive* in 1874). His father, Mohammed et Taki, had three other sons called Ya'qub, Yusef, and Sammani, as well as a daughter called Fatma. In contrast to Muhammad Ahmed, Abdullahi al-Taishi was not well-educated in terms of the Islamic faith, despite the fact that his own father had been a religious teacher. With his son unable to recite more than a few passages of the *Quran*, and then only those necessary for prayer, Mohammed et Taki encouraged the future *Khalifa* to leave Sudan and travel to Mecca in order to find someone to teach him the ways of his religion, a desire he repeated in his dying days. It is said, however, that Abdullahi al-Taishi never really did acquire much expertise in Islam, despite one day succeeding the devoutly religious *Mahdi* as leader of the *Mahdiyya* in Sudan.

Abdullahi al-Taishi was said to be both tall and physically strong, although his face was heavily pitted due to suffering from smallpox as a child. He was also known for his fearless courage, having displayed acts of great bravery as he fought against Zubair *Pasha*. During the campaigns in Darfur, he would be taken prisoner and sentenced to death by the governor, but he narrowly escaped execution due to the timely intervention of a number of influential religious men, who no doubt once knew his father. Oddly, watching Zubair *Pasha* grow ever victorious and more powerful, he developed an admiration for him, despite the sufferings the governor had inflicted on him and his people.

With Egyptian control over Sudan steadily on the wane in the early 1880s, Abdullahi al-Taishi began his quest to seek out the true *Mahdi*, who, allegedly according to a dream he once had, he believed was none other than Zubair *Pasha*. Upon conversing with the governor by letter, the official bluntly informed him that he was not the redeemer of Islam, and that he must look elsewhere. A somewhat disappointed Abdullahi al-Taishi reluctantly gave up the idea but nevertheless continued his search, during which he heard of a religious man on the island of Aba. Eventually, after an arduous journey to find him, the two men met, and, according to Slatin, who later conversed with the *Khalifa* during his time as his prisoner:

> ... *Sheikh* el Koreishi died, and Mohammed Ahmed and his disciples lost no time in going at once to Mesallamia, where they erected a tomb, or dome, to his memory.
>
> It was while here that a certain Abdullahi bin Mohammed, of the Taaisha section of the Baggara (cattle-owning) tribe of southwestern Darfur, presented himself to Mohammed Ahmed and sought permission to be admitted into the Sammania Tarika; his request was granted, and Abdullahi swore eternal fidelity to his new master.

Slatin also later claimed that Abdullahi al-Taishi once told him:

> At length I reached Messallamia, and here I found the *Mahdi* busily engaged in building the tomb of the late *Sheikh* el Koreishi. On seeing him I entirely forgot all the troubles I had suffered on my journey, and was content to simply look at him and listen to his teaching. For several hours I was too timid to dare speak to him; but at length I plucked up the courage, and in a few words told him my story, and about the sad condition of my brothers and sister, and I begged him, for the sake of God and His Prophet, to allow me to become one of his disciples. He did so, and gave me his hand, which I kissed most fervently, and I swore entire submission to him as long as I lived.

Thus, Abdullahi al-Taishi joined the Mahdist cause.

The Baggara tribesman would follow his new master throughout the events described in the previous chapters, eventually becoming one of his most trusted lieutenants. When the *Mahdi* died in 1885, he vied to become the rightful successor of Muhammad Ahmed, along with Muhammad Sharif of the Ashraf tribe. However, the *Mahdi* had personally long favoured Abdullahi al-Taishi to become his successor, and the decision was made to respect the dead leader's wishes—the *Mahdi*'s words were, after all, unquestionable. Despite this, Muhammad Sharif would later mount several serious challenges for the leadership of the *Mahdiyya*, but the newly recognised *Khalifa* would defeat each one in turn.

For the next fourteen years, Abdullahi al-Taishi would reign over Mahdist-controlled Sudan, although during most of this period he was forced to devote much of his time and energy to maintaining his personal powerbase. This resulted in his attention all too often being taken away from the expansion of Mahdism, which had the effect of the power and influence of the Mahdists going into a slow but steady decline, despite its successes in Abyssinia. While the *Mahdi* had managed to unite the fractious tribes of Sudan, the *Khalifa* conversely saw them begin to fragment; Abdullahi al-Taishi simply did not have the charisma of his predecessor.

The *Khalifa* rightly feared that Muhammad Sharif was working against him, and so he gave orders for those suspected of being supporters of his rival to be removed from positions of power or authority, many of which were either put to death or sentenced to long terms of imprisonment on a mere whim. He even ordered Muhammad Ahmed's wives and children to be kept under close surveillance, showing the high-levels of paranoia that were already setting in. Just about everyone who had served the *Mahdi* closely, including cousins and leading military figures, were affected at some point by these purges; the only exception was Osman Digna, who was, perhaps, so far away that he managed to escape the *Khalifa*'s attention.

In November 1891, in what appeared to be an attempt to usurp the *Khalifa*, supporters of Muhammad Sharif and Abdullahi al-Taishi clashed in a brief skirmish near the *Mahdi*'s tomb in Omdurman, which led to the Mahdist leader ordering the arrest of those suspected of plotting against him. A number of alleged conspirators were quickly executed or banished into exile; Muhammad Sharif aggressively protested against this, and so Abdullahi al-Taishi also had him arrested and put on trial. Unsurprisingly, he was found guilty of plotting to depose the *Khalifa* and given a four-year term of imprisonment.

It is said that Abdullahi al-Taishi maintained a personal staff of twenty eunuchs to tend to his personal needs, as well as at least a dozen male slave children who, once they reached puberty, were later sent to serve in the army and replaced with new, younger boys. It is also said that he preferred Christians to Muslims to act as close servants, since he believed they were less likely to plot against him; a fact that may help explain why the likes of Ohrwalder and Slatin survived as his prisoners for so long. The *Khalifa* also maintained a large harem, the women of which were sourced from all over Sudan, or sometimes even further afield. However, under Sharia law he was limited to only four wives, so he simply divorced the ones he no longer wanted in order to marry new women. He led the good life, despite the previous ban on worldly pleasures by his predecessor, and began to grow slow and fat.

During the latter years of his reign, shortly before his defeat at the Battle of Omdurman, Abdullahi al-Taishi became increasingly distant from his people. He built a wall around his home—as well as the homes of his close family members—and became ever more despotic, issuing orders for the people to pray more often at the central mosque in Omdurman; this move was made in an attempt to soak up more of their spare time so they had less chance to meet to plot against him. Execution by hanging, long ago banned by Muhammad Ahmed—who much preferred to behead people—as being un-Islamic, was reintroduced as a form of public execution that, it was reasoned, had the additional benefit of deterring others from committing crimes against the *Khalifa* and his rule of law.

Understandably, resentment against Abdullahi al-Taishi steadily grew; it reached such a level that the entire Batahin tribe actively turned against him. The response was swift as well as brutal, with many of the tribe being rounded up to die while prisoners or otherwise publically put to death; first by hanging, then, as the ropes broke after the strain of killing so many, by beheading. Those who escaped immediate execution had their hands and feet cut off by the local butchers; most would be left to bleed to death, while those who managed to stay alive had no recourse but to beg on the streets of Omdurman, although few survived for long. Such was the growing cruelty of the *Khalifa* in the lead up to his confrontation with the *Sirdar*.

Much of what we know about Abdullahi al-Taishi, of course, comes from Ohrwalder and Slatin, both of whom were heavily influenced in their writing by Major Wingate, who, as we have seen, wanted to wage a propaganda war against the Mahdists to galvanise public opinion against what he portrayed as the bloodthirsty *Khalifa* and his savage followers. There is little doubt that the *Mahdi*'s successor was indeed often cruel and brutal in his methods, but this was the way of life in the region at the time and long before, and thus not that unusual. In more recent years, 'Ismat Hasan Zulfo, in his book *Karari*, has sought to point out the more positive aspects of Abdullahi al-Taishi's reign, such as the introduction of a centralised state with its own fiscal and legal systems. The Mahdist leader even introduced a postal service and began rebuilding Omdurman along more modern, sanitary lines. Zulfo also argues that the *Khalifa* was a good organiser with great capacity to plan strategically, and that he was never quite the dictator as we tend to view him today. The *Mahdi*, he concedes, was certainly a dictator, since what he said was considered sacred and unquestionable, whereas Abdullahi al-Taishi made use of councils in an attempt to legitimise his decisions. The important point to remember here is that the *Mahdi* and the *Khalifa* were two very different men—the former bold, self-assured, and feared; the latter lacking in self-confidence and, in later years, suffering the effects of paranoia regarding his precarious hold on power.

Following the *Mahdi*'s death, the organisation of the *Ansar* remained largely the same for a while; as time went by, Abdullahi al-Taishi would eventually introduce a number of important and major changes. The predominate reason for these changes was to enable the Mahdist army to meet not only external threats but also address internal issues, effectively acting as a police force as well as a military one. All men capable of bearing arms were considered eligible for service in the *Ansar*. Full-time warriors—who we today would consider as regular soldiers—would be deployed to man the numerous garrisons established along Sudan's borders to guard against invasion. The part-time volunteers, who were effectively every other able-bodied male not in full-time military service, were used to form a reserve. When a military expedition was required, or when Sudan was threatened from an external aggressor, as it would be in 1896 through to 1898, warriors would be drawn from both the regulars and volunteers to form an army.

The *Khalifa* had also sub-divided Sudan into six administrative districts called *imalas*, and the senior *amir* of each *imala* would take command of military forces from that district in times of mobilisation. However, if Sudan was invaded by an external power, the *amirs* would stand aside for a more senior military commander appointed by the *Khalifa*. Supplies for the *Ansar* were the responsibility of the *bayt al-mal* (treasury), which was tasked with collecting taxes and securely storing any items of value that belonged to the Mahdist state. The treasury was further divided into departments that were responsible for stores of arms and ammunition, transports (camels and mules), as well as the granaries from which the *Ansar* would be fed. Each district of Sudan had its own *bayt al-mal*.

As with any army, the *Ansar* was organised into units, the most basic of which was known as a *rub*. Unlike most European armies at the time, *rubs* did not have any fixed number of men and often varied considerably in size, although they normally numbered no fewer than 800 warriors and could be as large as several thousand. A *rub* would also be sub-divided into four sections, three containing fighting men while the fourth was responsible for administrative tasks. The first of the three fighting sections included spearmen, the second riflemen, and the third cavalry or horsemen.

Spearmen would usually perform the majority of the fighting and bear the brunt of most battles. These warriors, as their title suggests, were only armed with bladed weapons—usually one long and three short spears, as well as a sword—and did not generally have modern, nor obsolete, firearms in their inventory. They would also be split into further sections along tribal lines, each having its own banner or standard under the command of a mounted *amir*. Again, there was no fixed number of these sections, nor fixed number of warriors within them, since each district would have unequal male populations from which to recruit to the army. However, larger sections would be divided into hundreds, each of which would be commanded by a *rasmiya*, with the hundred being further sub-divided into four equal quarters, again each of which were commanded by a *muqaddam*.

Riflemen were known as the *jihadiya*, and were also divided into further sections of one-hundred men under the command of an *amir* with its own standard. Again, each hundred would be sub-divided into sections of twenty-five men under a *muqaddam*. All members of the *jihadiya* were armed with rifles, most of which were captured Remingtons taken as booty from the previous victories against the Egyptian Army. Interestingly, the *Khalifa* later distributed a number of riflemen across other fighting units to increase the fighting ability of the non-firearm armed formations.

Cavalrymen came predominately from the Baggara, while their horses were also from Darfur. The number of horsemen varied within each *rub*, with each being armed with swords and long spears, although some would also carry rifles if they had possession of one, especially for reconnaissance purposes.

Mention should also be made of the *Khalifa*'s bodyguard, which, at the time of the Omdurman campaign, numbered around 2,000 warriors. This guard was divided into two *rubs*, with every man of the first *rub* being armed with a rifle. In contrast, the second *rub* would be divided into sections, some, known as *khashkhashans*, were armed with elephant guns, while the *mushammaratiya* were made up of particularly tall men armed with long spears. Another section was made up of musicians, itself sub-divided into three sub-sections, who played various brass instruments; all musicians were men taken prisoner in battle and forced to serve the *Khalifa*.

Finally, the *Ansar* also consisted of the elite *muluazimayya*, under the command of Osman al-Din; this was a specially selected group of warriors who received a higher-level of training and were issued with the best weapons available, mostly Remington rifles of the best condition. The *muluazimayya* was made up of eighteen *rubs*, each of which was sub-divided into eight to twelve sections of 100, again each having its own banner or standard. As a result of their high-status, these warriors, who were full-time regulars, were housed in barracks, drew regular pay and were serviced by their own individual *bayt al-mal*.

Before considering the weapons and tactics employed by the *Ansar*, it is perhaps useful to briefly examine the different coloured-flags or standards that will be mentioned in later chapters—in particular, the Black and Green Flags.

The Black Flag, under the *Mahdi*, had incorporated the entire Mahdist army. Later on, the *Ansar* was divided into three under three separate flags, at which point the Black Flag became considered the most important. It principally became a reserve of irregular troops and was commanded by *Amir* Ya'qub, one of the *Khalifa*'s half-brothers, who was responsible for calling up large numbers of warriors in time of war, and who acted as the overall leader of all Mahdist forces throughout Sudan. It was also the principal recruiter of men to the *Ansar*, and included the elite *muluazimayya*. The Black Flag would be sub-divided into sections under other flags or standards, which were again organised along tribal lines and further divided into hundreds in the fashion already mentioned above. There was no specific *bayt al-mal* for Ya'qub's command, since he had authority to draw weapons and other supplies from across stores in Sudan as required. Generally speaking, the vast majority of men under the Black Flag were poorly armed with swords and spears.

The Green Flag was only permitted to recruit warriors from tribes that inhabited lands in the area around the White Nile, including men from the Dighaim, the Kanana, and the Lahiwiyin. It had previously absorbed the Red Flag, and, like the Black Flag, it was generally poorly armed. It need be noted here that this Green Flag should not be confused with the personal Green Flag of Osman al-Din, which was of a darker shade.

The warriors of the *Ansar* used a variety of weapons of numerous type and description, but perhaps the most common was the spear. This took the form of an approximately six to ten-foot-long, broad-bladed weapon that was literally used to stab an enemy at close range. The actual blade was usually shaped like a leaf but could vary widely in terms of width—commonly three to nine inches—and be anything up to around fifteen inches in length. Surviving examples are sometimes seen with basic decoration to the blade, such as etched diamond patterns or even inlaid with copper or brass. In addition to his long spear, the average Mahdist warrior also carried three short spears, the latter of which were used for throwing at an adversary from a distance. Mounted warriors, however, would generally carry longer spears than those on foot.

Warriors would also be issued with a double-edged sword—known as a *kaskara*—for close-quarter combat, the weapon being carried in a red leather scabbard or bag worn over the shoulder using a strap. The blades of the swords had mostly been imported into Sudan from Europe over a period of many years prior to the rise of the *Mahdi*, although a few were made in Sudan itself, the latter usually being of much lower quality than the former.

A few tribesmen might carry knives or use shields for personal protection, but the majority of warriors did not use the latter, since the archaic shields could not hope to stop a high-powered round from a Martini-Henry or a Lee-Metford, and they could also be a burden to carry on long marches. The knives came in a wide variety of designs and sizes, although they were usually double-edged with wooden handles, the shaft of which were often covered in a leather grip. The blades were either straight or curved, although some were also hooked for use against horses or camels to bring down its rider in battle. The shields again came in varying designs, although the most common was probably the round type and made of buffalo, elephant, hippo or rhino hide with a leather strap fitted to the reverse to hold it.

Less commonly used, although they certainly made an appearance on the battlefield, were axes and throwing sticks known as a *trombash*. Again, the design of the axes varied but would consist of a metal head and wooden shaft, while the throwing sticks usually had a curved end, being designed to be used against horses or camels to bring them crashing to the ground.

The riflemen, of course, were armed with firearms, the vast majority of which were acquired from the dead bodies of defeated Egyptian troops or otherwise gathered up off the battlefields of the 1880s. It has been said that the Mahdists recovered an incredible 21,000 such rifles, most of them breech-loading, rolling-block Remingtons. At the time of Muhammad Ahmed's victories, this weapon was considered modern, but by the time of Kitchener's reconquest of Sudan, they had become obsolete, although Egyptian Army troops were also armed with older rifles compared to their British counter-parts. Nevertheless, the Remington, the design of which dated back to the mid-1860s, was both simple to use and robust.

This allowed the largely untrained tribesmen at least a chance to become relatively proficient with a firearm for which they received no expert instruction on its use or maintenance; although in reality many had the bad habit of firing too high and regularly missed their targets. In addition to the Remington, some warriors were also in possession of the Martini-Henry rifle, albeit in very small numbers, which had somehow found their way into Sudan, most likely via gun traffickers. Others were armed with even older muzzle-loading rifles and muskets, left over from a previous era. Riflemen would carry their ammunition in bandoliers, which were worn over the shoulder and were usually of local manufacture.

Incredibly, at the time of the Omdurman campaign, the *Ansar* had developed its own artillery arm of eleven batteries, each being made up of six guns. These included a variety of guns captured from the Egyptians over the preceding years, such as Krupp guns, Gatlings, rocket tubes, brass mountain guns, machine guns (including Nordenfelts and a Remington), and others that were of a more exotic nature. These heavy weapons, as we have seen, were serviced by troops once trained to use them in the Egyptian Army, with the artillerymen usually being prisoners forced to serve the *Khalifa*. Despite all this, only three Mahdist artillery pieces would actually be used on the battlefield of Omdurman, although others were found nearby, apparently abandoned *en route* to the action after their crews learned the battle was already lost.

Commanders of the *Ansar* knew they were heavily out-gunned by both Egyptian and British troops, and so they had to develop their tactics accordingly. The dominant tactic was to achieve surprise, then encircle an enemy before launching a rushed assault in order to shock. The hope was to use the overwhelming numbers of warriors to carry the day and quickly inflict defeat before their adversary could properly prepare and respond. As part of this strategy, the riflemen would take up positions some distance away and maintain fire on their targets, while the spearmen worked their way to closer positions from which to launch their massed rush. The fire from the riflemen, it was hoped, would soften up the enemy, allowing the spearmen to attack at close quarters before too many were gunned down.

Another common tactic in use throughout the time of the Mahdists was for their warriors to make use of natural cover and lie low, out of sight of an advancing enemy force. Once the enemy was within a short distance, the warriors would suddenly rise up as if from nowhere and launch their frenzied attack. It was noted by both the Egyptians and the British that the Mahdists could cover distances extremely quickly, and, in doing so, were also well-organised into formations, ahead of which would be a mounted *amir* leading his warriors in the charge, shouting words of encouragement and other religious phrases.

Again, we finish this chapter with a brief look at some of Abdullahi al-Taishi's principal military commanders who were present at the battles fought during the 1896–98 campaign. These include: Ya'qub Muhammad Turshain, Osman al-Din, Ibrahim al-Khalil, Osman Azrak, and Osman Digna.

Amir Ya'qub Muhammad Turshain was the overall military leader of the *Ansar*. He was noted for being kind, tactful, and charitable, but his ability to appeal to members of all tribes was, perhaps, his most useful and effective skill as a military commander. He was also well-educated, unlike his half-brother, since his father had one day hoped Ya'qub would directly succeed him as a religious teacher, and so heavily encouraged him in his studies. It was also Ya'qub who transformed the mass rabble of Mahdist followers into a well-organised army, developing and maintaining intricate records of men, arms, and supplies. In addition to his duties as a military commander, he was also responsible for protecting the power of the *Khalifa*, seeking out those who might oppose him, as well as maintaining internal security across Sudan. He had some limited experience of war, having taken part in the sieges of El Obeid and Khartoum under the *Mahdi*, and was well-respected by many who served under him. In contrast, others have criticised him as being too inexperienced for such high command, since he failed to modernise the weapons used by his troops, who, in 1898, would be faced with an adversary armed with far more modern equipment. Ya'qub was fiercely supportive of his half-brother, the *Khalifa*; however, as the years wore on, his influence with the Mahdist leader went into decline as Osman al-Din, Abdullahi al-Taishi's son, became increasingly the favoured one. In fact, a personal feud developed between uncle and nephew, but Ya'qub would still remain in command of the Black Flag by the time of the Battle of Omdurman.

Osman al-Din, the *Khalifa*'s eldest son who was born in 1873, had been mainly brought up in Omdurman and benefited from an education that his father had not. This privileged upbringing, however, resulted in him being far withdrawn from his fellow Baggara tribesmen, who generally lived away from large settlements such as Omdurman. Indeed, it is said that Osman al-Din spoke with a different accent to his fellow clansmen and had a much softer lifestyle, enjoying frequent late night parties and other forms of pleasure denied the ordinary Sudanese. Such a frivolous lifestyle brought him into conflict with his father, who once had him put under effective house-arrest in an attempt to make him take his responsibilities more seriously. Although he would take a senior command at Omdurman, he was totally inexperienced in the way of war, which would later become apparent during the battle where he commanded the *muluazimayya*.

Ibrahim al-Khalil, who was a year younger than Osman al-Din, was a far more able military commander with the ability to think on a much more strategic level. He was a cousin of Abdullahi al-Taishi, who had lived with the *Khalifa* and his own sons from the age of ten. He also benefited from a good education, and, at only twenty years of age, led a military expedition to put down a rising that had broken out in the Nuba Mountains in 1894, a campaign that ended in success for the young commander. Ibrahim al-Khalil, however, tolerated no nonsense and could be prone to spontaneous outbursts of anger if others did not agree with his military thinking. Following such a clash with Osman al-Din, the two developed feelings of bitter hostility towards one another, which would last for some time.

Osman Azrak was born in El Obeid, and had worked for the Sudanese postal service before coming into the employ of the Mahdists in a military capacity. His main role was to keep watch along Sudan's northern frontier, although it is said he personally led over 100 raids into Egyptian territory, which caused the Egyptian Government to spend considerable amounts of money in an attempt to counter his annoying intrusions. Although the Mahdists possessed cavalry, it was Osman Azrak who saw the true potential in such a fast-moving and mobile arm. At the Battle of Hafir in September 1896, he personally directed a gun manned by an Egyptian artilleryman—again, a prisoner in the Mahdist army—in an attempt to hit one of Kitchener's armoured steamers. After missing his target three times, Osman Azrak dismounted from his horse and approached the gunner, who he believed was missing his target on purpose, and struck the man with the flat of his sword, cutting off part of the artilleryman's hand as he instinctively raised it to protect his head. The trembling Egyptian, despite his terrible wound and rapid loss of blood, went straight back to his gun and fired a fourth round, this time hitting the steamer in its boiler. Osman Azrak would command—following the demotion of Hammuda Idris, the Mahdist commander in northern Dongola—the *Ansar* forces at the Battle of Firket in 1896.

Osman Digna was, undoubtedly, the most well-known of the *Khalifa*'s military commanders at the time. It is not known where he was born, although some believe it was Suakin, but it is known he spent time living in Alexandria, Egypt where he worked as a slave trader under the name of Osman Ali. He would later take part in Arabi *Pasha*'s rebellion before joining the Mahdists. As has been seen, he opposed the British during both their expeditions to Suakin, and fought against them at the Battles of El Teb and Tamai. Although he would be beaten in action a number of times, the British were unable to inflict upon him any meaningful defeat, allowing him to remain a threat for years. Following the *Mahdi*'s death, he continued to serve the *Khalifa*, fighting against the British again at the Battle of Gemaizah in 1888, and it would not be until the British captured Tokar in 1891 that he retreated from the area. He would, however, yet again oppose the British in 1898 at the battles of Atbara and Omdurman. It is said that Osman Digna often delivered fiery speeches to his warriors, which could last a number of hours, and that he understood the importance of the psychological aspect of warfare. He also had great physical endurance, being able to walk many miles carrying his weapons and supplies, as well as those of others when they became too weary on the march. In battle, he learned to identify and exploit the weak spots of British and Egyptian squares, particularly to their rear, a number of which he was able to penetrate.

6

The Dongola Campaign

In March 1896, the Mahdists had begun to turn their attention to the Italian garrison at Kassala in eastern Sudan. This presented the British with the need to move quickly, since not only was the enemy concentrating its efforts elsewhere, thus taking their eyes off the border with Egypt, but it was also imperative to do something to help prevent another humiliating defeat of European troops, who were now cut off from their comrades retreating towards Massowah. While fear of the French claiming new territory on the Upper Nile—the Belgians were also sending an expedition from the south—was the prime motivator in British policy, it was the predicament of the Italians that laid out the timetable.

This schedule began so rapidly that it took many by surprise in both London and Cairo. In fact, orders for an initial advance to Akasha from *Wadi* Halfa were forwarded to Archibald Hunter—then a colonel and commandant of the Egyptian Frontier Field Force—at midnight on 12 March. Additional instructions would also be sent to Kitchener, ordering all available troops to be pushed on up the Nile with a view to advancing towards Dongola itself. As the Egyptian troops began their movements, the 1st Battalion of the North Staffordshire Regiment was given orders to advance to *Wadi* Halfa, where it would take the place of the departing local Egyptian garrison.

It appears that the decisions being taken in London were not properly communicated to the Egyptian Government, the *Khedive* being largely unaware of events until after they had begun. So unexpected were the orders, according to Victorian author Charles Royale, who was writing of these events in 1900, that:

> It is said that Colonel [Leslie] Rundle, Chief of the Staff of the Egyptian army, was aroused to hear the news by stones thrown at his window in the middle of the night, and that no one could be found bold enough to awake and inform the *Sirdar*, who remained in ignorance until the morning.

Despite this sudden rush to action, neither Kitchener nor most officers and government officials in Egypt would have been surprised such events were now taking place. It had been long assumed by many that the time would come to face the Mahdists once again and—although this was not yet sanctioned—retake Khartoum in order to avenge the killing of Gordon, an event that had by now occurred over a decade earlier. Indeed, much of the effort expended in the rebuilding and retraining of the Egyptian Army during the previous years had been done in the belief of an eventual reconquest of Sudan. However, for the moment, operations would remain limited to a demonstration in the Dongola province in order to take pressure off the Italians.

Nevertheless, the forces being assembled for the coming campaign in Dongola—known as the Dongola Expeditionary Force—were considerable. In total, Kitchener would lead an army of over 9,000 Egyptian and Sudanese troops into the province, including infantry, cavalry, and artillery. It should be understood that no substantial number of British troops were initially mobilised for operations, with the exception of the British officers commanding certain battalions of the Egyptian Army. However, the men of the North Staffords, which was over 900 strong, were to remain in a state of readiness at *Wadi* Halfa in case they were needed, while small detachments from the regiment and the Connaught Rangers would also be employed to man a number of Maxim guns for the expeditionary force. The expedition was to advance to *Wadi* Halfa by rail and river, after which it would disembark and continue its march on foot. The Sudan Military Railway would be considerably extended by Captain Édouard Girouard of the Royal Engineers.

Kitchener, in company with Major Wingate and Slatin *Pasha*, left Cairo on 21 March and travelled to *Wadi* Halfa via Assouan with the North Staffords. Meanwhile, the Egyptian Government, now fully aware of the intended operations, again turned to the travel company Thomas Cook to supply it with a number of river steamers to facilitate the transportation of men and equipment down the Nile. These vessels, usually used to transport wealthy European tourists in great comfort, were stripped of all their niceties and temporarily converted into mini-troopships. The work of the steamers began on the same day the *Sirdar* left the Egyptian capital, and within five days, an incredible 4,500 men, 750 animals, and large quantities of other equipment and supplies had been moved up from their concentration point at the village of Belianeh in Upper Egypt. This settlement would remain in use as a storage depot in support of the expedition, and so a detachment from the Connaught Rangers was stationed there to both guard and service it.

Hampering the preparations, however, was the weather. According to Andrew Hilliard Atteridge, a special correspondent for *The Daily Chronicle* newspaper, who was travelling with the expeditionary force:

> The thermometer in the shade in the hospital at Alimula marked 129 degrees. At Melik-en-Nasr the air was like a furnace. About three o'clock there were heavy

peals of thunder, and then came a storm of wind, with driving clouds of hot dust and sand. Melik-en-Nasr happened to be between two thunderstorms; north and south of us we could see the dark rain clouds, and later on we heard that north of us at Ambigol and to the south at Tanjor there had been a regular deluge—a rare event in the Soudan. Six miles of poles and wires on the telegraph line were blown down, and many of the *khors* [dry watercourses or ravines] were flooded.

Along with the discomforts brought by the bad weather, Atteridge also experienced first-hand some of the earliest horrors of the campaign:

At five we had the camels loaded and started for Tanjor. We made a short cut, diverging at times from the regular convoy track. Vultures were exceptionally rare this year in Soudan, but in one of the *khors* there was perched on a rock one of the largest birds of the kind I have ever seen, and another black vulture rose wheeling from the sandy hollow below. A couple of hundred yards in front of the point we had reached, no fewer than nineteen dead transport camels lay in a straggling line across the *khor*. They were in every stage of decay, in every attitude of grimly grotesque distortion. The air was sickening. My horse, which generally took no notice of dead animals, shied badly, and our camels had to be almost dragged past the ghastly group of their dead comrades.

Hunter, meanwhile, had been able to reach and take Akasha without encountering any resistance from the Mahdists, who were probably as surprised by the sudden commencement of operations as were those carrying them out. A number of outposts were established between *Wadi* Halfa and Akasha, which would act as concentration points for the advancing Egyptian units. Another, the 9th Sudanese Battalion, would march across the desert from Kosseir on the Red Sea coast in eastern Egypt to Kenah on the Nile before joining the expedition; this unit had formed part of the garrison at Suakin. Girouard had also begun his work to extend the railway line towards the small settlement of Ambigol in Sudan, which was located between the second and third *cataracts*.

Thanks to the assistance of the Ababda (a subgroup of the Beja tribe who were friendly towards the British), intelligence came in that suggested the Mahdists had no more than about 400 men at Abu Hamed; a much more substantial force, estimated to comprise of 6,000 warriors and horsemen, was located at Berber, a settlement on the Nile near its junction with the Atbara River. It was now only a matter of time before the first major action of the Dongola campaign would take place, on 7 June, at Firket. However, the first actual clash of arms would take the form of a much more minor skirmish at the beginning of May.

At about midday on 1 May, Major John Burn-Murdoch, a cavalry officer who was a veteran of earlier campaigns in Egypt, was leading a reconnaissance of three squadrons of Egyptian cavalry—a small force totalling around 240 men. With him were Captains V. G. Whitla, W. H. Persse and H. G. Fitton, while Lieutenant Alexander Murray (also known as Lord Fincastle) was acting as his galloper. At about four miles out of Akasha, they came across a Mahdist force estimated at around 1,300 strong. Some 300 men of this force, believed to be Baggara tribesmen, were mounted on either horses or camels, while the remainder marched along on foot. Upon sighting the Mahdists, the major gave the order to retire back to Akasha, since he had no infantry support and his own force was simply too small to give battle. However, as the cavalrymen withdrew, the tribesmen also spotted the Egyptian troops.

Setting off in pursuit of the Egyptians, the Baggara were able to catch up with Burn-Murdoch's small force as it began to enter a narrow defile, and set about attacking the cavalrymen who were forming the rear-guard. This sudden clash quickly resulted in several casualties among the Egyptians, most of them being speared as they attempted to get away from their attackers. The leading elements of the major's force then turned around and conducted a head-on charge towards the Mahdists, the two opposing sides smashing violently into one another, at which a fierce hand-to-hand struggle ensued.

After about twenty minutes of close-quarter combat, the mounted Baggara tribesmen suddenly broke off from the fight and made off at speed back towards their fellow Mahdists who had been advancing on foot. The Egyptian cavalrymen were then ordered to dismount by Burn-Murdoch, who realised the ground was unsuitable to conduct another effective charge. The major instructed his men to commence fire at the enemy with their carbines. A hail of fire was poured down onto the Mahdists for some time, only ceasing at about 3 p.m., when the 11th Sudanese Battalion under Major G. W. Jackson came marching into view. Realising they themselves were now heavily out-gunned, the Mahdists conducted a speedy retirement and the skirmish came to an end.

This first clash of arms of the Dongola campaign resulted in two Egyptian cavalrymen being killed, while a further ten were wounded, including Captain Fitton. It was later determined that the Mahdists suffered eighteen of their number killed and more than eighty wounded.

Although not strictly part of the Dongola campaign, it is perhaps useful to briefly consider another minor clash of arms that would occur elsewhere in Sudan involving Osman Digna, who had arrived near the Red Sea Littoral with a force of 370 mounted men—including 300 horsemen and seventy camelmen—and 2,500 spearmen in early April. The Hadendowa chief had begun to threaten a number of outposts around Suakin, but he had been kept largely in check by Omar Tita, a tribal chief who was friendly towards the British. However, Osman Digna continued to pose a threat in the region, and so a force from the Anglo-Egyptian garrison at Suakin was required to march out and deal with him.

This force would consist of: the 8th Squadron of Egyptian Cavalry; two mountain guns; one company of the Camel Corps; three companies of the 5th

Egyptian Battalion; a composite company formed by men from the depot of the 9th and 10th Sudanese Battalions; and a company of mule transports. In total, over 1,200 fighting men were assembled, of which command fell to Major (temporary Lieutenant-Colonel) G. E. Lloyd of the South Staffordshire Regiment, who was also the governor of the district.

Lloyd wanted his men to be as mobile as possible, and so ordered every available camel in and around Suakin to be requisitioned. However, the force found itself to be around 180 camels short, and so the gap had to be made up by the use of mules and donkeys. The men assembled outside Suakin on 14 April, but since it was already 5 p.m., orders were given to bivouac for the night, with the actual advance beginning the following morning. It soon became apparent that the journey would be fraught with problems, mainly due to the fact most of the irritated camels had never been ridden before and attempted to throw off their riders. However, Lloyds' men pushed on, albeit at a slow pace.

After marching for four to five hours towards the water wells at Teroi, advance scouts came into contact with some of Osman Digna's own scouts, the latter of who quickly made off to inform their chief of the presence of the Egyptian column. As a precaution, Lloyd now ordered his men to form square before continuing; the men of the 9th and 10th Sudanese formed the leading face with the two mountain guns in the centre, while the Camel Corps guarded the rear and flanks. The terrain made the advance hard going, but by midday the square had finally arrived at the wells. With no enemy in sight, the column bivouacked and the cavalry was sent out to conduct a reconnaissance of the surrounding area. Some of the cavalrymen were also ordered to make for the post at Tokar, where the 10th Sudanese Battalion under Major H. M. Sidney was located, to update them as to the current situation.

Omar Tita had been holding the pass and adjacent heights of *Khor* Wintri. Captain M. A. C. B. Fenwick and thirty-eight cavalrymen set out for the pass, but before they could reach it, they came under attack from an estimated 200 Mahdist cavalrymen, who were also supported by a substantial number of spearmen and a few riflemen on foot. Outnumbered, Fenwick gave orders for his men to retire, but as they withdrew, the Mahdists quickly began to gain on them. The Egyptian cavalry increased to a gallop in a desperate attempt to outrun their pursuers, but they soon became entangled in bush and were slowed by terrain that proved difficult for their animals to traverse. Some of the cavalrymen even fell off their mounts, being instantly speared to death by the nimble Mahdist warriors.

Fenwick and the rest of his little force now began to pour volley fire into the ranks of their attackers, which, despite the small number of surviving cavalrymen, managed to keep the Mahdists at bay throughout the evening and into the night. Fortunately for the captain, his enemy were in possession of only a few rifles, and those that had them proved to be poor marksmen. Eventually, the Mahdists broke off their attack, and so Fenwick and his remaining men quickly set off back to the main force camped at the Teori Wells.

The following morning, the 16th, Lloyd resumed his advance to *Khor* Wintri, which was located some eight miles away. Due to the rough terrain, it was decided to conduct the final march on foot only, and so the camels and supplies were sent up into some nearby hills—which were known to be under the control of Omar Tita—where they would be safe. It would then take until the evening for Lloyd's column to reach their intended destination, and, to their surprise, they found 250 men of the 10th Sudanese under Major Sidney already in possession of the pass. The major had surprised the Mahdists the previous afternoon, and, despite several attempts to dislodge him from the pass, a 700 strong force of warriors had been repeatedly repulsed, losing forty killed and many more wounded during the fray. As Lloyd's cavalry had failed to reach Tokar, the lieutenant-colonel had been unaware of Sidney's own advance.

With the Mahdists driven off, it was decided that the column would return to Suakin, arriving back on the 18th. Osman Digna's army, although still largely intact, no longer presented an immediate threat. As such, operations in this part of Sudan came to an end, although in May the Suakin garrison would be asked to send troops to assist the Dongola Expeditionary Force. This necessitated replacement troops to keep the garrison up to strength, which were provided by the Indian Army; a contingent of Indian cavalry and infantry arrived on the 30th under the command of Colonel Charles Comyn Egerton of the Corps of Guides. The Indian Army, however, would play no part in the Dongola campaign.

By 2 June, the Dongola Expeditionary Force was fully concentrated at Akasha, and Kitchener now felt ready to continue his advance. Four days later, orders were given to begin the march to Firket, which was situated on the east-bank of the Nile some sixteen miles to the south. It was at this time that the *Sirdar* ordered his force to split into two parts, which would include a River Column under Hunter and a Desert Column under Burn-Murdoch. Both columns would need to arrive near Firket at the same time, a task that was not easy to achieve. In an attempt not to give this away to the enemy, the timings were kept secret by Wingate and Slatin, with the latter now acting as the former's deputy. Also, in order not to give the enemy prior warning that the advance was about to begin, regular cavalry patrols were pushed out to prevent Arab spies getting close enough to observe preparations.

Hunter's River Column would consist of three brigades, each made up of three battalions of infantry. The column would also be supported by two field batteries and two Maxim guns, the latter of which were operated by a detachment of the Connaught Rangers. Burn-Murdoch's Desert Column would be made up of seven squadrons of cavalry, the Camel Corps, and a battalion of infantry that had been mounted on camels for mobility. This column would likewise be supported by the Horse Artillery battery and two Maxims manned by men of the North Staffordshire Regiment. In all, the two columns totalled in excess of 9,100 men of all arms, the bulk of which, about 7,000, made up the River Column.

Although the main body of the *Ansar* in the Dongola province were at Dongola itself, Kitchener was well aware that considerable numbers of Mahdist warriors, possibly 2,000 to 3,000, were believed to be at Suarda. Others still were at Firket under the command of Hammuda Idris, although he would, on orders of the *Khalifa*, be replaced by Osman Azrak on account of his previous poor performance, and be demoted to command of a *rub*. Kitchener, therefore, needed to deal with these before considering any advance on Dongola. The taking of Akasha had been to cover the construction of the railway, with the extension of the line following as close behind the advancing troops as possible. Using the Nile River as a route to transport supplies was fraught with problems, particularly due to the *cataracts*, which were shallow lengths of rapid moving water that heavily laden supply vessels simply could not navigate. At low Nile it was also too shallow for such boats, and at high Nile, when they could sail, they still needed to be towed most of the way, itself an arduous task under the burning sun. Sending supplies across the desert would require a huge number of camels to maintain even a small force. The roads were usually bad and any movement would again have to be done under the hot sun. The answer to these supply problems was, of course, to build a railway, which would mean maintaining a gradual but slow advance.

Once Firket was taken and the Mahdists driven out, the railway line would be extended to reach it while the troops advanced further. The inevitable gap between the railhead and the advancing force would have to be supplied by camel transport, but, because of its relatively short distance, this posed only a minor problem. Also, once the line to Firket was completed, a large amount of supplies could be transported there for loading onto boats on the Nile, which could then easily sail from Firket to Dongola, due to a suitable stretch of the river between the two. Gunboats and armoured steamers would also sail ahead up the river, being used to shell enemy fortified positions and harass any Mahdists located along the banks. To get around impassable sections of the river, some of the gunboats were to be dismantled and transported on the railway; these could then be reassembled at a suitable point to continue their sail up the river. With a sturdy supply route established and full command of the river achieved, the Dongola Expeditionary Force could then bring the Mahdists to battle and inflict a heavy defeat upon them before taking the settlement of Dongola. This was Kitchener's basic plan of campaign.

For the advance on Firket, the River Column was instructed to move up the Nile along its bank, while the Desert Column headed towards the east. The intention was for both columns to converge on Firket together for the attack, the former attacking from the north while the latter was to position itself in order to block any route of retreat the Mahdists might take to the east and south. A body of irregulars would also take up positions to the west to likewise block any possible escape in that direction. Once the assault was underway, it was hoped to pin the Mahdists in place until they were ultimately defeated by superior Egyptian firepower. On the night of the 6th, the River Column advanced to within four miles of Firket, where it bivouacked at about 11.30 p.m., and the men were given strict instructions—under threat of being shot at dawn if they failed to comply—to maintain noise and light discipline, so as not to alert the enemy of the impending attack.

This pause, however, would be a short one, since orders to form up and begin the final advance to attack came at 1.30 a.m. on the 7th. The 1st Brigade under Colonel D. F. Lewis was positioned next to the riverbank, while 2nd Brigade under Brigadier-General Hector MacDonald advanced next to it in parallel. Bringing up the rear was 3rd Brigade under Colonel John Grenfell Maxwell. At the same time, the Desert Column crossed the desert in the dark, getting into position as planned without mishap. As the River Column marched through a narrow defile, Kitchener could hear the noise of drums in the distance, and he feared that the enemy was marching to meet his advance, leaving his men highly vulnerable to attack while still in the defile. However, he soon realised that the noise was in fact merely calling the Mahdists to prayer, and that they had no idea the attack was coming. The *Sirdar* and his troops pushed on.

The Action of Firket began at approximately 5 a.m. when a warrior of a small detachment of about five Mahdist riflemen fired a single shot from *Jebel* Firket, a mountain situated near the Nile River to the north of Firket itself—a feature that formed the defile Kitchener's River Column had had to march through. A temporary halt was made while a Maxim gun swiftly dealt with these warriors, but the warning of the Egyptian advance had now been given. It also soon became quickly obvious to the Mahdists that all possible routes of retirement were blocked, but, undeterred, they set about preparing a defence of their camp. The warriors of the Jaalin tribe took up positions near the banks of the Nile in the northern section of the camp, while the Baggara did the same in the southern portion. In effect, however, the Mahdists had been taken by surprise.

After clearing the mountain, Kitchener's advance resumed, and the 1st and 2nd Brigades slowly marched past the mountain onto open ground *bey*ond, where they began to fan out. Both brigades pushed forward two of their battalions, keeping the third positioned slightly behind to act as a reserve. 1st Brigade then manoeuvred to engage the left-wing of the enemy and 2nd Brigade to the right-wing. A gap then began to form between the two brigades, which would later be filled by Maxwell's 3rd Brigade following from the rear.

Eventually, the three brigades of the River Column were advancing on the Mahdist camp along a broad front. As they did so, they delivered a heavy and accurate fire into their enemy, inflicting an increasing number of casualties on the tribesmen. Burn-Murdoch's Desert Column also became engaged, with his artillery opening fire on the Mahdists from the south, the shells of which landed in the rear of the area held by the warriors. Despite their precarious position, the Mahdists conducted a number of charges at the oncoming Egyptian infantrymen, only to be gunned down and repulsed by heavy rifle fire on each occasion.

Lieutenant H. L. Pritchard of the Royal Engineers, who was serving with the Egyptian Army during the campaign, described some of the fighting during this part of the action:

> Just to the north of Ferket village was a low line of rocks. The Dervishes kept up a brisk fire from these, and clung to them till they were shot and bayoneted by the advancing troops. About forty horsemen suddenly dashed out of the houses and tried to charge, they were mowed down in ten yards. The Dervishes on the east side, finding themselves taken in front by the desert column and in flank by MacDonald and Maxwell, tried to fly back to the houses. To do so they had to cross an open bit of ground. Few survived the independent fire that was opened as they tried to get over the bare space.

The Maxim guns also opened fire on the Mahdists, targeting their reserves and preventing them from joining in the massed rushed attacks on the Egyptian infantry.

According to Atteridge, who was watching the action from his position with 3rd Brigade:

> The volley firing of our troops was wonderfully good. The rifles seemed to go off with one report. But neither the rifle nor the artillery preparation for the attack were allowed to last long. The word was given to storm the village. The whistle of the officers stopped the firing, and in our fellows went with the bayonet, first at the north end of the village, then nearer its centre. It was thus cleared from north to south.

When the Egyptian troops of Lewis' brigade entered the village, the battle turned into a bitter hand-to-hand struggle among the huts and other buildings that made up the Mahdist camp. Now broken down into smaller groups, Osman Azrak's men continued to resist, but were progressively driven out at the point of the bayonet. It soon became apparent that the warriors were no longer under any unifying command or orders, rather small parties were fighting isolated and on their own initiative. It was now only a matter of time before the Mahdists began an attempt to flee, and, indeed, a rout eventually ensued, many of them heading south only to be intercepted by the Desert Column. Warriors could be seen scrambling to escape the curtain that had been laid around their former position, and the few who did manage to get through were relentlessly hunted down by the cavalry. Meanwhile, the troops under MacDonald's command were pursuing large numbers of tribesmen across a swampy piece of narrow land that led onto an island in the Nile. As Kitchener watched from a nearby hill, he realised the action was now won and gave orders to the Maxim crews to cease fire; he was loathed to see ammunition wasted.

The action, which had lasted little over two hours, came to an end in victory for the Egyptian force. Egyptian casualties amounted to twenty men killed and a further eighty-three wounded; the latter number included Captain N. Legge of the 20th Hussars, the only British casualty of the day. Conversely, the *Ansar* were estimated to have lost 800 to 1,000 killed or wounded and around 500 taken prisoner. Hammuda Idris would be one of those killed. The action had been almost entirely fought by the Egyptian and Sudanese troops, save for a few British officers and Maxim gun teams. They performed so well in combat that Atteridge later positively commented on the soldiers:

> The battle of Ferkeh had been won. Hammuda's army had ceased to exist, and all doubt as to the fighting qualities of our Egyptian troops was at an end.
> The Soudanese had already made themselves a splendid reputation as fighting men, but in many quarters it had been the fashion to sneer at the *fellahin* battalions. No one who saw their ideal steadiness in action could doubt for a moment their sterling value. From the officers who led them I heard nothing but praise of their conduct.

Kitchener rode into the village with Wingate and Slatin, the latter encountering the dead body of Hammuda Idris, recognising him from a previous meeting at Omdurman during his days as a prisoner of the *Khalifa*; Slatin was to prove invaluable in identifying many of the fallen Mahdist senior leaders. Rather bizarrely, some of the *Sirdar*'s Sudanese troops also recognised old friends among the captured enemy warriors; there were scenes of men, who had, moments before been trying to kill one another, embraced and chatted as if they were long lost friends, which some undoubtedly were. A substantial number of these captured Mahdists would later volunteer to serve in Kitchener's Sudanese battalions.

A stretch of fifty miles of the Nile Valley had now been cleared of the *Ansar*, and they no longer had an effective fighting force near the border with Egypt. Kitchener next took possession of Suarda, which became his advanced post. However, there would now be an operational pause in the campaign for the next three months.

Despite the break in operations, many men of the Dongola Expeditionary Force would remain busy. The railway needed to be further extended and stores as well as other supplies had to be brought forward, not to mention the additional miles of telegraph cable that needed to be laid. Such work at the best of times was not easy, but it was made immeasurably harder by the fact the heat of the summer was now at its hottest. The post at Suarda was also strengthened, both in terms of physical fortification and additional men, the latter comprising of the 2nd Brigade supported by artillery. Meanwhile, the mounted men, including both the cavalry and the Camel Corps, conducted regular reconnaissance work.

While the men toiled in the heat, information was obtained that Osman Azrak was at the village of Kidden with a force of Mahdist cavalry. It was believed that he was on the hunt for men to take up arms to assist in the defence of Dongola; he desperately needed these men, since he had lost so many warriors at Firket.

Orders were, therefore, issued for a detached force of two squadrons of Egyptian cavalry and a company of the Camel Corps, all under the command of Captain D. Mahon, to advance on the village and drive Osman Azrak and his horsemen out. The captain and his men duly arrived at the village on 17 June, where their enemy retired without offering any notion of resistance. As well as the taking of the settlement, a total of eleven boats full of grain were seized, representing a sizeable supply of food for the *Ansar*.

The majority of the villagers of Kidden were not loyal to the *Khalifa*, and a stream of refugees from the settlement now headed off to seek safety with the *Sirdar* and his army. The British officers were keen to speak to these villagers, who were able to shed much light on the activities of the *Ansar*. It became apparent that the Egyptian victory at Firket had greatly worried the governor of Dongola, Muhammad Wad el-Bishara, who desperately asked the *Khalifa* to send him more warriors to protect the town. It also became known that the Mahdist governor was doing all he could to fortify Dongola, including the rounding up of all available able-bodied local men to be placed under arms.

A series of near-disasters, however, now struck the expeditionary force. Torrential rains, which were unusual in Sudan at that time of year, were so heavy that it swept away a length of the railway line near the village of Sarras on 25 August. Repair work began immediately, with over 5,000 men working throughout the day in a desperate attempt to get supplies moving again. Kitchener himself would be seen in his shirtsleeves, helping with the manual work as well as riding up and down the line giving words of encouragement—a task for which his command of the Arabic language greatly helped.

The Nile, too, had unusually not risen as expected, which meant the steamboats could not pass the second *cataract*, which in turn meant no general advance would be made until the vessels could eventually be moved up. The *Zafir*, a purpose built 135-foot long armoured steamer that had been co-designed by Kitchener and Burn-Murdoch for the campaign, suffered a broken cylinder following her transportation in sections and subsequent reassembly at Kosha. The vessel, which the *Sirdar* had once said was worth more to him than a battalion of infantry, would remain inoperable for a number of weeks until repairs were finally complete.

However, perhaps the most serious problem facing Kitchener was an outbreak of the deadly disease cholera. The first recorded case of cholera in Egypt had been noted late the previous year, but it had now managed to spread to Assouan in early June 1896. The British military doctors there, knowing how quickly the disease could devastate a fighting force, immediately took steps to eliminate it, which they successfully did at the post. However, it appeared at *Wadi* Halfa—possibly taken there by infected soldiers of the 5th Egyptian Battalion—where it again began to spread like wildfire. Unlike at Assouan, the doctors were unable to quickly isolate the disease, since all troops and supplies for the expedition had to pass through *Wadi* Halfa, and it was almost impossible to stop it being passed on to the healthy men.

Atterbridge, who was at *Wadi* Halfa, described some of the precautions and difficulties the medical officers experienced in combatting the disease:

> No one was allowed to travel south unless he belonged to the army or some department connected with the expedition, and every one embarking was medically inspected at the beginning of his voyage, at some point during its progress, and on landing. But it was impossible to keep the native boatmen under such strict supervision, and transport necessities forbade the entire cessation of boat traffic. Then, too, in the riverside villages there was a conspiracy of concealment. The natives did not believe in the white men's precautions against cholera, and only regarded them as irksome formalities to be evaded at any risk. Officers who had been in the villages on cholera duty told me that it was not uncommon for the Arabs and Berberis [people from Berber] to bury a dead cholera patient under the earthen floor of their huts, and then try to make out he had simply left the village—anything to avoid the quarantine regulations. No wonder that under these circumstances the pestilence made its way past all our barriers.

Fearing the loss of the only full British infantry battalion in Dongola, the North Staffords were moved out of their camp to a new one about six miles away at Gemai. Despite this wise precaution, some of the soldiers of the regiment became infected. By 15 July, it had reached the post at Kosha, where the camp was moved 2,000 yards out into the surrounding desert in the hope of protecting the troops. Eventually, however, the disease was eradicated, but not before it claimed the lives of four British officers and two engineers, as well as 235 Egyptian troops.

Further needless deaths occurred in August when 2nd Brigade marched out from Suarda under an oppressive heat unaccompanied by water camels. The men were in full-marching order, the weight of their kit, in addition to the weather conditions, resulting in an incredible 1,700—out of a total force of 3,000—falling out during the march; ten soldiers would die from their ordeal. This 'death march', as it was later dubbed, appeared to be carried out without any good reason, and MacDonald, albeit privately, later pointed the finger of blame at Kitchener.

On 10 September, intelligence was obtained to the effect that Muhammad Wad el-Bishara was concentrating his warriors at Kerma, and had begun improving the defences of the town. Kitchener immediately gave orders for his own forces to begin concentrating and prepare for an advance, with the troops transported up via rail and aboard steamers. The men of the North Staffords arrived on the 15th, after which the advance commenced in earnest. Every available fighting man was called forward, and the expeditionary force—now totalling around 13,000 men—consisted of the three brigades engaged at Firket, plus a fourth brigade of three Egyptian infantry battalions under the command of Colonel B. F. David, as well as the North Staffords. Small detachments, however, had to be left along the line of communication, while the 6th Egyptian Battalion remained at Khosha to guard the all-important railhead.

Kitchener's army arrived at Bagri on the 17th, then reached a point on the Nile called Abu Fatma, opposite the island of Imbos, the following day. As the expedition advanced, it was protected on its right-flank by the steamers *Tamai*, *Abu Klea*, and *Metemma*, under the command of Commander Stanley Colville of the Royal Navy. Another steamer, the *et-Teb*, had become stuck on some rocks lower down the river at the Hennek Cataract and had to be left behind, while two companies of the North Staffords were moved up aboard two unarmoured vessels called *Dal* and *Akasha*. The *Sirdar* planned to attack Muhammad Wad el-Bishara at Kerma on the 19th, but after commencing an advance at daybreak, he was disappointed to find the town deserted of the enemy; the Mahdists had made off the previous evening for the village of Hafir. Undeterred, Kitchener pushed on determined to catch up with his foe.

From the top of some high ground, the *Sirdar* could see large bodies of the *Ansar* on the west-bank of the Nile; he could also see a steamer, the *et-Tahira*, which was in use by the Mahdists along with about thirty other smaller boats. He now decided it was time to attack, and the Action of Hafir began at 6.30 a.m. when Kitchener's artillery, under Lieutenant-Colonel Charles Sim Bremridge Parsons, opened fire, while Colville's armoured steamers passed by Hafir along the river. As the vessels sailed by, they received heavy fire from Muhammad Wad el-Bishara's warriors, who had placed a number of concealed batteries along the bank as well as deployed riflemen in pits near the water's edge.

Lieutenant Pritchard of the Royal Engineers again described some of the action:

> The gunboats were steaming along side, and as they came opposite Hafir puffs of smoke and the report of guns revealed the Dervish position on the other bank. It was an excellent position. The navigable channel of the river at this point is not very wide, and to get through the gunboats would have to pass close by the Dervish position. As soon as the gunboats saw the Dervishes they steamed up and engaged them. The Dervishes were occupying some excellently placed low trenches connecting six earth gun emplacements. Several Dervishes could also be seen firing from the tops of the palm-trees, from which they were soon dislodged by the Maxims, and if they were not killed by the bullets, they certainly must have been by their fall to the ground.

Shells and bullets repeatedly struck the boats, but the men on the steamers stood to their positions and continued to shell and machine gun a number of fortifications. Colville, however, was wounded in the wrist by a bullet, while Armourer-Sergeant Richardson of the Royal Marine Artillery was killed and a number of others wounded. The *Abu Klea* was struck just above the waterline with the shell passing into her magazine, but fortunately for those on board, it failed to explode. The *Metemma* was also hit three times, one shell slicing through her smoke stack, a second through the main cabin, and a third into her bow.

The wounded Colville, who was aboard the *Tamai*, ordered his steamer to temporarily withdraw from the action in order to ask Kitchener for more artillery support, leaving the other two steamers to continue the attack. Once this task was completed, the commander came steaming back up the Nile to rejoin the fight. Although the flotilla now received increased cover from the artillery positioned ashore, the steamers simply could not get passed the heavy fire that the Mahdists continued to pour onto them. Eventually, the battered *Metemma*, much to the delight of Muhammad Wad el-Bishara's warriors, was forced to break off and head back in the direction of Kerma. The action had now been fought for over two and a half hours, and it seemed the Mahdists had gained the upper-hand.

Kitchener, meanwhile, in an attempt to finally turn the action against Muhammad Wad el-Bishara, gave orders for three artillery and one Maxim battery (under Parsons) to take up positions on the island of Artaghasi, a piece of land located about 1,200 yards from the main enemy position and connected to the bank via a narrow strip of land. Colville's boats had failed to silence the enemy's guns, but it was hoped positioning the batteries on the island would achieve the desired effect. Within moments of taking up their new positions, the guns roared into action, and after an hour of relentless shelling and sweeping of the enemy with Maxim fire, the Mahdists finally fell silent. As well as knocking out the enemy artillery, one of Parsons' guns had also hit the *et-Tahira*, which, taking on water, eventually sank into the river. Seeing the battle was won, Colville ordered his steamers to sail past Hafir one last time, delivering a final salvo as they did so. It was now just after 10 a.m. and Kitchener was again victorious.

Although not known until sometime later, both Muhammad Wad el-Bishara and Osman Azrak had been wounded in the Action of Hafir, but some of their riflemen persisted in keeping up a sporadic, yet ineffectual, fire on the Egyptian troops. Kitchener responded by shelling the trenches in which the Mahdist marksmen were hiding, until eventually they gave up and made off for Dongola under the cover of darkness. Kitchener's casualties included two killed and twelve wounded, while Muhammad Wad el-Bishara was thought to have lost around 200 of his warriors.

The following morning, it became clear that Hafir had now been completely abandoned by Muhammad Wad el-Bishara and his men. Upon speaking with some of the residents of the village, it also became known that the governor had made off for Dongola, which would be next on Kitchener's list to capture. However, he first needed to get his force across the river at Hafir before he could continue his march, not an inconsiderable task given the large number of men, animals, and equipment. With only the steamers and a few boats available, this would take some time, and the *Sirdar* was not able to begin his final advance to Dongola until late on 21 September.

Nevertheless, Kitchener was able to cover some twelve miles on the 21st before ordering his men to bivouac for the night near the island of Argo. As the men settled down, the *Abu Klea*, under Lieutenant David Beatty of the Royal Navy, sailed on towards Dongola to observe what was happening at the town. The following day was uneventful, but the expedition was able to march to Zowerat while the remaining two steamers caught up with the *Abu Klea*.

Finally, at about 4.30 a.m. on the 23rd, Kitchener's force began its last march for Dongola. Lewis' 1st Brigade advanced along the river bank while Maxwell's 3rd Brigade marched in parallel next to it. Following behind the two leading brigades were the artillery and Maxim guns along with the men of the North Staffords. MacDonald's 2nd Brigade, the Camel Corps, horse artillery, and cavalry were also following. Forming the rear-guard was David's 4th Brigade. As the Dongola Expeditionary Force advanced, the entire army presented a two-mile wide front.

It would be at 7 a.m. that a body of *Ansar* warriors would be spotted; orders were given for the Egyptian infantry to move forward to engage them. However, the Mahdists failed to engage in battle and made off, only to reappear as if now ready to fight, but again retired before committing; they would do this a number of times. The advance slowly continued, and, by 9.30 a.m., Kitchener could see the main camp of his enemy that was located to the north of the town—to their surprise, the Egyptian flag could also be seen flying above the settlement.

Although Kitchener's men had not been able to fire a shot in anger, Colville's steamers—which had just been joined by the recently repaired *Zafir*—had managed to shoot off a few shells at the Dongola garrison, who promptly surrendered to the commander by running up a white flag. The steamers also fired upon the *Ansar* camp, but the warriors were already in full retreat. Colville then ordered a detachment of his men to go ashore and raise the Egyptian flag in order to let Kitchener know the town had been taken. Although the cavalry and horse artillery would pursue the retiring Baggara, no sizeable action would be fought that day; Dongola had, almost disappointingly for the *Sirdar* and his men, fallen without a fight. During the pursuit by the cavalry, the Baggara did, however, put up some limited resistance by mounting several charges in the hope of assisting their spearmen on foot to escape. Pritchard later related part of this brief skirmish:

> Some of the Dervish cavalry turned at bay to cover the retreat and charged towards our cavalry. Captain Adams's squadron charged to meet them. Just as Captain Adams was within a few lengths of the leading emir, Adams's horse fell, throwing him to the ground. The emir galloped over him, slashing at him with his sword, but missed him. The Egyptian squadron defeated the Dervish one, and continued the pursuit. It soon became patent to all that we were not going to get a fight.

Many of the unmounted *Ansar* warriors would be overrun by the Egyptians, and over 900 were eventually taken prisoner. As previously, many of these men would later be recruited into the Egyptian Army and serve in the Sudanese infantry battalions. The Egyptian force would now spend the night in the town, which itself appeared to be in a state of almost ruin. On the 26th, the North Staffords, who were no longer needed, departed and embarked on their long journey back to Cairo.

In his despatch of 30 September 1896, a triumphant Kitchener concluded:

> The result of these operations has been to completely stop the constant Dervish raids and attacks on the villages between Assuan and Haifa, to add some 450 miles of the Nile Valley to Egyptian territory, 300 miles of which may be described as of great fertility, and to relieve, to their intense delight, the large and suffering population of the province of Dongola from the barbarous and tyrannical rule of savage and fanatical Baggaras.

He also issued praise for his Egyptian troops:

> These operations have, moreover, demonstrated the troops of the Egyptian Army to be possessed of high qualities of endurance and bravery, and I have only to add that no case of want of discipline or attempt to shirk duty has occurred—indeed the high spirit and eagerness which the troops have displayed under many very trying circumstances is *bey*ond praise. Egyptian soldiers have frequently been found to have concealed sickness, and in spite of severe footsores to have marched uncomplainingly in order to be present with their comrades when an engagement was imminent.

Kitchener had achieved his objective of driving the Mahdists completely out of Dongola province and his campaign had come to an end. The previously maligned Egyptian troops had proved their mettle in battle, and the once invincible Mahdists had lost swathes of their previously hard won territory. However, it would not be long before an extension of the campaign was ordered, and a full reconquest of Sudan authorised—a campaign led by the *Sirdar* against the *Khalifa* himself.

7

The Campaign Extended

Following the capture of Dongola, both Lord Salisbury in London and Lord Cromer in Cairo considered the *Sirdar*'s operations in Sudan a complete success and at an end, at least temporarily. The prime minister had no immediate desire to advance further, while the consul-general felt a pause of three or four years in order to consolidate was now necessary before considering any additional action. Perhaps unsurprisingly, Kitchener was of the opinion that the advance should continue soon, and that leaving the Egyptian Army to stagnate in Dongola province while the Mahdists gathered their own forces was a mistake. The *Sirdar* did, however, recognise the fact that he needed many more troops than currently available—by which he meant British troops—if he was to face the *Khalifa*'s main army in battle. He now felt he had no other option than to leave Sudan and return to England, via Cairo, to argue his case.

In truth, Cromer had little objection to extending the campaign further south into Sudan, to ultimately retake Khartoum. His main concern was how to finance it, since the Egyptian Government, who had funded the Dongola Expedition, was unlikely to be able to afford additional military operations for some time. The consul-general, therefore, knew the money must come from London, and that meant asking the British people, through the taxes they paid, to be prepared to underwrite it. To Kitchener's credit, he had completed the advance to Dongola without spending all of the money that had been set aside for it; Cromer later noted that the campaign had cost a total of 715,000 Egyptian pounds. Cromer told Kitchener that if he could persuade the British Government to pay for it, he would support him.

Arriving back in Britain in November 1896, Kitchener was given a hero's welcome, and, perhaps more importantly, a promotion to major-general. The press adored him, as did Queen Victoria, and a knighthood quickly followed. This new level of fame and respect, of course, served to help the *Sirdar* in his quest for the renewing of operations, and he intended to use it. He also had the support of the Duke of Cambridge, who willingly exerted his influence wherever he thought it would help. Kitchener's primary target, however, was Sir Michael Hicks-Beach, the then chancellor of the exchequer, who was known for his reluctance to spend public money.

However, despite all his efforts, the decision he sought was ultimately achieved through events *bey*ond even the newly promoted major-general's control. News had reached London that the French Government had issued instructions to one of its own military officers and explorers, Captain Jean-Baptiste Marchand, to conduct an expedition to the Upper Nile in order to stake a territorial claim for France. To make matters worse, the Frenchman was already in the Congo and needed only a few months to prepare for his journey. Time, again, was of the essence. Thus, on 16 November, Salisbury authorised an extension to the campaign in Sudan and instructed Hicks-Beach to make the necessary funds available, which would amount to £798,802. The prime minister also agreed to the potential deployment of British troops should Kitchener ask for them, which, as we will see, he eventually would.

Writing in 1908, Cromer appears not to have had any doubts on the issue:

> In the autumn of the same year [1896], it was not possible to adduce a single valid argument in favour of remaining inactive and delaying the completion of the work [i.e. the reconquest of Sudan], which had already begun. A certain amount of hesitation was, however, in the first instance displayed before the inevitable conclusion was accepted that the British Government had committed themselves to a policy, which involved the reconquest of the Soudan. This hesitation was probably due more to financial timidity, and to reluctance always felt by British Ministers to decide on anything but the issue of the moment, rather than any failure to realise the true facts of the situation. It was not till February 5, 1897, that the Chancellor of the Exchequer (Sir Michael Hicks Beach), speaking in the House of Commons, publically recognised that 'Egypt could never be held to be permanently secure so long as a hostile Power was in occupation of the Nile valley up to Khartoum,' and that the duty of giving a final blow to the 'baleful power of the *Khalifa*' devolved on England.

A delighted Kitchener returned to Egypt and set about planning his new advance. If Girouard's railway had been of immeasurable help during the Dongola campaign, it was about to become even more important for the coming one. The *Sirdar* did not want to use the same route Wolseley had taken during his failed attempt to rescue Gordon in 1885; instead, he wished to build a straight line from *Wadi* Halfa direct to Abu Hamed, greatly reducing the distance by about 330 miles by avoiding the need to follow the winding route of the Nile. Transporting men and supplies over a shorter distance by rail would, of course, greatly reduce the amount of time required to get them to the front.

Actually building the railway, however, was another matter. The proposed route was largely unknown to Kitchener and his staff, although it was generally believed that it would involve laying track over mostly sandy and rocky terrain; many railway builders in Britain felt that this would render the construction of the line virtually impossible. In addition to the physical difficulties, a substantial amount of the territory through which the proposed line would run was under control of the Mahdists. No maps existed and so survey teams would need to scout out the area of the route, a task made particularly difficult when the surveyors were likely to be attacked.

All of this, of course, did not put off Kitchener, who was determined to push on with his plans regardless of what his critics thought. He instructed Lieutenant Edward Cator of the Royal Engineers to complete the survey work and find places where water could be drawn along the route. Incredibly, the lieutenant, along with an escort of friendly Ababda tribesmen, did just that, identifying several sites where wells could be dug. More importantly, it turned out that the terrain along the route, while far from perfect, was not as unsuitable for the laying of track as first feared.

Meanwhile, Girouard travelled back to Britain in order to acquire suitable locomotives for use on the new line. Having met Cecil Rhodes—the well-known former prime minister of Cape Colony and businessman, who just happened to have some locomotives in Britain earmarked for South Africa—the two men agreed the loan of several engines for the extended campaign in Sudan. To the *Sirdar*'s surprise, Girouard returned to Sudan with the news that Rhodes asked for no money for the locomotives, no doubt thanks to his ardent imperialist nature. The captain had, however, spent some of the £240,000 set aside for railway equipment on other engines and several hundred wagons. On 1 January 1897, work on the extended Sudan Military Railway began.

Kitchener, of course, was not the only one making preparations for the impending campaign. Abdullahi al-Taishi, still reeling from the shock of losing Dongola, had hurriedly set about strengthening the defences of Omdurman, including sending out instructions to all the *amirs* to call up all able-bodied men and bring them to the Sudanese capital. To his surprise, the Anglo-Egyptian army did not come sraight away, but he knew it was only a matter of time before it would.

During Kitchener's absence, command of the Egyptian force in Sudan fell to Archibald Hunter, who established his headquarters at Merowi. The entire province of Dongola was placed under military law, although a new police force was established to maintain order and a civil rebuilding program introduced for its capital. Efforts were also made to encourage the former inhabitants of the province, who had previously fled persecution from the Mahdists and the subsequent fighting, to return and recommence their long-practiced cultivation of the land. The population of the province had decreased from 75,000 to 56,000 in only a decade; of those who remained, the greater portion were women and children. Thus, the area lacked the male workforce required to make it prosper, which was needed to ensure it remained stable.

After Kitchener's return from England, the building of the railway progressed rapidly from *Wadi* Halfa, although it would not reach its peak speed until May. Once July arrived, the work came to a near-grinding halt, not because of any technical problems but because it had advanced so near to Abu Hamed that it was now deemed too unsafe to go any further until the enemy had been driven out. Thus, on the 29th, Hunter marched out of Merowi ahead of a column including: the 3rd Egyptian and the 9th, 10th, and 11th Sudanese Battalions, a battery of field artillery, two Maxim guns, and a detachment of cavalry.

It took Hunter and his men eight days to march across 132 miles of desert in what was the hottest time of year for the region. During the advance, the column would pass close to the old battlefield of Kirbekan, fought in 1885 in the immediate aftermath of the killing of General Gordon. Upon arriving near Abu Hamed, on 6 August, he ordered his force to bivouac for the evening with the intention of attacking in the morning. The men now rested before what would be the first action of the extended campaign.

As the morning daylight broke, Hunter's men advanced on the village, in front of which the Mahdists had entrenched themselves. Behind this obstacle was a large mud-brick building of a simple rectangular design, within which were the watering holes and other stores of the garrison. Around the village were also a number of other smaller mud-huts, between which were walls connecting them to form a strong defensive position. Along these walls were loopholes, through which the defenders could fire their rifles. It was estimated that the *Ansar* garrison numbered around 1,350 footmen—of which about 500 were armed with rifles—and 150 horsemen.

Now ready to make his assault, Hunter gave orders for his infantry to extend into line, and, as soon as the maneuverer was complete, another order was given to begin a frontal advance on the village. The field battery was located over to the infantry's right, from where it would provide a covering fire as the Egyptian and Sudanese troops marched forward. At first little resistance was encountered, and some high ground in front of the village was taken with ease. However, once within 300 yards of the village boundaries, the Mahdist riflemen opened a heavy fire on Hunter's leading troops, inflicting a number of casualties on the Egyptians and Sudanese. Fortunately for many of Hunter's men, the enemy riflemen fired high and missed their targets.

Lieutenant Pritchard was again present at the action:

> Colonel MacDonald's intention was to rush the place with the bayonet, but without any word of command, first the Eleventh and then the other battalions broke into rapid independent firing, and no one could advance without getting shot by their own side, so there were our troops on the sky-line with the enemy shooting them from a trench eighty yards off. In the first few seconds four out of the five mounted officers of the Tenth Battalion were brought to the ground, two

killed and two with their horses shot; every man of the colour party was either killed or wounded. It was a most unpleasant position. Colonel MacDonald immediately came out in front swearing at the men and knocking up their rifles. The other officers did the same, and in a few minutes our firing ceased.

At that moment, the Mahdists in the trenches suddenly bolted and made off into the huts behind. The order was then given to charge, and the whole of the infantry lunged forward until they were in among the enemy. Bitter hand-to-hand fighting ensued, with hut after hut having to be painstakingly emptied of warriors who opposed the Egyptian and Sudanese troops across the entire village. To better assist the infantry, the field battery was moved forward to a new position closer to the settlement.

As the action dragged on, an increasing number of the mounted *Ansar* warriors became casualties until their nerve finally broke. The surviving horsemen then decided to make a run for it, a move which caused panic among some of the spearmen and riflemen on foot, of which about 100 then suddenly abandoned the fight and fled. Soon the village fell completely to Hunter's determined troops, after which a number of Mahdist warriors were taken prisoner. The most significant prisoner was the leader of the garrison, Mohammed Zain Hassan, who surrendered to an Egyptian officer. He was at once sent to Hunter who asked the Mahdist why he chose to stand and fight against such overwhelming odds; his reply was that since his fighters were worth four of the enemy, he believed he had an even chance. This young and committed Mahdist would remain a prisoner at Rosetta until 1901.

Egyptian casualties were high, including twenty-three killed and sixty-four wounded, the result of frontally attacking an entrenched position. Those killed-in-action also included Major Henry Sidney—who had captured the *Khor* Wintri Pass the previous year—and Lieutenant Edward Fitzclarence, both of the 10th Sudanese Battalion. *Ansar* casualties are a little less easy to determine, but it was estimated at the time that around 250 to 450 were killed, with many more wounded or taken prisoner. The few of the Abu Hamed garrison who did manage to escape made off in the direction of Omdurman.

With Abu Hamed occupied, the work on the railway recommenced. Kitchener now sought to advance and take Berber, and so orders were issued for all available troops to move up from their current positions at Merowi and Dongola. By 29 August, all of the *Sirdar*'s gunboats, including the *Tamai, Feteh, Nasr, Metemma,* and *Zafir*, had arrived at Abu Hamed—the *El Teb* under the command of Lieutenant David Beatty had become wrecked at the Fourth Cataract—along with a number of other vessels carrying troops and supplies, the Nile now having risen enough to permit their passage.

Berber, located about 130 miles further down the Nile, was the next major stronghold of the Mahdists along the river, where the local *Ansar* commander was Zaki Osman. News of the loss of Abu Hamed had already reached Berber, and frantic messages had been despatched to the *Khalifa* at Omdurman requesting reinforcements. Unfortunately for Zaki Osman, no additional *Ansar* warriors were forthcoming, and so he decided to evacuate the position on the 24th and retired to Shendi.

This evacuation came to the attention of Hunter, who immediately asked Abdel-Azim and his brother Ahmed *Bey Khalifa*, of the friendly Ababda tribe, to advance on ahead and seize Berber. These irregulars, numbering about forty, arrived at the town on the 31st to find the Mahdists had gone, and thus encountered no resistance. A few days later, on 5 September, four of the gunboats also arrived, and Hunter, with the main body of his force, entered the town on the 13th, being soon joined by Kitchener who rode across the Bayuda Desert from Merowi. The original site of Berber, a once prosperous settlement, was now nothing more than a ruin. The Mahdists, however, had built their camp several miles to the north and several miles from the river. Although an easy victory, the *Sirdar* was concerned that his lines of communication had now become stretched, since the railhead was over a hundred miles away. He was also acutely aware that the *Khalifa* could send a force to retake Berber long before the railway could be extended to the settlement. However, despite these concerns, Kitchener was very pleased with the success of his extended campaign so far.

Prior to Hunter's arrival, two of the gunboats pushed on ahead along the Nile to a place called Ed Damer, a village located a little way past the river's junction with the Atbara River. As the vessels came close they could see a number of *Ansar* warriors along the banks, who were most likely some of those who had fled Berber earlier, and an exchange of fire took place. A short while later, the gunboats seized several boats filled with grain, further depriving the Mahdists of some of their food stocks. The warriors then continued their retirement towards Shendi, and the gunboats put ashore a small party which raised the Egyptian flag over the village. Later, half a battalion of infantry was sent up to Ed Damer, which became the advanced post of Kitchener's force.

Elsewhere in Sudan, Osman Digna had gathered together 5,000 warriors at a place called Adarama, located about ninety miles from Ed Damer. Learning of this, Hunter planned to lead out his force to confront the Hadendowa chief, but delays in transporting supplies up from Abu Hamed to Berber meant that he had to postpone his plans until 23 October. Eventually, however, the major-general was able to advance with 400 men of the 11th Sudanese, a detachment from the Camel Corps and several artillery pieces. Alerted to this move, Osman Digna abandoned Adarama some two full days before Hunter could arrive, crossing the Nile at Guidi and making for Abu Deleh out in the desert. Although the major-general had failed to engage the chief, he had forced him to withdraw, leaving eastern Sudan effectively free of Mahdists.

Unbeknown to senior British officers at this time, a rift had occurred between Osman Digna and a senior *Ansar* leader by the name of *Khalifa* al-Sharif Mahmud

Ahmed; the dispute apparently being over a number of women taken by the latter from the former's tribe. This dispute resulted in the two refusing to cooperate by joining together their respective armies in order to oppose Kitchener's advance. Abdullahi al-Taishi, meanwhile, also made matters worse by continuing to refuse to send out reinforcements from Omdurman through fear of the perceived threat to his seat of power. The *Ansar*, therefore, remained impotent at a time it should have being taking to the offensive against the invading British and Egyptian troops.

Mahmud Ahmed, who commanded an army of about 10,000 warriors, thus remained on the defensive in and around Metammeh, while Osman Digna likewise stayed put at Abu Deleh. Kitchener, however, was aware of the current location of the former, and three steamers, the *Zafir*, *Fateh*, and *Nasr*, under the command of Commander Keppel, had been ordered to carry out a reconnaissance up the Nile to Metammeh on 15 October. Upon their arrival at 7 a.m. the following morning, the fortifications of the town could be clearly seen; the defences consisted of a total of seven circular forts constructed of mud-brick.

Keppel decided to open a bombardment of the forts, and, when within about 4,000 yards of the nearest, his 12- and 6-pounder quick firing guns, manned by members of the Royal Marines, began firing high-explosive and shrapnel shells. A number of Baggara horsemen could be seen along the banks, and were similarly fired upon by the Maxim guns, mowing many of them down; the survivors were forced to make off for their lives. Each of the forts appeared to be armed with a brass artillery gun, with each one returning fire on Keppel's little flotilla as it passed them by. These old guns seemed unable to strike their targets, with most of the shells falling into the river some distance short of the gunboats. However, possibly due to luck rather than the skill of the gunners, two or three Mahdists shells eventually found their mark, hitting one of the steamers and mortally wounding a Sudanese soldier.

The bombardment was kept up for an hour, after which the gunboats began targeting anywhere the gunners thought their enemy was taking cover. This fire seemed to be having an increasingly negative effect on the Mahdists, since the intensity of their return fire began to greatly decrease. Nevertheless, as the vessels sailed closer to the banks, a group of *Ansar* riflemen suddenly appeared and started to pour rifle fire into the gunboats from only 100 yards range, the bullets repeatedly hitting the sides of the armoured vessels. Keppel's men responded by sweeping the positions held by these riflemen with their Maxims, the rapid fire of which quickly drove the warriors off again. Having by now sailed passed the town, the gunboats turned around and steamed back up the Nile in the direction they had come, continuing to shell and machine gun the Mahdists and their defences as they did so. The firing continued until around 2.30 p.m., when the skirmish eventually came to an end.

On the 17th, Keppel resumed his reconnaissance, during which he ascertained that the Mahdists had brought up two additional guns to their battered forts at

Metammeh. The commander again ordered his gunboats to sail slowly past these forts and begin shelling, more or less replaying the events of the previous skirmish. After several hours of bombarding the defences, the flotilla finally moved off and sailed down river. As they withdrew, the guns in the forts continued to fire on the vessels, keeping it up long after the gunboats had got well out of range.

A short while following his departure from Metammeh, Keppel suddenly noticed a man sitting on a white horse, who came galloping down the bank of the Nile behind the boats. Following him were large numbers of *Ansar* warriors, all shouting and jeering at the gunboats as if they had won a victory and forced the vessels to withdraw. Ignoring these, the commander sailed steadily on, leaving the warriors far behind. It is not known who the mounted chief was, but it may have been Mahmud Ahmed himself, or, if not, it was certainly someone of note from his army. Whatever the Mahdists might think, Keppel had lost only one man and inflicted an unknown number of casualties on his enemy, having expended over 650 shells during the two brief skirmishes.

Yet another reconnaissance was made on 1 November, this time as far as the Sixth Cataract. As the gunboats steamed past Metammeh, they again opened fire on the forts and at any Mahdists spotted on the banks. This they then repeated on the return journey. These exchanges of fire, of course, had little real effect on either side, but it did allow Hunter to determine that Mahmud and his army were still very much in and around Metammeh in force. Furthermore, his men took to conducting raids on nearby villages in an attempt to find food and other supplies, hinting at the levels of desperation that had arisen while staying put for too long. It was at around this time, on 31 October, that the railway line from *Wadi* Halfa to Abu Hamed was completed, amazingly with only seventeen miles of track to spare; however, Kitchener had no intention of allowing it to stop there. Work was soon resumed, once further track and building supplies arrived—this time to push the line on from Abu Hamed to Berber.

While the gunboats were shelling anything that moved around Metammeh, political talks were taking place between the Anglo-Egyptian authorities in Cairo and the Italian Government. The basis of the talks was Egypt's desire to re-acquire Kassala from Italy; the latter formally agreed to transfer the territory to the former on 25 December 1897. This agreement necessitated Kitchener's attention, and so he temporarily left Merowi and returned to Cairo to work out the military arrangements for the withdrawal of Italian troops and their replacement by men of the Egyptian Army.

The prosperous town of Kassala had fallen to Osman Digna's army in 1885. The Egyptian authorities desperately wanted the settlement back, but at the time, the Egyptian Army was still far from ready to conduct a military operation of the type and size to drive the Mahdists out and retake it by force. The British, however, came up with another plan, asking the Italians, who had forces not far away at Massowah, to take it as theirs until such a time Cairo and Rome could negotiate its return to Egypt. However, it would not be until 1894 that Italian forces, under the command of Baratieri, finally took possession of Kassala following a bitter contest with Osman Digna's warriors. Any celebrations on the part of the Italian troops regarding their victory were short-lived, for the garrison stationed at the town had become besieged in early 1896.

In anticipation of the formal agreement to transfer Kassala back to Egypt, Cairo instructed a column of Egyptian troops to make preparations to begin an advance to the town. This force consisted of the 16th Egyptians and some artillery—a total of 850 men under the command of Lieutenant-Colonel Parsons. Following a review by Kitchener, Parsons' force left Massowah and marched to Kassala, where it arrived on 18 December. Their arrival was warmly welcomed by the Italians, who gave the Egyptian troops a twenty-one-gun salute and agreed to raise the Egyptian flag over the town next to the Italian flag. However, Parsons had to wait until the 25th, the agreed date, before he could formally take possession of the town, with his troops making camp for a few days at a location a mile away from the fort at Kassala.

Little occurred during this wait; as the Italians departed, they transferred over to Parsons command of a 700 strong battalion of locally raised levies, who had bolstered the Italian garrison during the siege. Knowing of this transfer of troops in advance, Parsons asked to march them out of the town in order to assault El Fashir and Osobri, both of which were held by warriors of the *Ansar* some fifty miles out of Kassala. The first was taken without much effort, but the latter held out for six days before it finally fell to the levies. Nevertheless, the levies had proved themselves in action, much to Parsons' delight. The Italians were now finally free of their predicament at Kassala, and Egypt had recovered her lost territory.

With the little, but not insignificant, matter of Kassala dealt with, Kitchener could now turn his attention back to his reconquest of Sudan. His next concern was that of the size of the enemy force he must soon defeat in battle. He knew the *Khalifa* had an estimated 40,000 warriors at Omdurman, and those of Mahmud Ahmed and Osman Digna combined—it appears that the two had resolved, or at least put aside, their differences in early 1898 under orders from the *Khalifa*—now numbered 20,000. Faced with a possible enemy army some 60,000 strong, the *Sirdar* knew he needed more men of his own.

To render matters more urgent, intelligence was received that indicated Mahmud Ahmed was planning to advance on Berber after being put under pressure from the *Khalifa* to take action, and before his army suffered further deterioration due to continuing desertions. In order to meet this advance, Kitchener could only muster 10,000 Egyptian and Sudanese troops, so he sent a request to Cairo asking for a brigade of British troops to be moved forward to reinforce those of the Egyptian Army. This request was authorised by Sir Francis Grenfell, who now held the position of commanding officer of the Army of Occupation. Thus, on 2nd January 1898, the 1st Battalions of the Royal

Warwickshire Regiment, the Lincolnshire Regiment, the Cameron Highlanders and the Seaforth Highlanders were ordered to form a brigade and proceed to the front. The first three of these regiments were already in Egypt, but the Seaforths were in Malta, and so had to embark on troop transports and sail to Egypt; it would, therefore, arrive a little later than the other regiments. Command of the British Brigade was given to Major-General William Forbes Gatacre.

While the British regiments were awaited, Kitchener gave orders for all available Egyptian and Sudanese troops in Dongola province to make their way to *Wadi* Halfa then on to Abu Hamed and Abu Dis, the movement of the troops being facilitated by the railway. At the same time, the small flotilla of gunboats under Keppel were instructed to conduct a number of reconnaissances up the Nile to Metammeh and Shendi to keep an eye on the activities of Mahmud Ahmed's army. In addition, the Ababda irregulars likewise conducted mounted patrols of the area around Ed Damer in the hope of bringing advanced warning of any *Ansar* advance.

It would not, however, be until 10 February that Mahmud Ahmed finally began his operations, moving his warriors across the Nile to Shendi. Whether he knew of the impending arrival of British troops or not is unclear, but the commencement of his advance on Berber appeared to be timed to confront the Egyptian and Sudanese troops before the reinforcements arrived. Unfortunately for the Mahdists, the lack of suitable vessels with which to transfer their warriors across the Nile meant that the crossing would take almost two weeks to complete, greatly slowing their intended advance. Another problem facing Mahmud Ahmed was the differences between his Baggara and Osman Digna's Beja tribesmen, the latter believing themselves superior to—and looking down on—the former, a situation that caused much friction between the two. Mahmud Ahmed, unlike Osman Digna, had never experienced action against the British, but he was loathed to seek advice from his more experienced colleague and preferred to do things his own way. Unsurprisingly, the two Mahdist commanders failed to work together to the benefit of their common cause, something which would later greatly reduce their fighting potential against Kitchener's army.

The delay experienced by the *Ansar* in crossing the river allowed the majority of Gatacre's brigade to get close to the front by the time the 20,000 warriors under Mahmud Ahmed's command were finally over it and ready to continue their advance. Indeed, by the middle of February the Warwicks, Lincolns, and Camerons were at Abu Dis. The Mahdists had lost the initiative and the British troops, who benefited from high-morale, were spoiling for a fight. On the same day as the Mahdists completed their crossing of the Nile (25 February), Gactacre received orders to march his brigade to Berber; the journey was made to Sheriek by train, then the onward march to Berber on foot, the latter of which being reached on 2 March. Bennet Burleigh, the war correspondent from the *Daily Telegraph*, remembered the warm reception that greeted the British troops upon their arrival at Berber:

Men and women alike, they rushed up and shook hands with the British soldiers as they passed, and gave them such small presents as they could afford of dates, water, onions, and tomatoes. As for the Soudanese and Egyptian troops quartered in Berber, they turned out to a man and welcomed the brigade most loyally.

Here, they joined the two Egyptian brigades under the command of Hunter. It would be during the march to Berber that the British troops first encountered problems with their boots; the footwear fell apart too easily due to poor stitching, leaving several hundred men with sore feet.

Further intelligence as to Mahmud Ahmed's movements came in on the 13th, when it became known that he had left Shendi the day before and had advanced to Aliab, which was roughly the halfway point between Shendi and Berber. It was now clear to Kitchener that his enemy was most certainly planning to attack his position at Berber, and so he issued orders for his army to advance to Kenur, an abandoned village located about ten miles north of Atbara, in an attempt to intercept him. He would, however, leave behind an Egyptian battalion at Berber to garrison it and another half-battalion to guard the railhead. Gatacre's brigade arrived at Kenur on the 15th, with the Seaforths finally catching up with the other British regiments the following day.

Kitchener also learned that Mahmud Ahmed had resumed his advance on the 19th and was heading towards the east in the direction of Atbara. The Mahdist leader intended to cross the river at Hudi, a point where it was easier for his warriors to ford, then continue his advance on Berber across the desert. In response to this, the *Sirdar* ordered his army to begin a march to Hudi the following day, where, upon arrival, he would be joined by Colonel Lewis' 3rd Brigade, which had formed the garrison at Fort Atbara. This combined force offered Kitchener a total of over 13,000 men organised into four infantry brigades supported by 800 mounted troops, four batteries of artillery, and ten Maxim guns.

Once at Hudi, Kitchener ordered the cavalry, under the command of Lieutenant-Colonel Robert George Broadwood, to scout out the surrounding area in the hope of finding Mahmud Ahmed's army. While they conducted their search, the infantry began gathering in suitable materials for the building of a *zariba*. With this built, they were then ordered to bivouac for the night. The night was a cold one, and every soldier slept—if he could—in his uniform with his equipment and rifle next to him in order to turn out immediately in the event of a surprise attack. Despite Kitchener's belief that Mahmud Ahmed was heading for Hudi to cross the river, he had in fact marched thirty miles further up on the 20th to a place called Nakhila, where his warriors crossed over. It is possible that the Mahdists had learned of the advance of the Anglo-Egyptian troops with the intention to intercept him, and so chose this new location instead. Once across,

Mahmud Ahmed instructed his army to begin entrenching itself and make preparations for the expected attack.

Realising his enemy was not now heading for Hudi, Kitchener resumed his march along the Atbara River to Ras-el-Hudi, where he again made camp and built a *zariba*. Several days would pass while the *Sirdar* pushed out his cavalry in another attempt to locate the Mahdist force. Positioning his army here, however, prevented Mahmud Ahmed advancing on Berber, and so he knew it was only a matter of time before the two opposing armies finally met in battle, unless the *Ansar* took the unlikely decision to retreat. However, it would be on the 22nd that Broadwood's cavalry finally found a large force of Baggara tribesmen camped at Abadar. These mounted tribesmen also spotted the Egyptian cavalry and conducted a charge, forcing Captain the Honourable E. Baring and his squadron to retire.

Returning to the Anglo-Egyptian camp with the news, Kitchener was now sure the cavalry had located Mahmud Ahmed's main army. He next ordered Major John Collinson to march out with a battalion of infantry, supported by a squadron of cavalry and several Maxims, and advance towards Abadar. The *Sirdar* hoped that the sight of the major's modest force would encourage them to come out from their camp and leave the safety of the *zariba*, after which he could engage them in the open to his advantage. After advancing for about six miles, a party of 300–400 Baggara tribesmen suddenly appeared near Collinson's squadron of cavalry, who opened fire on the Mahdists before quickly withdrawing back towards the infantry and Maxims. Chased by the Baggara, the cavalry arrived to find the major had ordered his men into square, who, upon seeing the Mahdists, opened fire with rifle volleys and Maxim fire. Faced with the ferocity of this fire, the Baggara beat a hasty retreat. The brief skirmish over, Collinson formed up his men and returned to camp.

Having failed to tempt Mahmud Ahmed to come out, Kitchener next ordered Keppel to sail with three of his gunboats to Hosh Ben Naga, a village three miles upriver from Shendi, on the 25th. On board the vessels the *Sirdar* placed the 15th Egyptian Battalion with orders to capture the depot and seize the Mahdist stores he knew to be located there. The following day, the infantry, under the command of Major Thomas Edgecumbe Hickman, disembarked the gunboats a short distance from their target and advanced to the attack. In the ensuing action, the Egyptian infantrymen had little trouble in driving off the relatively few *Ansar* warriors that Mahmud had left to guard his supplies, killing about 150 and capturing another 650, the latter number also including some women and children who were later released. One of the captured men, a clerk in the employ of Mahmud Ahmed, informed the British officers during his subsequent questioning that the Mahdist leader had left Shendi with 18,941 fighting men, a figure that was reported back to the *Khalifa*. With the stores secure, the battalion marched on to Shendi, where the few warriors there also quickly surrendered. All fortifications were then burned and the infantrymen re-embarked on the steamers, along with their booty, for the return journey.

On the 30th, Kitchener ordered out another reconnaissance, this time in force, under the command of Hunter, which included: two battalions of infantry, eight squadrons of cavalry, the horse artillery battery under Major N. E. Young, and four Maxims under Major Charles Edward Lawrie and Captain M. Peake. Hunter, who personally approached the Mahdist camp to within 250 to 300 yards, finally located Mahmud Ahmed's main army at Nakhila, where it was found to be strongly entrenched within a *zariba* on the north bank of the Atbara River, which was by now almost dry. Armed with the information he needed, he instructed his force to return back to camp, although he ordered the horse artillery to fire several shells into the *zariba* before departing.

At about the same time as Hunter was conducting his reconnaissance of the *zariba*, a number of Mahdist deserters arrived at the Anglo-Egyptian camp. They revealed that their army was greatly suffering from the lack of available food—much of it having being seized earlier by Kitchener's troops—and was existing on a limited supply of vegetables and nuts that could be found near to their camp. The increasing suffering of the warriors had led to the desertions, although Mahmud Ahmed had introduced strict measures to prevent his warriors leaving the *zariba*.

It is likely that Mahmud Ahmed was procrastinating due to the fact he knew his advance to Berber was blocked by the Anglo-Egyptian army, which he believed would, due to their superior firepower, wipe out his own army during a battle in the open. In this he was almost certainly correct, and so he determined it wiser to wait for the *Sirdar* to attack him, thus benefiting from the defences of the *zariba*, which in turn would prove a serious disadvantage to his enemy. Falling back to Omdurman to join with the main Mahdist army was also not an option, since he knew the *Khalifa* would be angry with him, with severe punishment likely to follow, perhaps even death. In short, his situation was an unenviable one, and one in which he could not possibly hope to win. However, it did mean that any hope Kitchener may have had that the Mahdists would come out into the desert for a fight was highly unlikely; he would have to go to him before his own army deteriorated by sitting in the desert doing nothing for too long.

Thus, on 4 April, after some consultation with Cromer via telegraph, Kitchener gave the order for a general advance to be made to Abadar. The following day, in a final attempt to draw Mahmud Ahmed out of his *zariba*, Hunter, in company with Major William Francis Henry Style Kincaid of the Royal Engineers, with the same force he commanded on the 30th, as well as the addition of eight Maxim guns, marched to within 1,000 yards of the Mahdist camp. Finally, at 9 a.m., Mahmud Ahmed's warriors began to stir, and two large groups of Baggara tribesmen came riding out of the *zariba*, one advancing towards Hunter's left and the other to his right. A third group of horsemen then appeared, this time advancing directly towards Hunter's centre, the Egyptian troops responding by almost immediately opening fire. The major-general, who had previously ridden on ahead of his force to get a better look at the *zariba*, now had to frantically gallop back to his men, who were by now engaged in a violent struggle with their opponents. The Maxim guns, which had been positioned to the left of the cavalry, also opened fire, while the British officers were forced to draw their revolvers and fire at the Baggara tribesmen at close range.

Meanwhile, another body of *Ansar* warriors marched out from the *zariba* on foot, placing Hunter's force under such a threat that he decided it wise to order a retirement. The *Ansar* had met the Anglo-Egyptian reconnaissance in force, but the majority of the warriors still remained entrenched behind their defences. Hunter's retirement increasingly became desperate, the Baggara exerting much pressure on the cavalry, but thanks to the murderous fire of the Maxims the initial withdrawal was completed successfully. Nevertheless, the Mahdist horsemen continued to press the Egyptian cavalrymen, who, in squadrons of two, dismounted and held their pursuers at bay by firing volleys with their carbines while the other squadrons fell back. Two other squadrons would dismount and cover the retirement of the two that earlier dismounted to give fire.

As the retirement continued in this fashion, the Baggara also relentlessly continued to apply pressure on the retreating Egyptians. Broadwood, therefore, ordered the squadrons under Major P. W. J. Le Gallais and Captain William Horsley Persse to turn around and conducted a charge head-on at their enemy at about 10 a.m., a full hour after the action had begun. This sudden assault had the effect of temporarily driving the enemy horsemen off. However, the action would not finally come to an end until 1 p.m., when both the Egyptians and the Baggara moved off in opposite directions, the latter having followed the former for eight miles.

Broadwood's cavalry action had been a short but sharp affair. Total losses for the Egyptians amounted to eight killed and fourteen wounded—the latter including Captain Persse, who received a bullet to his left forearm—while Mahmud Ahmed was thought to have lost around 200 warriors. The action, although indecisive, did confirm to Kitchener that his enemy had no intention of fighting a major battle outside of his *zariba*, and so the following day he again ordered his men to strike camp and resume their advance. The Anglo-Egyptian army next arrived at a deserted village called Umdabbia, located approximately seven miles from Mahmud Ahmed's position, where they again bivouacked for the night. Both sides now made preparations for what they knew would be one of the most significant battles of the campaign—the Battle of Atbara.

8

The Battle of Atbara

For the next two days, Kitchener remained in camp and made preparations for the coming assault on Mahmud Ahmed's *zariba*. Then, at around 5 p.m. on 7 April, the troops of the Anglo-Egyptian army slowly began to march out for the long anticipated attack, the baggage and supplies being left behind under guard of half a battalion of Egyptian infantry. The advance was conducted in echelon, with Gatacre's British Brigade leading, behind which followed MacDonald's 1st Brigade of the Egyptian Division, then Lewis' 3rd Brigade along with the Camel Corps. Finally, acting as reserve, Maxwell's 2nd Brigade brought up the rear.

Although it was soon dark, the way ahead was lit by a bright moon; the route itself being parallel to the Atbara River, which consisted of marching over predominately broken and sandy terrain. A strong wind, however, began to hamper the movement of the troops, which blew sand around so violently that it made seeing even the man directly ahead difficult. In order to retain the formation and prevent the soldiers getting lost, a series of halts were ordered in an attempt to keep everyone in place. For the next three hours, Kitchener's men would march steadily on until they arrived at a place called Mutrus, which was a mere three miles from Mahmud Ahmed's position. Here they were told to get some rest, many of them simply laying down on the sand in the hope of drifting off to sleep.

This short rest would be interrupted at 1 a.m., on the 8th, when orders were given to the men to fall in. Within thirty minutes the advance, now conducted in squares, resumed, this time without the wind, but still with the moon lighting up the way ahead. Noise and light discipline was strictly observed, and the men obediently refrained from talking and smoking, the only sounds heard being the tramping of thousands of feet and the occasional murmured order from the officers when necessary. George Warrington Steevens, the war correspondent of the *Daily Mail* attached to the Anglo-Egyptian army, recalled this part of the final advance to battle:

> It was one o'clock. The square rustled into life and motion, bent forward, and started, half asleep. No man spoke, and no light showed, but the sand-muffled

trampling and the moon-veiled figures forbade the fancy that it was all a dream. The shapes of lines of men—now close, now broken, and closing up again as the ground broke or the direction changed—the mounted officers, and the hushed order, 'Left shoulder forward,' the scrambling Maxim mules, the lines of swaying camels, their pungent smell, and the rare neigh of a horse, the other three squares like it, which we knew of but could not see,—it was just the same war-machine as we had seen all these days on parade. Only this time it was in deadly earnest, moving stealthily but massively forward towards an event that none of us could quite certainly foretell.

At around 3 a.m., the quietly marching army suddenly witnessed a bright fire in the distance, the flame of which burned hotly for a few minutes before simply disappearing. The officers wondered as to what the purpose of this flame might be; perhaps the army had been spotted by Mahdist scouts and it was a signal to their *zariba* as a warning of their advance, or perhaps it was merely the result of some bizarre accident. Whatever it was, Kitchener was never able to ascertain its cause or purpose for certain, but in any case, it did not seem to cause his army any immediate issues and so he carried on.

An hour later, the Anglo-Egyptian force finally came to within sight of Mahmud Ahmed's camp, where dimly lit fires could be clearly seen in the near distance. A halt was ordered while, for the next thirty minutes, the men changed from square to attack formation, after which the march was once again resumed. The British Brigade was now positioned on the left, with the 1st Egyptian Brigade in the centre and 3rd Brigade on the right. 2nd Brigade again followed in the rear as reserve, while the cavalry and horse artillery took up positions approximately half a mile out to the left of the infantry.

By 6 a.m., Kitchener's army was within 600 yards of the *zariba* when yet another halt was ordered. The morning sun was already beginning to rise, and the camp before them could be made out in great and clear detail. Looking down into the camp, the British and Egyptian troops could not, however, see much human activity, although it was clear that the defending warriors had made good their preparations for the defence of their position. Despite this lack of activity, the *Sirdar* realised that his arrival had not come as the hoped-for surprise to his enemy, and, perhaps, the bright flame of the night had indeed most likely been a warning of the advance after all.

With the eye of a military engineer, Lieutenant Pritchard described the Mahdist camp now sitting in front of him:

> It was more or less an oval resting on the river, honeycombed with trenches, and surrounded by a zeriba. It resembled Abu Hamed on a larger scale, in that it lay at the bottom of a kind of crater, of which the radius was about six hundred yards, so that it would be impossible to open fire at a greater range, which was evidently the reason which caused the Dervishes to take up such a position.

The Battle of Atbara

Also examining the *zariba* at this moment was Kitchener, who, in his despatch of 10 April 1898, later described the Mahdist camp:

> ... a large irregular inclosure [sic], strongly entrenched all round, palisaded in parts, with innumerable cross trenches, casemates, and straw huts, besides ten palisaded gun emplacements, the whole surrounded by a strong zareba. That portion of the camp nearest to the desert was fairly free of bush, but towards the centre it became thicker, and the rear and flanks closest to the river were concealed in a dense jungle of sunt trees, dom palms, and undergrowth.

The defences around the Mahdist camp presented a somewhat formidable sight to the officers and men of Kitchener's army, for they knew it would not be long before they would be ordered to storm the position at the point of the bayonet, an unenviable and daunting task for all concerned. Such an assault was the very thing the *Sirdar* had very much wished to avoid, because he knew it was likely to result in a far greater number of casualties among his men than a battle fought in the open. However, with Mahmud Ahmed unwilling to budge, the time had finally come to act; in an attempt to soften up his enemy's defences, thus reducing Anglo-Egyptian losses, Kitchener would open the battle with a sustained artillery bombardment.

Kitchener had placed two batteries of artillery over on the right-flank of the Egyptian brigades, together making a total of twelve guns. He also placed another two batteries of six guns each in the gap between the left of the Egyptians and the right of the British Brigade. At 6.15 a.m., all twenty-four guns—which included six Krupp and eighteen Maxim-Nordenfelt guns—roared into action and commenced firing directly into the *zariba*. Also supporting this bombardment was a detachment of the Egyptian rocket battery—operating 24lb rocket tubes—under the command of Lieutenant Beatty of the Royal Navy, while the cavalry and several 'galloping Maxim' guns were positioned further to the left of the line out in the desert.

Steevens was watching the bombardment; he witnessed:

> ... from the horse battery and one field battery on the right, from two batteries of Maxim-Nordenfelts on the left, just to the right front of the British, and from a war-rocket which changed over from left to right, belched a rapid, but unhurried, regular, relentless shower of destruction. The round grey clouds from shell, the round white puffs from shrapnel, the hissing splutter of rockets, flighted down methodically, and alighted on every part of the *zariba* and of the bush behind.

During the shelling, many of Mahmud Ahmed's warriors wisely opted to stay put in their trenches or other places of shelter, although a few dusty figures could, rather incredibly, be spotted strolling around as if totally unconcerned by the shells exploding around them. Occasionally, a few poorly-aimed rifle shots were fired at Kitchener's artillerymen, but only one of the bullets found its mark, an Egyptian gunner being wounded. At one point, one of the shells set fire to a palm tree, then another almost spontaneously began to burn next to it. Then, all of a sudden, a large group of Baggara horsemen came galloping out of the southern end of the *zariba* and began to form up as if to mount a charge towards Kitchener's left-flank. However, spotted by the eagle-eyed Maxim crews, these mounted Mahdists quickly came under heavy machine gun fire, which almost immediately forced them to abandon whatever attempt they were trying to make. If the Maxims had not done this work, the Egyptian cavalry would have, since they were spoiling for a fight and were on the very verge of charging the Baggara moments before they retired.

Shortly after the Mahdist horseman broke off, Steevens recalled:

By now, when it [the bombardment] had lasted an hour or more, not a man showed along the whole line, nor yet a spot of rifle smoke. All seemed empty, silent, lifeless, but for one hobbled camel, waving his neck and stupid head in helpless dumb bewilderment. Presently the edge of the storm of devastation caught him too, and we saw him no more.

In total, the artillery bombardment of the *zariba* lasted between eighty and ninety minutes—depending on the source consulted—after which the order to cease fire was given. For a brief moment, an eerie silence then descended over the battlefield, but this was soon shattered by the shouting of orders by British and Egyptian officers, who now instructed their men to rise to their feet—they had been lying down as protection from the Mahdist rifleman while watching the bombardment—and form up ready for the infantry assault.

Over at the position occupied by the British troops, the men of the Cameron Highlanders could be seen quickly extending into line across the whole front of the brigade. The other regiments of the brigade formed into columns of companies behind this line, including: the Royal Warwickshire Regiment on the left, the Seaforth Highlanders in the centre and the Lincolnshire Regiment on the right. To the right of Gatacre's Brigade was MacDonald's, with the 11th, 10th, and 9th Sudanese Battalions respectively to the front. Each of these three battalions had pushed forward three of their six companies, while the remaining three formed up directly behind. In support was the 2nd Egyptians who were formed up in column to the centre of the rear. To the right of MacDonald was Maxwell's brigade, with, from left to right, the 12th, 14th, and 13th Sudanese Battalions in line; each battalion pushing forward four of its six companies to form a broad front, with the remaining companies again directly behind. The 8th Egyptians were acting as support, and so formed up in column behind the rear companies. Of the eight squadrons of cavalry over on the extreme left of the Anglo-Egyptian line, one, under the command of Captain W. E. Peyton, was detached with orders to redeploy over to the right near the dry riverbed. Lewis's brigade remained in reserve to the left-rear of the British Brigade.

Kitchener and his staff had positioned themselves on high ground some 900 yards from the *zariba*, while Gatacre, MacDonald, Maxwell, and many other senior officers had taken up positions directly in front of their respective brigades, ready to lead their men into battle. At 8.15 a.m., the order to advance was sounded, and, with bayonets fixed, the Camerons moved forward in line, with the other British regiments following closely behind. The Egyptian brigades similarly began their respective advances at the same time. Directly in front of the British Brigade was Gatacre, along with Lieutenant-Colonel G. L. C. Money, commanding officer of the Camerons. As the brigade advanced, the bagpipes of the Highlanders played and a large Union Jack was unfurled and carried in the centre of the line by Staff-Sergeant Wyeth of the Army Service Corps.

After advancing a few yards, the whole line would temporarily halt and independent fire or volley fire by sections was directed at the *zariba*, after which the advance resumed before halting and firing again. This process would be repeated numerous times during the initial assault. The *Ansar* warriors, in the meantime, withheld their fire until the British and Egyptian troops came to within 200 yards of their outer defences, when, all of a sudden, a heavy rifle fire erupted from the *zariba* and hundreds of bullets hurtled towards the Anglo-Egyptian troops. Yet again much of this fire went high, the Mahdist bullets whistling over ahead with most causing no injury or damage. A few, however, did manage to hit some of the men in the leading ranks, and a number of troops, either alone or in small groups of twos and threes, could be seen crashing to the ground as the lines marched on regardless. There were many instances of soldiers experiencing close-shaves, including Lieutenant Samuel Fitzgibbon Cox of the Lincolns who had a bullet pass through his helmet before the man to his left, a Sergeant Malone, was shot in the mouth and fell to the ground. Nevertheless, the officer continued to advance, but later learned the NCO had been killed. Despite the growing number of casualties, Kitchener's men all relentlessly marched on, keeping to their formations throughout their advance.

The fire from the *Ansar* warriors, however, became increasingly effective as the Camerons reached a stretch of elevated ground, from which they had to advance down a slope towards the *zariba*. From a range of about 100 yards, the Mahdist riflemen also began to pour an increasingly heavier fire into their attackers, and so the Highlanders were again ordered to halt so they could return the fire with their powerful Lee Metfords. After a number of rounds were discharged, the order to advance was again given, this time the men running forward to conduct a final headlong charge at the *zariba*, and as they did so loud cheers could be heard along the entire line, accompanied by words of encouragement from the officers and NCOs.

Leading from the front, Gatacre was the first to reach the *zariba*, and he immediately grabbed at the obstacle in front of him in an attempt to tear his way through. It would be at that moment that a Mahdist warrior lurched forward with his spear raised ready to kill the major-general, but, fortunately for Gatacre, a soldier of the Camerons, Private Cross, saw what was happening and immediately thrust at the warrior with his bayonet, bringing the man down and, most likely, saving the major-general's life.

The whole of the Cameron Highlanders were now at the edge of the *zariba*, the men grasping and tugging at the thorn bushes. Moments later, the men of the Warwicks, Seaforths and Lincolns joined them, and they also began to tear the defences apart with their bare hands. Some of the British troops attempted to literally drag away the obstacles, while others took aim at the Mahdist defenders and fired their rifles repeatedly to keep them at bay while a way in was found. Eventually, a number of holes in the *zariba* where made, and the British troops finally began to pour into the Mahdist camp.

Prior to the attack, the plan had been for the Camerons to conduct the initial assault and clear a number of paths through the thorn bushes, after which they were to stand back to allow the men of the other three British regiments—who had avoided the burden of being in the front line during the advance—to enter and carry the *zariba*. However, in the confusion of battle and faced with the rifle fire and spears of the *Ansar* warriors, the Camerons, having accomplished their allotted task, entered the *zariba* regardless of their orders. Gatacre also had no intentions of watching the Camerons stand by as the other regiments finished the assault, and so he ordered the men of the regiment to continue to push on. Indeed, the first British soldier to actually enter the *zariba* was Captain Charles Findlay, an officer of the Camerons. With sword in one hand and revolver in the other, the captain jumped over the first trench behind the thorn bushes only to be shot by a Mahdist rifleman and come crashing to the ground; he would not survive. Once the Camerons were inside, the other British regiments followed through the gaps.

If the attack had been hard work so far it was about to get even harder, the real fighting of the battle now beginning as the British soldiers came face-to-face with their adversaries at close-quarters. In front of them were numerous trenches and rifle pits, most of them filled with warriors, many of the Mahdists holding rifles and firing at virtually point-blank range at the onrushing British troops. The fight quickly became a bitter contest between the two sides, the British desperately attempting to clear each trench they came to, and gunning down or bayonetting every Mahdist warrior before them.

The nature of the hand-to-hand fighting was particularly vicious, an example of which Lieutenant Ronald Forbes Meiklejohn of the Warwicks later recalled:

Pioneer-Corporal Jones of my regiment, a mighty giant well over 6 feet, unofficially joined my company armed only with an axe, which he had carefully

Above left: Muhammad Ahmed, the *Mahdi* of Sudan. (*Author's collection*)

Above right: Ismail *Pasha*, the *Khedive* of Egypt, who was forced to resign on 26 June 1879. (*Author's collection*)

Above left: Tewfik *Pasha*, the weak and unpopular *Khedive*, who ruled Egypt under the heavy influence of Britain. (*Author's collection*)

Above right: Arabi *Pasha*, the popular nationalist Egyptian Army officer, who would rebel against Tewfik, but was later defeated by the British at the Battle of Tel el-Kebir. (*Author's collection*)

Colonel William Hicks, known as 'Hicks *Pasha*', was a retired British Army officer who led an expedition on behalf of the Egyptian *Khedive* to put down the Mahdi's revolt. He was killed on 5 November 1883. (*Author's collection*)

General Charles 'Chinese' Gordon, who was killed by the Mahdi's men during the fall of Khartoum on 26 January 1885. The British would wait more than a decade to avenge his death. (*Author's collection*)

Sir Garnet Wolseley, who led the failed campaign to save Gordon at Khartoum. (*Author's collection*)

Evelyn Baring, 1st Earl of Cromer, the British consul-general of Egypt. (*Author's collection*)

Major-General Horatio Herbert Kitchener, Sirdar of the Egyptian Army. For his success against the Khalifa and the Mahdists in Sudan, he would later become known as 'Lord Kitchener of Khartoum'. (*Author's collection*)

Major Francis Reginald Wingate, the British intelligence officer who co-produced *Ten Years' Captivity in the Mahdi's Camp, 1882–1892* and *Fire and Sword in the Sudan*. Both books proved popular with an outraged British public. (*Author's collection*)

Right: Colonel Rudolf Carl von Slatin, the Anglo-Austrian Egyptian Army officer who spent over eleven years as a prisoner of the Mahdists. (*Anne S. K. Brown Military Collection*)

Below: Father Joseph Ohrwalder (right), the Austrian missionary taken captive by the Mahdists for ten years. (*Author's collection*)

Left: Major-General William Forbes Gatacre, who commanded the British Infantry Division at Omdurman. (*Author's collection*)

Below left: Brigadier-General Andrew Gilbert Wauchope, who commanded the 1st British Infantry Brigade at Omdurman. (*Author's collection*)

Below right: Brigadier-General Neville Lyttelton, who commanded the 2nd British Infantry Brigade at Omdurman. (*Author's collection*)

Right: Major-General Archibald Hunter, who commanded the Egyptian Division at Omdurman. (*Author's collection*)

Below left: Brigadier-General Hector MacDonald, who commanded the 1st Egyptian Infantry Brigade at Omdurman. (*Author's collection*)

Below right: A young Winston Spencer Churchill, who was present at the Battle of Omdurman with the 21st Lancers. He would later write *The River War: An Historical Account of the Reconquest of the Soudan*, in which he recounts his experiences of the campaign. (*Author's collection*)

Captain Paul Aloysius Kenna of the 21st Lancers, who was awarded the Victoria Cross for saving the life of Major Wyndham and going to the assistance of Lieutenant Montmorency during the cavalry charge at the Battle of Omdurman. (*Author's collection*)

Private Thomas Byrne of the 21st Lancers, who was awarded the Victoria Cross for going to the assistance of the wounded and disarmed Lieutenant Molyneux during the charge of his regiment at Omdurman, enabling the latter to escape certain death at the hands of Mahdist warriors. (*Author's collection*)

Lieutenant the Honourable Raymond Harvey Lodge Joseph de Montmorency of the 21st Lancers, who was awarded the Victoria Cross for going to the assistance of Second-Lieutenant Grenfell, who, having being unhorsed, was laying on the ground surrounded by Mahdist warriors at Omdurman. (*Author's collection*)

A single-shot rolling-block Remington rifle of the type used by the Egyptian Army before its reorganisation by the British. Many of these rifles would also be used by the Mahdists, being picked up from numerous battlefields in large numbers. (*Courtesy of Tim Rose*)

Men of the Egyptian Camel Corps practice forming a defensive square. (*Author's collection*)

Men of the Egyptian Horse Artillery on parade. (*Author's collection*)

Following a defeat, many ex-Mahdists, such as these Sudanese men, joined the Egyptian Army in order to fight against their former comrades. (*Author's collection*)

Above, below and opposite below: Sudanese recruits undergoing military training in the Egyptian Army. (*Author's collection*)

British troops, possibly in Malta, prepare to leave for Egypt and Sudan. (*Author's collection*)

The transport ship *Nubia* taking aboard men and equipment at Malta for the journey to Egypt. (*Author's collection*)

Above and opposite below: Baggage and troops being transferred to a transport ship in Malta for the journey to Egypt. (*Author's collection*)

Below: British troops disembark at Alexandria following their journey from Malta. (*Author's collection*)

Above and opposite: A British howitzer is unloaded from a transport ship at Alexandria. (Author's collection)

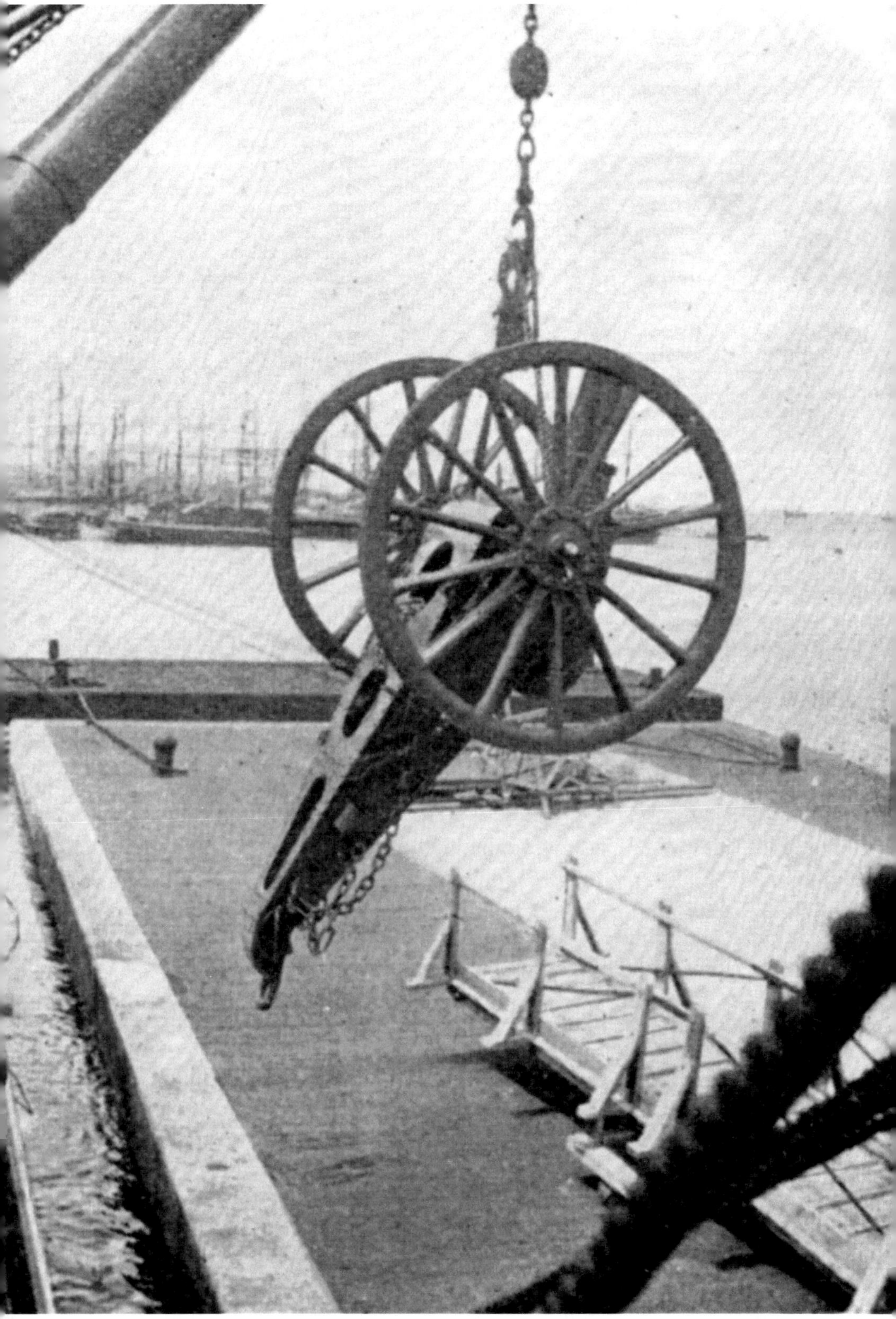

British troops stretch their legs during a brief halt *en route* to Cairo from Alexandria. (*Author's collection*)

British soldiers of the Lancashire Fusiliers in Sudan. (*Author's collection*)

Opposite above: Men of the Grenadier Guards are issued with ammunition in Sudan. (*Author's collection*)

Opposite below: British officers who took part in the Dongola campaign of 1896. (*Anne S. K. Brown Military Collection*)

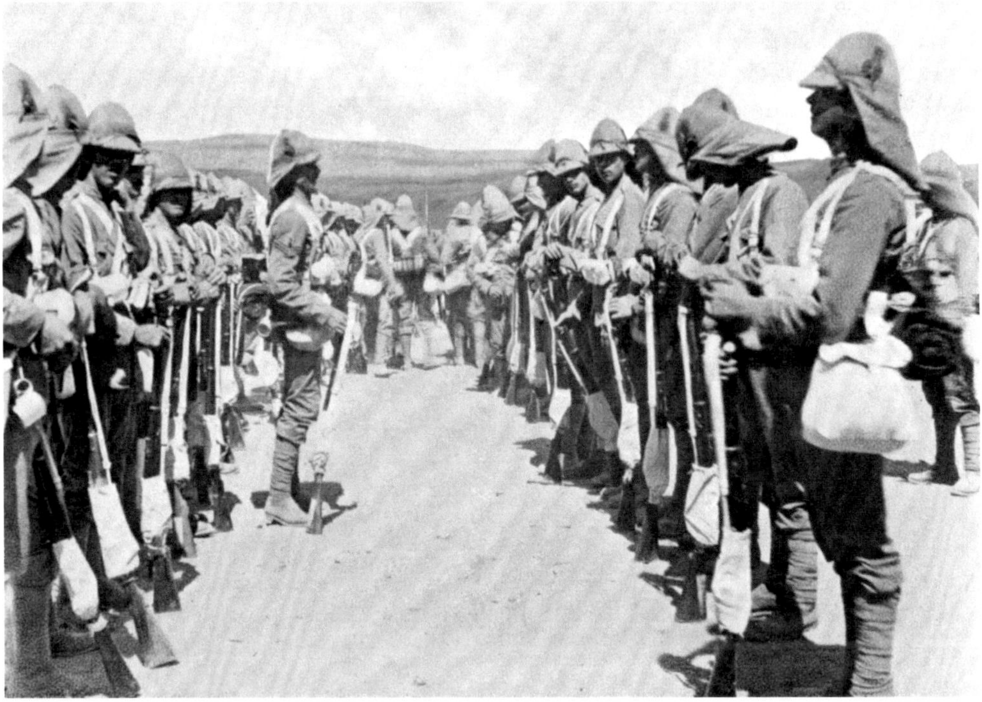

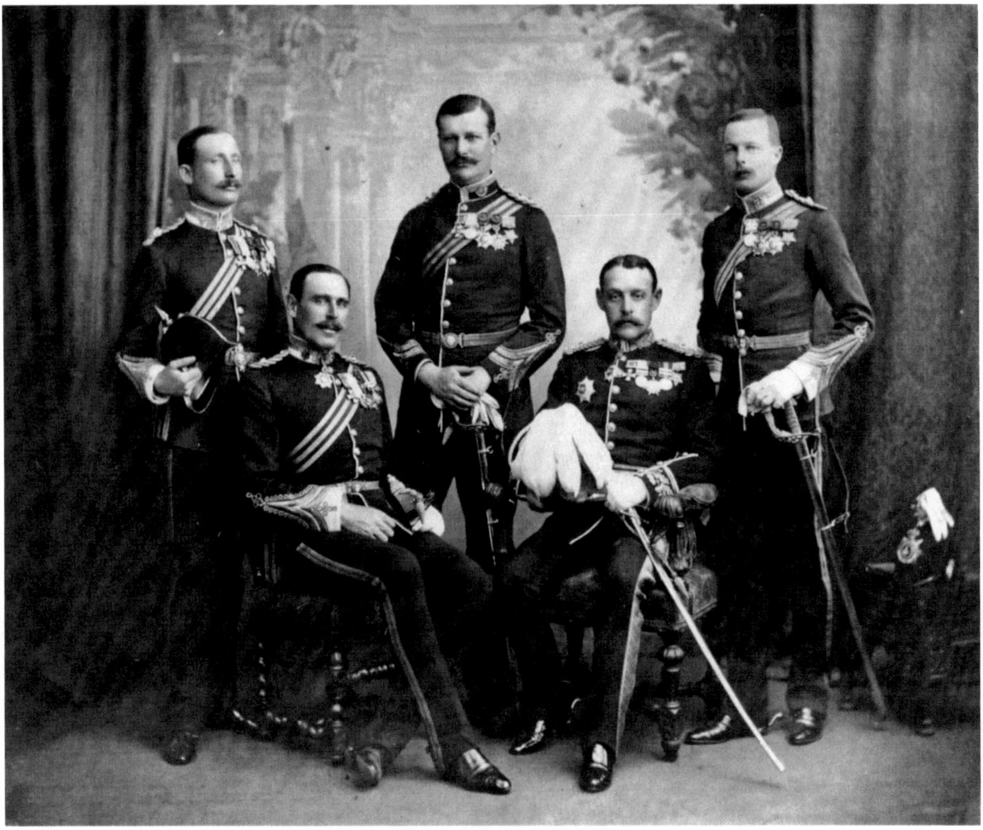

Above: Officers of the Grenadier Guards in Sudan. (*Author's collection*)

Below: Officers of the 21st Lancers who took part in the Battle of Omdurman. (*Author's collection*)

A soldier of the 21st Lancers in Sudan kit, by Richard Caton Woodville. (*Anne S. K. Brown Military Collection*)

A mounted Mahdist chief c.1896. (*Anne S. K. Brown Military Collection*)

Although depicting the charge of the Mahdists at the Battle of Abu Klea in 1885, the tactics of the *Ansar* changed little over the following decade. (*Anne S. K. Brown Military Collection*)

The building of the Sudanese Military Railway. The SMR was crucial to Kitchener's campaigns between 1896 and 1898. (*Author's collection*)

Above: A British war correspondent in Sudan in 1898. Although detested by Kitchener, the likes of Bennet Burleigh and George Warrington Steevens wrote invaluable first-hand accounts of the reconquest of Sudan. (*Author's collection*)

Below: Egyptian cavalry clash with Mahdist forces near Akasha, 1 May 1896. (*Author's collection*)

The Battle of Firket, 7 June 1896. (*Author's collection*)

The Action of Abu Hamed, 7 August 1897. (*Author's collection*)

The Cameron Highlanders attacking Mahmud's *zariba* at the Battle of Atbara, 8 April 1898. (*Anne S. K. Brown Military Collection*)

The scene inside the *zariba* after the Battle of Atbara. (*Author's collection*)

One of a number of brass cannons captured from the Mahdists during the Battle of Atbara. (*Author's collection*)

Mahmud is brought before Kitchener following his defeat at the Battle of Atbara. (*Anne S. K. Brown Military Collection*)

The 1st British Brigade begins its march to Omdurman. (*Anne S. K. Brown Military Collection*)

A Mahdist attack during the Battle of Omdurman, 2 September 1898. (*Author's collection*)

Above: British and Egyptian troops repel the Mahdists during the Battle of Omdurman. (*Author's collection*)

Below: The charge of the 21st Lancers during the Battle of Omdurman. (*Anne S. K. Brown Military Collection*)

Above: The 21st Lancers enter Khor Abu Sunt during their charge at the Battle of Omdurman. (*Author's collection*)

Below left: Mahdist warriors make a last desperate defence of the *Khalifa's* Black Flag towards the end of the Battle of Omdurman. (*Author's collection*)

Below right: Kitchener enters Khartoum following the fall of Omdurman. (*Anne S. K. Brown Military Collection*)

The ruins of the *Mahdi's* tomb at Omdurman as it appeared sometime after the fall of the city. (*Author's collection*)

The *Khalifa's* house at Omdurman. (*Author's collection*)

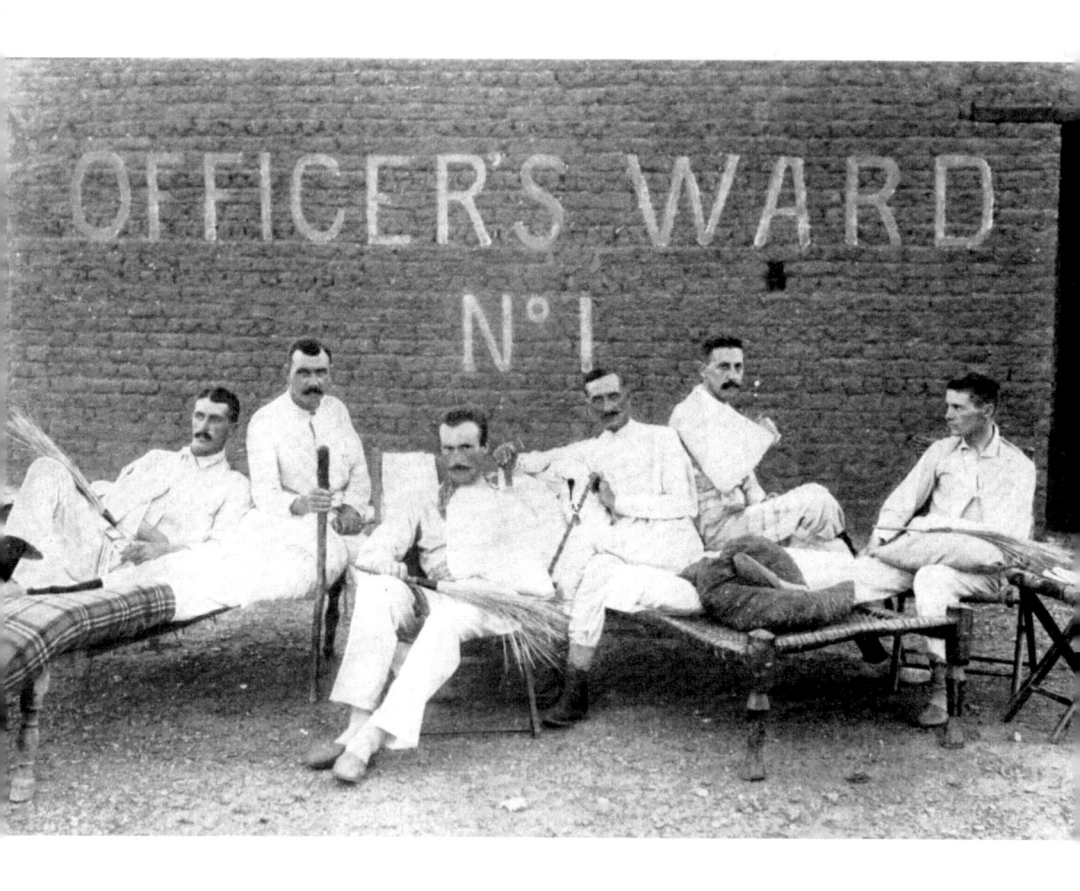

Above: Wounded British officers convalescing at Cairo in 1898. (*Author's collection*)

Right: The death of the *Khalifa* at the Battle of Umm Diwaykarat, 22 November 1899. (*Author's collection*)

Above: Obverse and reverse of the Queen's Sudan Medal, awarded to recognised service during the reconquest between 1896 and 1899. (*Courtesy of Mark A. Reid*)

Below: Obverse and reverse of the *Khedive's* Sudan Medal. (*Courtesy of Mark A. Reid*)

sharpened. A dervish met him and thrust at him with his spear. This he dodged, then, swinging his axe over his head, brought it down on his enemy's head, almost severing half his head and shoulder.

Despite the seemingly unstoppable Anglo-Egyptian onslaught, the Mahdists showed no signs of fleeing from their attackers; the men of the *Ansar* fought back equally as viciously, contesting every bit of ground as the mass of British soldiers pushed ever forwards.

Watching the developing action was Steevens, who, rather colourfully, recalled the moment the British troops gained access to the *zariba*:

> For now began the killing. Bullet and bayonet and butt, the whirlwind of Highlanders swept over. And by this time the Lincolns were in on the right, and the Maxims, galloping right up to the stockade, had withered the left, and the Warwicks, the enemy's cavalry definitely gone, were volleying off the blacks as your beard comes off under a keen razor. Farther and farther they cleared the ground—cleared it of everything like a living man, for it was left carpeted thick enough with dead.

Leading a group of men of the Camerons was Major Beauchamp Colclough Urquart of the same regiment, who would lose his life fighting his way into the Mahmud Ahmed's camp, being shot in the back by a Mahdist rifleman who had concealed himself under a pile of dead bodies, and thus missed by the officer as he rushed by. Another officer of the regiment, Major Robert Francis Ladeveze Napier, was also severely wounded by a shot from what later turned out to be an elephant gun. Although he survived the battle, he would later die of his wounds back in Egypt some six weeks later.

Casualties also occurred among the men of the Seaforths, with both Lieutenant-Colonel R. H. Murray and Lieutenant Paul Alexander Gore being shot, the former in the arm and the latter mortally through his heart. Murray's wound was bandaged up by Mr Seudamore, the correspondent of the *Daily News*, while under a 'distracting fire'. Captain Alan Charles Duncan Baillie, also of the regiment, suffered a shattered leg, dying of his wounds five weeks later in hospital in Cairo. Sergeant-Major Mackay narrowly escaped death when a Mahdist warrior attempted to stab him with a spear but only managed to catch and tear the NCO's kilt. Mackay then pointed his revolver at the warrior and shot him at point-blank range before finishing him off with his claymore.

The men of the Lincolns were also in the middle of the fray, with the soldiers frenziedly shooting and stabbing with their bayonets, slaughtering every Mahdist they came across. The Lincolns' commanding officer, Lieutenant-Colonel Thomas Edward Verner, who was a rather large and tall gentleman, had a bullet graze along the side of his cheek, which also cut the chinstrap of his helmet. This may have been a lucky escape, but another round hit him in the mouth, tearing off his upper lip and moustache. Incredibly, despite his horrendous injuries, the lieutenant-colonel carried on, pausing only for a few moments for a medical orderly to bandage his head before resuming to fight alongside his men.

As the soldiers of the Warwicks entered the *zariba*, one of the officers of the regiment heard someone shout: 'Now you're into them Warwichshire lads. Stick every mother's son.' The experience of the Warwicks was, naturally, the same as the other British regiments, with officers shooting warriors at point-blank range with their revolvers or sticking them with their swords, while the enlisted men made great use of their bayonets and rifle butts, killing every adversary they came upon. Lieutenant Meiklejohn had a narrow escape when he spotted a warrior raising his rifle in an attempt to shoot him. Spinning round to face him, the officer fired his revolver, but the bullet missed and hit the ground near his intended target. The warrior then fired his rifle, but the bullet similarly missed its target, passing close by the lieutenant's head with what he later described as a 'loud whizz'. Fortunately for Meiklejohn, several men of the Warwicks quickly put an end to the Mahdist with their bayonets, leaving his dead corpse slumped in his trench.

It was not only the British troops who were fighting hard against the *Ansar*, the Sudanese and Egyptian troops having also reached and entered the *zariba*. Leading them was Major-General Hunter mounted on horseback, who had actually managed to get inside just prior to the Camerons. Their experience of the close-quarter fighting would be very similar to that of the British troops, and a number of their British officers had also quickly become casualties. However, it would be as they approached what appeared to be a second *zariba* that Hunter's men would see their hardest fighting of the battle. This inner defensive position was resolutely defended by Mahmud Ahmed's hand-picked bodyguards, who kept up an intense rifle fire on the Sudanese troops as they steadily fought their way towards them. The *Ansar* fire was so intense that a full company of Major Jackson's 11th Sudanese Battalion was almost annihilated trying to take the inner-*zariba*. The position finally fell to the regiment, but only after additional companies added their weight to the attack.

Under the immense pressure of the Anglo-Egyptian assault, the Mahdists eventually began to buckle and give ground. Increasing numbers of warriors then started to flee, although some would occasionally halt, turn around and open fire on the pursuing British, Egyptian and Sudanese soldiers. Such acts of resistance soon came to an end, and large groups of warriors could be seen running to the dry riverbed which they used as an escape route.

Lieutenant Pritchard noted what happened next:

> As soon as the position was taken the cavalry attempted to pursue, but the dense bush was absolutely impracticable for them, and they were obliged to give up, but pursuit was unnecessary. The Dervishes were entirely broken up. They could

not go to the Nile, for the gunboats were watching it; they could only go up the Atbara, and then try and strike across the desert to hit the Nile higher up.

Once the *zariba* was cleared of any remaining warriors, orders were issued to the men to cease firing and discontinue any attempt at pursuit of the enemy. Their objective had been met, Mahmud Ahmed's camp was now firmly in Kitchener's hands, and the Battle of Atbara was over.

Kitchener's losses for the battle were quite severe. The British Brigade alone suffered three officers and twenty-two NCOs and men killed, while a further ten officers and thirty-two NCOs and men were wounded. As we have seen above, a number of the wounded later died of their injuries, adding to the death toll. Of those to later die were Staff-Sergeant Wyeth, who had carried the Union Jack that was shot through at least three times, and Private Cross, who had saved Gatacre's life. Cross had been suffering badly from dysentery but took part in the battle nonetheless, only to be badly wounded for his efforts; had he lived, it was said he would have been recommended for the Victoria Cross—the medal was not awarded posthumously at the time.

Of the Egyptian Division, a total of fifty-seven NCOs and men were killed, while five British and sixteen Egyptian officers as well as 365 NCOs and men were wounded. Again, others would later die of their wounds in the coming days and weeks. To treat the wounded, the *Sirdar* had established a nearby field hospital where they were dressed before being taken to Fort Atbara, where they were then made as comfortable as possible. Some of the wounded were later sent back to Egypt via boats, then on to hospital in Cairo.

Ansar casualties were estimated at around 3,000 killed and an unknown number wounded. According to Steevens:

> In the *zariba* itself *Bimbashi* [James Kiero] Watson, A. D. C. to the *Sirdar*, counted over 2000 dead before he was sick of it. There were others left: trench after trench was found filled with them. A few were killed outside the *zariba*; a great many were shot down in crossing the river-bed. Altogether 3,000 men must have been killed on the spot; among them were nearly all the Emirs, including Wad Bishara, who was Governor of Dongola in 1896.

Mahmud Ahmed had managed to survive the battle, but had not been fortunate enough to escape along with some of his warriors across the dry riverbed. In fact, he had been taken prisoner by men of the 10th Sudanese, who, rather oddly, found him inside his inner-*zariba* sat on a carpet with his personal weapons next him, in what was described by Steevens as after 'the manner of defeated war-chiefs who await death'. Other accounts claim he was hiding under a bed, but this is unlikely. A dispute, however, erupted between the men of the 10th and 9th battalions about who should take him to the *Sirdar*, since the major-general had offered a

£100 reward for his capture, a considerable sum for an ordinary soldier. With the argument boiling over, it seemed for a moment that they would rather kill their prisoner instead of allowing each other to claim the money, but Captain Franks of the Royal Artillery, realising what was happening, quickly intervened and ordered the prisoner to be taken at once to the *Sirdar*. After a brief exchange of words, Kitchener ordered the Mahdist to be placed in custody for further questioning later. Hunter had also offered a reward of £100 to any soldier who captured Osman Digna, but the chief had managed to escape along with the Baggara horsemen; he would fight the British again at the Battle of Omdurman.

The battlefield of Atbara now presented the Anglo-Egyptian force with a major health hazard, since the thousands of bodies of those killed were fast deteriorating under the hot sun, as were the carcasses of many dead animals unwittingly caught up in the action. Even without the dead, the Mahdist camp had been a filthy one, since little in the way of sanitary arrangements had been made by its original occupants. Even the pools of water sprinkled across the otherwise dry riverbed were said to have been polluted and unfit to drink or wash. All-in-all it was a very unpleasant place to be. Initially, the men were told to get out of the camp and rest further away in the desert, but this was found to be rather uncomfortable due to the hot sand and scorching sun. Eventually, however, the order was given for the fatigued men to march back to Fort Atbara, the wounded being carried on stretchers by the men of Lewis' brigade, who had not been involved in the initial assault.

A triumphant Kitchener, however, still had one more task to complete. The people of Berber had expected the Mahdists to achieve victory over the Anglo-Egyptian force, a belief probably born out of their personal fear of the *Khalifa* and the *Ansar*, a result of the harsh treatment previously meted out to them. The *Sirdar*, therefore, thought parading the captured Mahmud Ahmed through the streets would make the people believe that the *Ansar* was not invincible and that it could ultimately be defeated throughout Sudan. In order to prepare for the spectacle, Captain Doran, who was the officer in charge of the depot at Berber, was ordered to decorate the town with flags and bunting—a somewhat bizarre order since such items were unlikely to be found in the town—but he failed in this task. However, the captain would be saved by the local women, who produced a plethora of different brightly coloured dresses which were used to decorate the streets.

On the day Mahmud Ahmed was paraded through the streets, the local populace turned out in huge numbers, and upon seeing their enemy now a prisoner it is said it brought them much pleasure. Some of the local *sheikhs* even approached Kitchener to offer him their personal congratulations. The *Sirdar*, however, knew that Atbara and the capture of Mahmud Ahmed was but a small victory in his renewed campaign, and a much more difficult fight against the *Khalifa* and his powerful army was yet to come.

9

The March to Omdurman

Kitchener now set his sights on Omdurman itself, where he knew he would fight the decisive battle of the entire campaign against the *Khalifa* and his *Ansar*. Preparations for the advance to Abdullahi al-Taishi's seat of power began in earnest in May 1898, during which time the *Sirdar* moved the headquarters of his Anglo-Egyptian army to Fort Atbara. It would also be to here that an incredible amount of supplies was moved up via rail—and other methods of transport—in order to stockpile at least three months' worth of provisions for the 25,000 men who would undertake the march. The British commander similarly established an arsenal and a number of workshops at Abadieh near Berber, the latter to service Keppel's small fleet of gunboats.

Other preparations also included keeping the men physically fit for the coming operations. In particular, the British soldiers—who were less used to working and fighting in the heat compared to their Egyptian and Sudanese counterparts—were instructed to conduct a number of long route marches, a physical task made easier by the fact the men were by now becoming acclimatised. While these tasks were carried out, Kitchener travelled back to Britain for a brief visit, as did a number of other officers, knowing this would be their last chance to see families and home before the final part of the long advance began.

By July, the British Government took the decision to add a second brigade of British troops to the *Sirdar*'s army, which included infantry, cavalry and artillery. The two brigades together would form the British Division, which would be placed under the command of Major-General Gatacre; the 1st Brigade would be commanded by Brigadier-General Andrew Gilbert Wauchope and the 2nd Brigade by Brigadier-General Neville Lyttelton. Wauchope would command the British regiments that fought at the Battle of Atbara, while Lyttleton would be given newly arrived battalions, which included: 1st Grenadier Guards, 1st Northumberland Fusiliers, 2nd Lancashire Fusiliers, 2nd Rifle Brigade, four Maxim machine guns of the Royal Irish Fusiliers, and a detachment of Royal Engineers. Again, some of these regiments would already be in Cairo or

Alexandria, whereas others would arrive from Malta and Gibraltar. In addition, the Anglo-Egyptian force would be joined by four squadrons of the 21st Lancers, under the command of Lieutenant-Colonel Rowland Hill Martin, and the 32nd and 37th Field Batteries of the Royal Artillery, as well as detachments of men from the Army Service Corps and Royal Army Medical Corps.

The Egyptian Division, which remained under the overall command of Major-General Hunter, was also increased in size, receiving an additional infantry brigade. The original brigades remained under control of their previous commanders, including: 1st Brigade under Brigadier-General MacDonald; 2nd Brigade under Colonel Maxwell; and 3rd Brigade under Colonel Lewis. The new brigade, which was designated 4th Brigade, was placed under command of Lieutenant-Colonel John Collinson, and consisted of the 1st and 5th Egyptians and the 17th and 18th Sudanese battalions. There would also be nine squadrons of Egyptian cavalry, eight companies of the Camel Corps, a horse artillery battery and four field batteries.

Orders were given for all the above to concentrate at Fort Atbara in August, although Lewis' 3rd Brigade had been instructed to move on ahead to Nasri Island in order to establish a supply depot, after which he advanced to Wad Habeshi. From here, once the other brigades were brought up, it was intended to advance to Wad Hamid, itself only a short distance from the former. In order to help facilitate the transport of troops, equipment and supplies, the railway was extended to within only a short distance of Fort Atbara.

On 3rd August, the main advance from Atbara began when six of the Sudanese battalions and the cavalry marched out of camp. The six Egyptian battalions would also advance, boarding the steamers and journeying along the Nile. As the Egyptian Army battalions vacated Atbara, the additional British regiments arrived to take their place before they themselves later followed the line of advance. One of these regiments, the 2nd Rifle Brigade, had left Cairo on the 27th and 28th of July and travelled via rail to Shellal, after which they disembarked the trains and boarded steamers for the move to *Wadi* Halfa. From here, the troops again boarded trains for the journey to Atbara via Abu Hamed. This was the typical experience of many of the British troops as they made their way to join Kitchener's army at the front.

Wauchope and his brigade staff arrived at Atbara on 5 August, with the remainder of the 2nd British Brigade also arriving over the next few days. Gatacre's 1st Brigade, however, by-passed Atbara by advancing direct from their camp at Darmali to Wad Hamid, although they were travelling on steamers and so passed close to Fort Atbara on the 13th. As Gatacre's men sailed by, Kitchener left Fort Atbara and made his way towards Wad Hamid to join his troops now pouring into the area. This, however, was not the end of troop movements at Atbara, since further Egyptian Army troops began to arrive regularly up to the 21st from both Merowi and Suakin, often marching all the way on foot. Once the empty steamers returned from Wad Hamid, these troops were quickly embarked on the vessels for their trip up the river. By the 23rd, virtually all of Kitchener's army was now in Wad Hamid, save for the Camel Corps that journeyed separately across the Bayuda Desert to the concentration point via Metammeh.

While troop numbers were building up at Wad Hamid, a reconnaissance was ordered to scout out the area around the Shabluka Cataract, through which the mounted men had to first ride through a menacing looking gorge guarded by four stoutly built forts. Thankfully, both the gorge and Shabluka turned out to be long deserted by the Mahdists. Pushing on, the men of the reconnaissance reached the island of *Jebel* Royan, a mere thirty-four miles from the city of Omdurman itself. Climbing to the top of some high ground, the tomb of the *Mahdi* could just be made out in the distance, its white walls and dome seemingly looming over the other buildings of the city. Perhaps ironically, the first to cast his eyes over this impressive sight was Major Staveley Gordon of the Royal Engineers, the nephew of General Gordon. The island of *Jebel* Royan proved to be an excellent position at which to establish a forward depot, and large quantities of supplies were brought up by steamers from Nasri Island. A field hospital with 200 beds was also established on the island.

Meanwhile, Kitchener had conducted a review of his troops on the 23rd, after which orders were issued to resume the advance in successive divisions towards Omdurman, and within two days no men were left at Wad Hamid. The order in which the advance was made included the Camel Corps followed by the Egyptian Division then the British Division. This part of the arduous journey, however, proved too much for the newly arrived British troops of Lyttelton's brigade, who began to fall-out in large numbers due to the fact they had not yet properly acclimatised to the oppressive heat of Sudan.

By the 27th, the main body of the Anglo-Egyptian force arrived at *Jebel* Royan and made camp at nearby El Hajir in order to rest for the night. The advance was then again resumed at 5 p.m. the following day, this time marching to a place called *Wadi* Abid, where, due to the close proximity to the Mahdist capital, the troops were instructed to build a *zariba*. While this defensive work was carried out, Kitchener drafted a letter to the *Khalifa*, informing his adversary that he intended to bombard Omdurman, and advised him to remove all women and children from the city for their safety.

The short stay at *Wadi* Abid turned out to be an awful one for the men, since, on the 29th, a heavy rainstorm thoroughly drenched every man, animal and piece of equipment. Nevertheless, it would be at 3 a.m. the following morning that the troops again packed up their kit and resumed their march in wet clothes. They would arrive at Sayal the next day.

On 31st, Kitchener's army yet again marched out, this time heading for Suruab, while Keppel's gunboats sailed for Kerreri and opened a bombardment of a Mahdist position there. Although now dried out, the British and Egyptian troops would experience another soaking during the night. So heavy was this downpour that it washed away sections of the field telegraph system, which would take a number of days to repair and bring back into operation. Finally, on 1 September, the Anglo-Egyptian expedition arrived at the village of Egeiga, located a mere six miles from Omdurman. Again the march was conducted under heavy rainfall, but no resistance to the advance was encountered. It should be noted that Kitchener's cavalry frequently encountered Mahdist horsemen throughout the advance to Omdurman. However, these scouts merely retired when spotted and no skirmishes took place.

As the infantry made their way into Egeiga, Kitchener ordered some of his cavalry to conduct a reconnaissance towards *Jebel* Surgham, which lay to the south-west. Upon reaching the slopes of this mountain, at about midday, a large number of Mahdist warriors could be seen at a distance of about a mile. The *Ansar* numbered, it was believed at the time, at around 40,000 to 50,000, and it soon became clear that the cavalrymen had located the *Khalifa*'s main army. It also soon became obvious that they were spoiling for a fight; their line slowly advancing along a three-mile-wide front. Faced with such overwhelming numbers, the officers ordered the cavalrymen to turnabout and make for Egeiga at best possible speed in order to inform Kitchener of what they had found. Kitchener decided to take a look for himself:

> At noon, from the slopes of *Jebel* Surgham, I saw the entire Dervish army some 3 miles off advancing towards us, the *Khalifa*'s black flag surrounded by his Mulazemin (bodyguard) being plainly discernible. I estimated their numbers at 35,000 men, though, from subsequent investigation, this figure was probably under-estimated, their actual strength being between forty and fifty thousand. From information received I gather that it was the *Khalifa*'s intention to have met us with this force at Kerreri, but our rapid advance surprised him.

Upon learning of the presence of the *Ansar*, the *Sirdar* had immediately issued orders for his men to fall in and form up ready to receive what he believed would be an attack. However, cavalry scouts observing the Mahdists returned with the news that the *Khalifa*'s army had halted at 2 p.m., and appeared to be making camp, where many little fires could be seen dotted across the desert. It now seemed that no attack was to come that day, but, according to Kitchener:

> Information was received that the *Khalifa* contemplated a night attack on our position, and preparations to repel this were made, at the same time the Egeiga villagers were sent out to obtain information in the direction of the enemy's camp with the idea that we intended a night attack, and, this coming to the *Khalifa*'s knowledge, he decided to remain in his position.

A few shots had been traded between Kitchener's scouts and leading elements of the *Ansar*, but it had become obvious that no major battle would be fought just yet; the long-awaited clash of arms would have to wait until the following morning.

Another clash of arms, however, was taking place elsewhere. Keppel and his steamers had advanced up the Nile towing barges carrying the guns of the 37th Field Battery of the Royal Artillery. A party of friendly Jaalin irregulars was following them along the east-bank; they were under the direction of Major Edward James Montagu-Stuart-Wortley, who cleared away a few pockets of Mahdist warriors as they advanced from one minor village to another. As Keppel approached Halfiyeh, three forts could be made out; they suddenly opened fire on the British flotilla. The commander ordered his gunners to return the fire, which quickly had the effect of silencing the enemy guns, after which the irregulars moved in and took each of the forts in turn.

Having taken Halfiyeh, Keppel continued to sail up the Nile to Tuti Island, where the gunboats again came under fire from the forts located at both Omdurman and Khartoum. None of the Mahdist shells, however, found their mark and the gunboats escaped damage. Keppel next ordered the guns of the 37th Field Battery to be landed on the east-bank in order to conduct a bombardment of the forts. Almost immediately after being set up, the howitzers, at a range of 3,000 yards, began shelling Omdurman. During this bombardment, the *Mahdi*'s tomb suffered serious damage, with the dome being mostly destroyed by lyddite shells. The skirmish soon came to an end, and, leaving both the *Tamai* and *Nasr* to watch over the artillery, Keppel ordered the rest of his fleet of gunboats to return to Egeiga.

The men of the Anglo-Egyptian army now settled down to what would be an uneasy night, the two opposing armies being less than five miles apart. The fear of a night attack, of course, was still very much in everyone's mind, and so the *Sirdar* again ordered his troops to sleep in their uniforms with their equipment and rifles next to them. The night would be a dark one, with thick clouds blocking out much of the moonlight, the darkness being punctuated now and again by the electric lamps of the gunboats as they tried to spot any movement on *Jebel* Surgham and the area surrounding the camp. Poor vision and nervousness did, however, result in two false alarms being raised by the sentries, but the night would otherwise prove to be an uneventful one.

The Battle of Omdurman: The First Attack

On the morning of 2 September 1898, Kitchener's Anglo-Egyptian expeditionary force occupied what was a favourable position for defence. Apart from the *zariba* and trenches that had been constructed around Egeiga, the crescent-shaped camp stood on slightly elevated ground with its back to the Nile River, where it was guarded by Keppel's gunboats. In front, facing towards the west, was an open plain of desert that stretched for five miles until it reached the foot of some hills, offering the troops a clear field of fire, save for a few scrub bushes dotted here and there. Two miles to the north were the Kerreri Heights, while to the south lay the slopes of the *Jebel* Surgham at a distance of 1,200 yards. The war correspondent of the *Daily Telegraph*, Bennet Burleigh, further described the Anglo-Egyptian camp:

> From the north to the south end along the river the camp was about one mile in length, and its greatest width about 1200 yards. There were a few mud-huts within the space enclosed by mimosa and the double line of shallow shelter-trenches. The cut bushes were piled in front of the British troops, who were facing Omdurman and the south; the trenches covered the approach from the west and north where the Khedival troops stood on guard. Neither extremity of the lines of defence, zereba or trench, quite extended to the river. Openings of about thirty to fifty yards were left. Besides these there were other small passageways left open during daylight, but closed at night. Near the river facing south the ground was rough, and there were several huts, so that the security of the camp was not imperilled by the failure to carry the hedge of trenches to the Nile's brink.

Burleigh also described, in considerable detail, the dispositions of Kitchener's troops in the *zariba*:

> Lyttelton's brigade were placed upon the left south front. Wauchope's men continued the line to the right. In the south gap were three companies of the 2nd

Battalion Rifle Brigade, their left resting on the river. On their immediate right were three batteries—the 32nd Field Battery of English 15-pounders, under Major Williams; two Maxim-Nordenfelt mountain batteries, 12½-pounders, respectively under Captains Stewart and de Rougemont; and six Maxims under Captain Smeaton. Later on these guns and Maxims during the first stage of the battle—for the action resolved itself into a double event ere the combat ceased—were wheeled out until they were firing almost at right angles to the zereba line. On the right of the guns, in succession, were the remainder of the Rifles, the Lancashire Fusiliers, the Northumberland Fusiliers, and the Grenadier Guards. In the interval between General Lyttelton's brigade and General Wauchope's, which stood next to it, were two Maxims. Then came the Warwicks, Camerons, Seaforths, and Lincolns. To the Lincolns' right, where the trenches began and the line faced nearly west, was Colonel Maxwell's brigade. Between Wauchope's and Maxwell's brigades were two Maxims, and, I think, for a time during the first attack made by the dervishes, the two-gun mule battery of six-centimetre Krupp guns. To complete the tale of the guns placed for defending the camp, there was Major Lawrie's battery of Maxim-Nordenfelts on the right of Maxwell's brigade next Macdonald's, and on the north side, near the right of the position facing west, Major Peake's battery of Maxim-Nordenfelts. These guns had done so well at the Atbara, that the *Sirdar* promptly increased his artillery by adding three batteries of that class. Maxwell's brigade was composed of three Soudanese and one Egyptian battalion, viz, 8th Egyptian, and 12th, 13th, and 14th Soudanese. Farther north, to the right of Colonel Maxwell's men, was Lewis *Bey*'s brigade of Egyptian troops—the 3rd, 4th, 7th, and 15th Battalions. The 15th Battalion was a fine lot, mostly reservists. Upon the farthest west and northern face of the protected camp was Colonel Macdonald's oft-tried and famous fighting brigade, made up of the 9th, 10th, and 11th Soudanese, with the true-as-steel 2nd Egyptians. Within the wall of hedge, trenches, and armed infantry, in reserve, was another brigade, the 4th Khedival, commanded by Major Collinson. It was made up of the 1st, 4th, 17th, and 18th Egyptian battalions.

On the morning of the battle, the 21st Lancers were initially deployed inside the *zariba* near Egeiga itself and the bank of the river, while the horse artillery battery, the Camel Corps and four Maxims were positioned on the ridge of the Kerreri Hills. They would later be joined by Broadwood's Egyptian cavalry.

In total, Kitchener's expeditionary force consisted of 8,200 British and 17,600 Egyptian and Sudanese troops, supported by forty-four guns and twenty Maxims. In addition to these land forces, Keppel's flotilla amounted to ten gunboats, including: three 1898-class armoured screw gunboats, three 1896-class armoured stern-wheel gunboats and four old-class armoured stern-wheel gunboats. Collectively, these vessels were armed with thirty-six guns and twenty-four Maxims. As well as the fighting men, there were also 2,469 horses, 3,524 camels, 896 mules and 229 donkeys, not to mention a large number of followers and a few civilians, the latter of which included the war correspondents attached to the force.

Abdullahi al-Taishi had divided his army into the following sections: 5,400 Degheim and Kehena tribesmen (of which about 800 were horsemen) under the Green Flag of *Khalifa* Ali wad Ullu; 28,400 warriors of the *muluazimayya* (of which 12,900 were riflemen and 2,900 horsemen) under the Dark Green Flag of Osman al-Din; 14,100 warriors (of which 1,050 were riflemen and 1,600 horsemen) under the *Khalifa*'s personal Black Flag and commanded by Ya'qub; 3,400 warriors (of which 360 were riflemen and 190 horsemen) under Osman Digna; eighty men under the Red Flag of *Khalifa* al-Sharif; and seventy men under Osman Azrak. These figures were determined by the Egyptian Army Intelligence Department at the time or shortly after the Battle of Omdurman, thus should be treated as estimates only. However, the *Khalifa* is said to have lost around 6,000 men through desertions the night before the battle. Whatever the true figures, it is reasonable to assume that Abdullahi al-Taishi had roughly double that of Kitchener on the day of the battle.

Thirteen years earlier, the Mahdists had conducted a successful night attack on Khartoum, a feat that Osman Digna, Ibrahim al-Khalil and Osman Azrak wished to repeat by assaulting Kitchener's force at Egeiga on the night of the 1st/2nd. However, Osman al-Din openly opposed the move, arguing—with some validity—that the warriors would be hard to control in the darkness and that his riflemen would be ineffective if they could not see their targets, while others would take the opportunity to use the cover of darkness to desert. This was the view that the *Khalifa* himself took, and so no night attack would be authorised, much to the dismay of the other senior Mahdist commanders.

In the intervening years since the Battle of Omdurman, Abdullahi al-Taishi has been criticised by some historians for his lack of willingness to conduct such a night attack, but there is little evidence to suggest that the *Ansar* could have inflicted defeat on Kitchener's force by attacking in the dark. It is, however, quite likely that Osman al-Din was correct in his fears about losing control over his warriors while others simply disappeared. Additionally, the misinformation Wingate and Slatin had sent out during the night—using a number of local villagers as messengers—which hinted at a British night attack on the Mahdist force, merely reinforced the *Khalifa*'s belief that it was best to stay where he was.

Naturally, Kitchener hoped that the *Khalifa* would attack him while still in his *zariba* during daylight. This would give him the chance to engage his enemy from a distance with artillery, Maxim machine guns and long-range rifle fire. However, he knew—as at the Battle of Atbara—he might in fact have to advance on his adversary and attack, should the *Khalifa* prove unwilling to make the first move. The latter prospect was again an unfavourable one, because it would likely result in higher casualties for the British and Egyptian troops, especially since the size of the *Ansar* now facing him was considerably bigger than that encountered at Atbara, although Kitchener did now have a bigger army himself. In the early hours of the 2nd, Kitchener sat pondering as to what his opponent might do next.

It would be at 4.30 a.m. that the order to 'stand-to-arms' was given; within thirty minutes, the men of Kitchener's entire force were ready and had taken up their allocated positions along the perimeter of the *zariba*. The soldiers now quietly peered into the darkness waiting for their enemy, but the *Khalifa* did not appear to be coming. An hour passed and the time that Kitchener had expected to be attacked (i.e. around 5.30 a.m.) drifted by without any sign of the Mahdists. The men of the 21st Lancers had earlier been given orders to be prepared to make ready, in the event of the enemy failing to show by dawn, to conduct reconnaissance patrols along the Kerreri plains. Thus, the troopers now readied their horses and got their kit together.

What the British and Egyptian troops did not know at this point was the fact that the *Khalifa* had already mounted his personal white Nubian donkey and began to lead his army forward towards where he thought the Anglo-Egyptian expeditionary force was now positioned. Abdullahi al-Taishi could no longer just sit and wait at his camp in the desert, since the morale of his own army was beginning to run dangerously low and there had already been thousands of desertions during the night. If he failed to act now, he would end up watching his army disintegrate before his own eyes, thus losing the war before he had even fought a major battle. Besides, there was still some hope that he would be able to defeat Kitchener's force, which was thought to be highly concerned and nervous about the number of Mahdist warriors it was about to face. This assessment, of course, was based on misinformation spread by Wingate and Slatin in the hope of encouraging the *Khalifa* to attack Kitchener in his *zariba*.

The *Ansar*, at about 5.20 a.m., was advancing behind *Jebel* Surgham out of view of Kitchener's men. The huge Mahdist army was spread across a front some four to five miles wide, with the Green Flag of *Khalifa* Ali wad Ullu on the left, to the right of which was the Dark Green Flag of Osman al-Din, then the warriors under Osman Azrak. Next came the Black Flag under the *Khalifa* himself and Ya'qub, while Osman Digna's tribesmen split off towards the eastern part of *Khor* Abu Sunt; those under Ibrahim al-Khalil headed for the eastern side of *Jebel* Surgham. The latter force is sometimes referred to as the White Flag in other histories, but it should be noted that no such flag officially existed at the time of the battle.

As the warriors of the *Ansar* marched forward to battle in their densely packed ranks, they are said to have chanted 'La Ilah illa' llah wa Muhammad rasool Allah', which roughly translates into English as 'There is but one God, and Muhammad is his prophet'. Leading from the front were the *amirs* and *sheikhs*, while the Baggara horsemen rode in line with the warriors on foot, the whole undoubtedly presenting both an impressive and fearsome sight to anyone who might be watching. It has been the subject of debate as to how confident the *Khalifa* was about securing victory over the *Sirdar* and his army. One story has it that Abdullahi al-Taishi claimed to have seen the *Mahdi* and the Prophet Muhammad in a vision, both informing him that he would indeed be victorious in the coming clash of arms. The story then adds that the *Khalifa* had promised all his warriors that any of them who died in action would ascend to paradise in return for sacrificing their lives while fighting the infidel. However, this, of course, was merely a front, since he knew the power of the Anglo-Egyptian force—which was a modern well-armed and well-trained army—from the defeat of Mahmud Ahmed at Atbara. He had also witnessed the near-destruction of the *Mahdi*'s tomb the day before, thus he could be forgiven for questioning whether God was really on his side.

Meanwhile, Lieutenant Winston Spencer Churchill, who was in command of several *vedettes* of the 21st Lancers, was sitting on the ridge of *Jebel* Surgham watching the advancing *Ansar* through the dim light of the early morning hours:

> There in the plain lay the enemy, their numbers unaltered, their confidence and intentions apparently unshaken. Their front was now nearly five miles long, and composed of great masses of men Joined together by thinner lines. Behind and near to the flanks were large reserves. From the ridge they looked dark blurs and streaks, relieved and diversified with an odd-looking shimmer of light from the spear-points. At about ten minutes to six it was evident that the masses were in motion and advancing swiftly. Their Emirs galloped about and before their ranks. Scouts and patrols scattered themselves all over the front. Then they began to cheer. They were still a mile away from the hill, and were concealed from the *Sirdar*'s army by the folds of the ground. The noise of the shouting was heard, albeit faintly, by the troops down by the river. But to those watching on the hill a tremendous roar came up in waves of intense sound, like the tumult of the rising wind and sea before a storm.

An awestruck Churchill knew he had to quickly inform Kitchener of what he had seen:

> It is now daylight. I slip off my horse, I write in my field service notebook 'The Dervish army is still in position a mile and a half south-west of *Jebel* Surgham.' I send this message by the corporal direct as ordered to the Commander-in-Chief. I mark it XXX. In the words of the drill book 'with all despatch' or as one would say 'Hell for leather.'

At 5.50 a.m., the men of the 21st Lancers on *Jebel* Surgham could clearly see the *Ansar* advancing at considerable speed. What was more, a number of Baggara horsemen were also seen peeling off from the main force towards the heights where the British cavalry *vedettes* were positioned, and it would not be long before one of the mounted Mahdists fired a shot at the ridge. At the time, it was thought that this shot was aimed at Hubert Howard, a war correspondent with *The Times*, rather than at any of the troopers, since the latter had concealed themselves among the rocks and other available cover along the ridge. After this initial round came many more bullets as the Baggara drew increasingly closer. This shooting alarmed Lieutenant-Colonel Martin, who, according to Lieutenant Robert Smythe—who was also on the ridge at that moment—was 'much excited and annoyed and very fussy, saying I was unnecessarily exposing myself'. The lieutenant, perhaps irritated for being told off as being responsible for drawing the enemy fire, later wrote 'It was the Correspondent's fault and after all it was only one private [who was holding Smyth's horse] and myself, no great loss if we had been hit …'

While the Baggara were taking pot-shots at a journalist, Osman Azrak and his warriors altered course and began to surge past *Jebel* Surgham towards Kitchener's *zariba*. At about the same time, those under Ibrahim al-Khalil manoeuvred around the south of the mountain and began to advance on the left-flank of the Anglo-Egyptian line. Curiously, however, the Dark Green Flag under Osman al-Din carried on towards the Kerreri Hills, where both the Egyptian cavalry and the Camel Corps had taken up positions. Thus, the bulk of the *Ansar* was not in fact heading for the position occupied by Kitchener's force, but rather it was advancing north and risked missing the main body of the Anglo-Egyptian army altogether. It still remains unclear exactly why the Mahdist army did not initially advance directly on the *zariba*, but it is highly likely that the *Khalifa* simply failed to understand exactly where his enemy was. It is also very likely that Abdullahi al-Taishi was under the wrong impression that Kitchener had abandoned his camp at Egeiga, and had moved off towards the Kerreri Hills.

Broadwood's cavalry was now about to face the full-force of the *Ansar*. Churchill ordered his four troopers to remount their horses and make their way down to a sand-ridge located below, where the men again dismounted, and, on the orders of the lieutenant, opened fire at the approaching mass of warriors with their carbines. Just exactly what Churchill was trying to achieve is not known for sure, but he probably wanted to be the first to have a shot at the enemy; if so, he certainly achieved this, since he and his men were indeed the first of the *Sirdar*'s army to open fire during the battle. Within moments, the riflemen of the *Ansar* returned fire, and so Churchill again ordered his men to mount and rode off up the slopes of *Jebel* Surgham, where he and his troopers took up a new position, despite the enemy now being only about 300 yards away. He had orders from Kitchener to remain as long as possible to keep the enemy under observation.

Although both the warriors of the *Ansar* and the British *vedettes* had traded a few distant shots, perhaps the first true shot to open the Battle of Omdurman came when the Mahdists opened fire at Kitchener's *zariba* using several old artillery pieces they were hauling along in their centre. Both shots, however, fell short and crashed into the ground some distance in front of Kitchener's infantry. Before the dust and sand thrown up by these shells could begin to settle, the British and Egyptian artillery responded by commencing their own bombardment of the Mahdists, who were now crowning the crest in front of them. Kitchener, in his official despatch of 5 September, recorded:

> At 6.40 a.m. the shouts of the advancing Dervish army became audible, and a few minutes later their flags appeared over the rising ground, forming a semicircle round our left and front faces. The guns of the 32nd Field Battery opened fire at 6.45 a.m. at a range of 2,800 yards, and the Dervishes, continuing to advance rapidly, delivered their attack with all their accustomed dash and intrepidity.

The Battle of Omdurman had finally begun.

Although the main body of the *Ansar* had been advancing north, sections of it now suddenly swerved to the right and came rushing down towards the southern face of the *zariba* where the British troops were positioned. The shells of Kitchener's artillery burst above and in the midst of the ranks of the Mahdists, causing numerous casualties, but the warriors rushed on regardless. More shots were fired by the *Khalifa*'s guns, but again the shells fell short of the *zariba* and caused no damage to the Anglo-Egyptian line. More *Ansar* warriors then came charging up from behind *Jebel* Surgham, heading for the left-flank, while the Mahdist riflemen appeared to be taking up positions on the heights, from where they fired down into the *zariba* below. The guns of Keppel's gunboats also now began to roar into action, shelling the *Khalifa*'s riflemen on the slopes. Churchill was watching this chaotic scene and was probably closer to the *Ansar* than anyone else in the Anglo-Egyptian army at that moment; he could plainly make out the grizzled faces of his enemy as they came under fire from the British and Egyptian artillery:

> About twenty shells struck them in the first minute. Some burst high in the air, others exactly in their faces. Others, again, plunged into the sand and, exploding, dashed clouds of red dust, splinters, and bullets amid their ranks. The white banners [carried by the Mahdists] toppled over in all directions.

The lieutenant had been ordered by Martin to retire, but he had chosen to ignore the instruction. However, Churchill was now in danger of being cut off, and, following a second order to retire, he at last told his men to mount their horses and make for the *zariba*, the British and Egyptian shells screaming over their heads as they did so.

For the men in the *zariba*, a two-mile-wide mass of warriors could be seen surging towards them, their battle cries now clearly audible. Another mass then appeared on the ridge of *Jebel* Surgham, although this second body seemed to be holding its position and advanced no further. In the words of Captain Alfred Edward Hubbard of the Lincolns, it looked as if 'the entire world was coming against us' and that the 'spectacle was the most magnificent & imposing I have ever seen'.

The men of Gatacre's division—on the left-flank—had taken up positions behind a rough fence made of thorn bush. Before the battle had begun, these men were ordered to fix bayonets and line the fence in two ranks, the front of which was kneeling while the rear rank remained standing. Captain F. A. Earle, the adjutant of the Warwicks, galloped up to the officers of his regiment and shouted to them: 'Get into your places please, Gentlemen, the show is starting!' As the *Ansar* advanced on this section of the *zariba*, Kitchener rode over and positioned himself behind Lyttleton's 2nd Brigade. From here, he watched the warriors under Ibrahim al-Khalil—who rode into battle on a horse called Aim, behind which was his second horse called End, the latter being led by a servant—advance to within 2,000 yards of the British line, at which point a single shot rang out from the ranks of the Grenadier Guards. This ranging-shot, believed to have been fired by Private G. E. Paragreen, was then followed by an eruption of rifle fire from the Lee Metfords of the battalion. The rest of 2nd Brigade then opened up, quickly followed by Wauchope's 1st Brigade.

Lieutenant Meiklejohn of the Warwicks recalled this part of the action:

Then the order came to open 'Company volleys' and I think the opening range was 1,500 yards. A volume of fire burst out from the whole length of the *zariba*. Continual repetition on my part of the words of command 'Ready'—'Present'—'Fire'—'Ready' in this rhythm, only varied by a shortening range.

Thousands of lethal .303 bullets were now hurtling towards the packed, massed ranks of the *Ansar*. Soon, the entire *zariba*, including the Egyptian and Sudanese troops, were pouring rifle and Maxim fire into their oncoming attackers.

Ibrahim al-Khalil's force was spread across a front of 800 to 1,000 yards, and had advanced on the *zariba* south of *Jebel* Surgham towards the eastern ridge, which acted to conceal their initial movements from the British. No fewer than 500 banners could be seen marking the positions of the *rub* commanders and other officers. The majority of these banners were concentrated in the centre-front of the surging mass of warriors, and, therefore, around Ibrahim al-Khalil himself, who was leading from the front. The leading *rub*, which was the largest, was commanded by Muhammad Ishaq al-Taishi, behind which were the *rubs* of Hamid Sabun, Hasab al-Daim, Khalil Hasan, Ismail al-Sahib, and Abd al-Latif.

Osman Azrak's force stretched over a front of two miles, and advanced on the *zariba* along the northern side of *Jebel* Surgham, forming a crescent shape parallel to Kitchener's position around Egeiga. This wide front consisted of a line of six *rubs* under the command of Masud, Abd Allah Adam, Abd al-Baqi, Ibrahim Jabir, Abd al-Majid Abu Saq and Muhammad Abu Sad (running south to north), while the mounted warriors were spread along the whole line. The right—or southern—

wing of Osman Azrak's line was the thickest, being eleven ranks deep, while the left—or northern—wing was the thinnest, at three or four ranks deep. Unlike the well-ordered advance of Ibrahim al-Khalil, Osman Azrak's line was less well organised, with gaps forming between his warriors.

As impressive as the British fire was, there was a distinct feeling of disappointment among the artillery officers regarding the effects their guns were having on the enemy. The shells were finding their mark on the *Ansar*, but the damage done was simply not stemming the onrush towards the *zariba*. However, it was the fire of the artillery that probably forced large sections of the *Ansar* to swerve from their northerly advance to the Kerreri Hills and swing towards Egeiga. Nevertheless, the guns continued to spew forth relentless shrapnel shells onto and into their adversaries.

Despite the disappointment of the artillerymen, the infantry—prior to opening fire themselves—had been watching the bombardment with a mixture of awe and concern. Awe because of the perceived death and destruction being rained down on the Mahdists and concern because many of the men, who were desperate to play their part in the action, feared the battle might end before they were given the opportunity to fire a shot. However, they need not have worried as there was plenty of hot work for them that day.

During the assault on the *zariba*, Ibrahim al-Khalil's horse, Aim, suddenly collapsed after being hit by a large splinter from a shell. Unhurt himself, the Mahdist commander got up on his feet and immediately mounted his other horse, End. Once remounted, the advance continued, but his force was greatly dwindling in number as a result of the murderous fire of Kitchener's army. The Mahdist riflemen did their best to return the fire, killing and wounding a handful of their targets, but there was little hope of inflicting the level of damage the Anglo-Egyptian troops were able to inflict upon them.

The second mass of *Ansar* warriors that had been seen on the ridge of *Jebel* Surgham were a section of the Black Flag under the command of Ya'qub and Abdullahi al-Taishi. Most of the Black Flag warriors, however, were in fact out of view of Kitchener's men down in the *zariba*, having taken to sheltering from the artillery fire on the reserve slopes. Not committing these warriors to an all-out assault of the main Anglo-Egyptian force was, perhaps, a mistake, since the *Khalifa* was now only engaging Kitchener with a portion of his available army. Holding these men back was probably born out of the mistaken belief that the *zariba* was not the main position of the *Sirdar*'s army; the *Khalifa* believed that the latter had marched out earlier, leaving only a strong garrison behind to guard the camp. It is not possible to know if committing these extra men would have turned the battle in Abdullahi al-Taishi's favour—although it is highly unlikely—but by assaulting the *zariba* with only the 10,000 warriors now engaged the *Khalifa* was merely helping to ensure his own defeat.

Perhaps the last of the 2nd Egyptian Brigade to open fire was the 12th Egyptians, under the command of Lieutenant-Colonel Charles Vere Ferrers Townshend of siege of Chitral fame. Being armed with the older Martini-Henry rifle, the Egyptian and Sudanese troops were unable to fire accurately at the long distances that were achieved by the British soldiers with their more modern Lee Metfords. The Egyptian Division, therefore, opened fire slightly later, but Townshend was determined not to order his men to commence firing until the Mahdists were within 400 yards, thus ensuring his men were able to bring down their attackers *en masse*. Despite this, he eventually gave the order to fire at 600 yards, possibly due to the look of disbelief on the faces of many of his men who were eager to pull their triggers.

Not all regiments, however, were engaged with the Mahdists; both the Lancashire Fusiliers and the Rifle Brigade, being on the extreme-left of the line, did not have any targets immediately to their front within a 3,000 yards range. Kitchener, therefore, ordered both to reposition behind the Camerons and Seaforths respectively. During this manoeuvre, however, several men of the Rifle Brigade were hit by Mahdist rifle fire. Once finally in position behind the Seaforths, at about 7 a.m., the men of the Rifle Brigade found they were now in an elevated and somewhat exposed position, and an almost constant stream of Mahdist bullets would come crashing in and around their ranks, causing a number of further casualties.

One of the first British casualties was Private P. Dillion of 'B' Company of the Northumberland Fusiliers, who was hit by a Mahdist bullet in the right-forearm; his wound was later described as 'slight'. Another was Lance-Corporal T. McKenzie of 'C' Company of the Seaforth Highlanders, who had been similarly hit in the right-leg by a ricochet; his wound was again recorded as 'slight'. Tending the wounded were, among others, Lance-Corporal H. H. E. Taylor and Private A. Davidson of the Royal Army Medical Corps. While both men were carrying a wounded man on a stretcher, the former was shot in the left-arm and the latter hit by a spent bullet in the head; both wounds were described as 'severe'.

Captain Guy Coldecott of the Warwicks, who was noted as being one of the strongest men in the army, was shot in the head; the bullet, however, must have also been spent because he was not killed outright. He was taken to the rear and lay unconscious for an hour, after which, it is said, he came to and shouted 'For God's sake, give me water!', but as he drank, he died. As the first attack (sometimes referred to as the first phase or phase one) of the battle progressed, a number of other British officers were also hit, as were several war correspondents. Captain Sir Henry Rawlinson of the Coldstream Guards, who was acting as a galloper for Kitchener, had his horse shot from under him and came crashing to the ground behind the Warwicks. A private in the Lincolns had a lucky escape when a bullet smacked into his haversack and became lodged in his prayer book; it was later extracted by his company commander, Captain Hubbard, and it was said to be still warm. Hubbard himself also had a narrow escape moments later, when another bullet passed under his foot and grazed the sole of his boot before burying itself in the sand; the officer then picked it up and placed it in his pocket as a souvenir of the battle.

Most of these casualties had been inflicted by a group of 200 Mahdist riflemen, who had managed to take up positions behind a bank about 300 yards to the front of the British section of the line. In an attempt to dislodge them, Major W. H. Williams, who was in command of the Royal Artillery, ordered a battery to fire a shell in among them, causing those not initially killed by the shrapnel to spring up out of cover and flee. These riflemen were then quickly gunned down by the Warwicks, Camerons, and Lincolns, until not a single one was left alive.

Kitchener had also proved to be a tempting target for the Mahdist marksmen, as Lieutenant Pritchard of the Royal Engineers remembered:

> The *Sirdar* had some close shaves. He and his Staff, being mounted, were rather prominent marks. One staff officer got a bullet through his shoulder-strap, General Rundle's horse was wounded, two gallopers [including Rawlinson] had their horses shot, so it was evident the enemy were firing at the Staff.

British casualties were, of course, minor when compared to those being inflicted upon the Mahdists. *Ansar* warriors fell in their droves, their bodies piling up in heaps with the ground in front of the British section of the *zariba* being painted almost completely white by the clothing of the dead and wounded. Yet despite this butchery, the warriors continued to make attempts to reach the *zariba*, and small groups here and there would seize whatever opportunities they could to get to the British lines, only to be shot down as they did so. Nevertheless, as one group perished another replaced it from behind. One old *sheikh* was seen waving a banner and leading a group of warriors in a rush to the *zariba*, within just a few seconds most of his followers were dead or wounded, and those who remained were likewise quickly brought down by .303 rounds. Now on his own, the *sheikh* charged on nevertheless, and when within 200 yards he suddenly dropped to the ground dead with his arms folded. Such was the bravery of the Mahdists.

The most notable Mahdist casualty during the first phase of the battle was Ibrahim al-Khalil, who, at 7.05 a.m., was hit in the head and chest by fire from a Maxim gun. His warriors watched in horror as their commander fell from his horse, itself now also wounded. He had managed to escape the artillery and rifle fire for some time, but it was perhaps only a matter of time before the inevitable happened. As Ibrahim al-Khalil hit the ground, four of his men rushed forward to pick up his body and attempt to carry him away from the fighting; it was, however, too late. Command of Ibrahim al-Khalil's *rubs* then passed to Muhammad Ishaq al-Taishi, but he, too, was fatally wounded by rifle fire moments later.

By 7.30 a.m., after almost fifty minutes of battle, the first attack of the *Ansar* finally began to falter. The warriors had been under a continuous bombardment of artillery—both from the British and Egyptian field batteries and the guns of Keppel's gunboats—and intense fire from the Maxim guns and thousands of rifles. It is, therefore, unsurprising that they should now begin to buckle in the face of such firepower. Kitchener's men were also feeling fatigued from keeping up their rate of fire, with their rifles becoming so hot that they had to exchange them for those of the men in the rear in support.

Before the Mahdist attack ceased altogether, however, about 150 to 200 horsemen and spearmen, led by Osman Azrak, made one last desperate attempt to charge the Anglo-Egyptian line in front of Maxwell's 2nd Egyptian Brigade. Forming up at a distance of about 1,200 yards, the mounted warriors charged headlong at the *zariba*. The whole attempt was, of course, a deadly and futile act, since the rifles of Maxwell's brigade ripped through the attackers while the Maxims swept along their line of advance. By the time the last of the horseman came within 200 yards, all lay dead or dying, men and horses alike. Osman Azrak was hit in the thigh during the attack, while his horse, also wounded, managed to carry on charging towards the *zariba*. However, at a distance of about 400 yards, the horse finally gave way and its rider hit the ground under a hail of rifle and Maxim fire, he would not survive. Soon, only Osman Azrak's standard bearer and five dismounted horsemen were left, but, as they continued their charge forward, they were also finally gunned down. The fire of the British and Egyptian troops now began to slacken as the Mahdist attack finally melted away. Kitchener, again never one to waste ammunition, then, at about 8 a.m., gave the order to 'cease fire!' and the roar of the guns quickly died down.

Interestingly, the Mahdists seldom managed to get within 800 yards of the British regiments (in any great number at least), while they managed to get within 500 of the Egyptian and Sudanese. The reason for this was predominately due to the smoke caused by the Martini-Henry rifles, which obscured the view of the infantrymen, allowing the warriors of the *Ansar* to get closer before being seen and shot. The Lee Metfords, however, used a smokeless cartridge, which resulted in a less obscured view for the British soldiers.

Babikr Bedri, a Mahdist warrior present at the battle, but yet to be engaged in the fighting, remembered feeling disillusioned as he watched fellow wounded *Ansar* warriors returning from this early morning part of the action:

> At about seven in the morning we heard the noise of fire-arms, both the enemy's and our own; and about eight the wounded from 'Uthmān Diqna's regiment began to pass by us to the rear. We noticed that for every one wounded man there were four others carrying or supporting him; so I said to our little group, 'Look here, if one of us gets wounded I shall get wounded too–with his blood; and the rest of you can carry us away, since that seems to be allowed.

It appears that not all of the *Khalifa's* warriors were so eager to give up their lives to earn their place in paradise. Indeed, the tradition of those to the left and right of a wounded man in carrying him off the battlefield was now acting to greatly reduce the number of fighting men available to continue the assaults.

The fighting during the first Mahdist attack of the battle was, however, not quite over yet. A party of thirty to forty *Ansar* riflemen under Ibrahim Jabir had managed to position themselves behind a small ridge several hundred yards from the *zariba* where the Camerons were standing. With a lull in the fighting seemingly underway, the Mahdists suddenly and unexpectedly opened fire at the British soldiers, whose only protection was the flimsy thorn bushes used in the construction of the *zariba*. Quite a number of British soldiers were hit, including twenty-five men of the Camerons and twelve of the Seaforths, all of who had to be carried to the rear under fire. The shooting lasted for around fifteen minutes, during which Kitchener suffered his greatest number of casualties for the first phase of the battle. To deal with the *Ansar* riflemen, an Egyptian field battery was rushed over, which commenced firing at the ridge. The men of the Camerons and the Seaforths also delivered volley after volley at the ridge at the same time. Eventually, the Mahdists had little choice but to attempt to flee their position in order to escape the shrapnel shells; when they did so, they were brought down by the British infantrymen. Ibrahim Jabir, wounded in the stomach, was somehow carried away to safety by two of his men.

With the action seemingly over, or at least experiencing a lull, a number of camp followers and others moved forward out of the *zariba* in order to pick up trophies from the dead Mahdists. Bennet Burleigh witnessed a group of four such trophy hunters picking up swords and other weapons laying on the ground. He then noticed Mr Bennett Stanford, an early filmmaker who was attached to Kitchener's army in the hope of capturing moving footage of the campaign, rode out to join this little group. Burleigh then decided, along with a colleague, to ride out and also join Stanford, since he was curious to see what effects the British fire had had on the dead Mahdists. As he grew nearer, he suddenly saw a warrior, who had apparently been pretending to be dead, suddenly rise up with spear in hand and charge at the trophy hunters. Unsurprisingly, the camp followers bolted back for the safety of the *zariba*, as did Burleigh's frightened colleague.

The war correspondent, however, did not turn back, since he was over 200 yards away from the incident and not immediately threatened. Burleigh next saw an Egyptian NCO—who had followed the camp followers from behind—drop down on his knee and level his Martini-Henry rifle at the warrior in an attempt to shoot him. Unfortunately for the NCO, the rifle misfired, but he was able to quickly load another cartridge and get off a shot, only to miss his target. The warrior next ran for the *zariba* coming close to Stanford, who, armed with a four-barrelled Lancaster pistol, took aim at the Mahdist and pulled the trigger, again only to miss his target. The warrior now charged at the filmmaker, but, quickly pulling on the reigns of his horse, he was able to avoid his enemy and gallop off.

Having failed to kill anyone, the unsuccessful warrior turned back to the NCO and made a rush towards him. At this moment—if Burleigh's account is to be believed—the war correspondent intervened by galloping in between the two men, pulling up his horse and taking aim at the Mahdist with his own pistol. The warrior immediately turned his attention to Burleigh, the latter firing his weapon at close range; this time, he hit his enemy, although the man somehow remained standing while a second shot missed him. Burleigh then decided it prudent to ride off and get away from the dangerous Mahdist as fast as he could.

Almost immediately as the correspondent made a run for it, Lieutenant Smyth of the 21st Lancers suddenly appeared galloping towards the warrior, who he then collided with. The officer, with revolver in hand, fired at the Mahdist, but yet again the bullet missed its target. The warrior then grabbed at Smyth and attempted to stab him with his spear, but the lieutenant managed to shoot the man at point-blank range directly in the face, finally killing him outright. Leaving his dead adversary, a calm Smyth trotted back towards the *zariba* where Burleigh asked him if he was alright, to which the lieutenant replied that he was 'untouched'. However, unbeknown to the officer, he had in fact been slightly wounded in the arm by the warrior's broad-bladed spear. For his actions in stopping the Mahdist warrior, Lieutenant Smyth would be awarded the Victoria Cross, the first of four for the battle. When the Mahdist's body was later examined, it was found that he had in fact been hit four times by bullets. It was not the first time that an *Ansar* warrior would act as if dead in order to ambush an unsuspecting enemy as he passed by, nor would it be the last.

The first attack of the action was now at an end; however, the Battle of Omdurman was far from over yet.

11

The Battle of Omdurman: Charge of the 21st Lancers

While the previously described events were taking place at the *zariba*, a Mahdist force—which has been stated variously at 10,000 to 25,000 in number, but in reality most likely at the lower end of the estimate—under Osman al-Din was advancing up the Kerreri Hills at considerable speed. Facing this juggernaut was the battery of horse artillery (armed with six out-dated 9-pounder Krupp guns), four 'galloping-Maxims', Major Robert John Tudway's Camel Corps, and Colonel Broadwood's Egyptian cavalry, the latter having formed up behind the former. It was at 7 a.m. that the horse artillery commenced firing at a range of about 1,500 yards, while the mounted men dismounted and began pouring volleys into the oncoming *Ansar* with their Martini-Henry carbines. However, it was an almost hopeless attempt to try and stop the mass of warriors, who, characteristically, simply continued with their advance despite the losses they were taking. It soon became apparent to Broadwood that his enemy was trying to encircle him, thus cutting him off from Egeiga.

Osman al-Din's force included the warriors of the *muluazimayya*, and was divided into six *rubs*. Leading was the *rub* commanded by Arifi al-Rabi, who was followed in turn—at 1,000 yard intervals—by the *rubs* of Jabir Abu Shilaykhat (who was a little to the right of the leading *rub*), Adam Ismail, Fadl Bishhara, Ibrahim Malik and Tahir Ali. As Osman al-Din's force advanced, instructions were given to the leading *rub* to slow a little in order for the one under command of Adam Ismail to overtake on the left, in hope of taking up position to prevent the Egyptian cavalry from withdrawing to the north.

The Kerreri Hills are actually made up of two natural knolls, known as *Jebel* Abu *Zariba* and *Jebel* Daham, which in certain places reach a height of about 300 feet. Between the two runs a 1,000-yard-long ridge, while *Jebel* Kerreri itself, from which the area derives its name, is nothing more than a small hillock not far from the Nile. The largest of the two knolls is *Jebel* Abu *Zariba*, a feature made up of three peaks, and the entire area of the Kerreri Hills is strewn with sharp, jagged rocks that are difficult for both horses and camels to traverse.

The Battle of Omdurman: Charge of the 21st Lancers

Colonel Broadwood had previously sent a messenger to Kitchener to inform him of the developing situation on the hills, to which the *Sirdar* replied by telling his cavalry commander to retire back to the *zariba* if he felt overly threatened. Despite this, Broadwood had no intention of doing so; if he did, he believed he would only bring with him the mass of warriors now coming up to his front, who, no doubt, would then launch a heavy assault on the *zariba*'s northern or right-flank, where it was held by the Egyptian infantry. This was the weakest section of Kitchener's position—a fact the cavalry commander was acutely aware of. Broadwood, therefore, decided to withdraw his cavalry towards the north in the hope the Mahdists in front of him would follow, and thus be led away from Kitchener. However, he instructed the slower moving Camel Corps to make towards the east before turning south for the *zariba* along with the horse artillery.

It should be noted that even if Broadwood had decided to comply with Kitchener's instructions to withdraw back to the *zariba*, such a movement would have proved extremely difficult. The reason for this was the fact that the *rub* under Arifi al-Rabi had already reached the southern peak of *Jebel* Abu *Zariba*, virtually blocking the route. The colonel, therefore, was forced to withdraw towards *Jebel* Daham instead, although Adam Ismail's *rub* was by then scaling the northern peak. It should also be noted, as will be seen later, that Broadwood's decision to defy his *Sirdar*'s orders would greatly assist the latter.

For the cavalry, the task of retiring would be a relatively easy one, since they were highly mobile and could out-run their pursuers. However, for the men of the Camel Corps the manoeuvre was much more difficult, the camels finding the rocky and bushy terrain harder to traverse than the horses. The horse artillery, hauling their heavy guns behind them, would similarly find the going both tough and slow. As such, the danger was that the *Ansar* would be able to over-run these units, slaughtering every soldier to a man.

Lieutenant Henry Hopkinson of the Camel Corps commanded the rear-guard that was to cover the retirement; unfortunately, as he formed up his men, the lieutenant suddenly heard and felt:

> ... a thud, like a fist sinking into flesh, and I felt my beast lurch under me. It sank down to its knees and twisted round its neck, so that its huge brown eyes flecked with a septic yellow seemed to be staring reproachfully at me. Its mouth was open in a grimace of pain and a thick trickle of black blood oozed from the corner and smeared the brown of its hide.

The dying camel then keeled over on to its side, giving out a 'half wail' and began 'twitching feebly' on the ground.

Supporting the retirement of the Camel Corps were the gunners of the horse artillery, who did their utmost to keep the *Ansar* at bay while the mounted men fell back, the latter pausing at intervals to fire volleys at their pursuers, the warriors being of Arifi al-Rabi's *rub*. The battery stayed in position firing shrapnel shells until the Mahdists were almost upon them, at which point they then scrambled to limber-up their guns and escape their attackers through the skin of their teeth. However, some of the artillerymen had left it too late, and one of their horses was brought down by a Mahdist bullet. Now unable to move one of the guns, the gunners desperately attempted to remove the dead animal; but a further disaster struck when a second gun, being closely pursued by the enemy, collided with and got stuck on the stricken 9-pounder. There was nothing for it—the two guns had to be abandoned, their crews jumping on the backs of other horses pulling the remaining four guns. Two to a horse, or desperately clinging to the stirrups of a mounted comrade, the gunners hurried to make good their escape.

The fighting withdrawal painfully continued, and the men of the Camel Corps would at times find themselves in hand-to-hand combat with their enemy. Eventually, however, they found themselves at a point not too far from the Nile, when almost out of the blue one of Keppel's gunboats—the *Melik*, under command of General Gordon's nephew—came steaming down the river in an attempt to help their comrades on land. Moments later, the gunboat began furiously shelling the *muluazimayya* who were pursuing the mounted Egyptians. *Ansar* warriors again fell in their droves, with some 450 later being counted as having perished in just one small area alone. Other steamers also soon arrived, and the ensuing bombardments from the river finally managed to check the advance of the *Ansar*, allowing the Egyptians to escape. The Camel Corps would arrive back to the relative safety of the *zariba*, while the Egyptian cavalry, still heading north, continued to be pursued. Curiously, the Mahdist warriors who had chased the Camel Corps towards the *zariba* at this point suddenly broke off their attack and retired under the cover of the hills, rather than commence the almost expected assault on the right-flank of Kitchener's line. It was without doubt that the gunboats had saved the men of the Camel Corps, who otherwise may have been over-run and suffered destruction. As it was, they had lost sixty men during their retirement from the Kerreri Hills.

Meanwhile, the Egyptian cavalry had carried on with their attempt to encourage the bulk of the warriors of the Black Flag to follow them towards the north. The troopers would ride a short distance before they would dismount, fire a volley at their pursuers, remount, ride on further, then repeat the process. The rear of Broadwood's retirement was covered by the squadron under the command of Major B. T. Mahon, who, at one point, ordered his men to conduct a flank attack of the pursuers on their right, an action that resulted in the successful checking of a group of mounted warriors.

Throughout the retirement of the cavalry, the Mahdists attempted to get round Broadwood's flank; by 8 a.m., after covering some three or four miles, the warriors appeared to break off their pursuit and began heading back towards the west of the Kerreri Hills. It quickly became clear that the *Khalifa* had finally realised that the main Anglo-Egyptian force was in fact at Egeiga, and that thousands of his warriors had been fruitlessly chasing but a small part of Kitchener's army. The Egyptian cavalry was now able to briefly come to a halt, after which it was decided to head south and return to the *zariba*. A small detachment, however, peeled off in an attempt to recover the two guns of the horse artillery battery that had been abandoned almost an hour earlier.

One British officer who had been seen confidently inspiring his Egyptian troops was Captain Douglas Haig, the future field marshal who would command the British Expeditionary Force in France throughout much of the First World War. Although the Egyptian cavalry was now enjoying a brief respite following the end of the first attack of the battle, the British cavalry—in the form of the 21st Lancers—was soon to conduct its famous charge at the Battle of Omdurman; one that would lead to the award of no less than three Victoria Crosses to the regiment.

Back at the *zariba*, Kitchener was pondering what to do next and what his adversary might also be contemplating. If the *Ansar* fell back to the city of Omdurman in the hope of defending it, the *Sirdar* knew he would have to send in his men to fight street by street until it finally fell into his hands. This would, of course, be an extremely costly affair, since both British and Egyptian casualty numbers would likely be high. On the other hand, the *Khalifa* might attempt another assault on the *zariba* at Egeiga, which would be a far more favourable outcome for Kitchener, because he would have another chance to inflict heavy casualties on the *Ansar* by engaging them from an entrenched position with a devastating combination of artillery, machine gun, and rifle fire. However, he simply could not wait to see if Abdullahi al-Taishi would take this course of action; Omdurman would have to be occupied, and quickly.

Kitchener, therefore, issued orders to Lieutenant-Colonel Martin to take out all four of his squadrons—amounting to around 320 men—of the 21st Lancers and reconnoitre from the southern end of the *zariba* up to the outskirts of the city. The intention was to ascertain what, if any, Mahdist forces lay between the main body of the Anglo-Egyptian army and Omdurman, and, if possible, drive off any warriors encountered so as to clear a way for the infantry to safely advance. Finally, after spending much of the first attack of the battle stood by their horses in the *zariba* as bullets relentlessly whistled over their heads, the men of the 21st were ordered to make ready and mount up, after which they trotted out towards the south within only two minutes of receiving their initial orders.

As the British cavalrymen approached *Jebel* Surgham, the ridge was found to be deserted and so was immediately occupied. However, when they rode past the eastern slopes they could see, at about three miles' distance, large columns of several thousand wounded Mahdists warriors who were seemingly heading towards Omdurman. Martin instructed the signalling officer to send a message, via heliograph, to Kitchener informing him of what they had seen, after which the regiment had to wait for a reply. As they sat motionless on their horses, they suddenly came under a distant fire from Mahdist marksmen hiding among the rocks on *Jebel* Surgham, forcing the lancers themselves to hide behind and between nearby mounds of sand. Several troops, however, were sent out to return fire on the *Ansar* riflemen.

Eventually, at 8.30 a.m., a reply was received from Kitchener with the order to 'Advance and clear the left flank, and use every effort to prevent the enemy re-entering Omdurman'. In turn, Martin instructed two patrols to scout towards the south-west along the slopes of *Jebel* Surgham. One of these patrols, led by Lieutenant Arthur Murray Pirie, headed towards the city and pushed through the scattered lines of Mahdist riflemen; the latter fired excitedly at the former with little accuracy. The other patrol, which was commanded by Lieutenant Robert Septimus Grenfell, speedily skirted around the slopes of *Jebel* Surgham in order to ascertain what lay ahead. They similarly came under fire, but, within two or three minutes, the men returned unscathed to report they had seen nothing of note laying ahead. However, Pirie's detachment had come across what appeared to be a force of 700 to 1,000 warriors holding position in a shallow *khor* (a *wadi* known as Abu Sunt or *Khor* Abu Sunt) that was located three-quarters of a mile away between the main body of the 21st Lancers and the retreating wounded Mahdists. It was clear that these had been posted by Abdullahi al-Taishi to protect his line of retirement to Omdurman. Hearing of this, at about 9 a.m., Martin quickly issued further instructions for his regiment to advance to attack in order to drive off the group of warriors.

This body of 700 to 1,000 *Ansar* warriors (most likely actually numbering no more than 700) was made up of Hadendowa tribesmen, and was led by Osman Digna and one of his early and trusted companions, Ibrahim Said. Most of these Mahdists were swordsmen or spearmen, but around thirty of them had been seen by Pirie brandishing Remington rifles. Earlier, as the men of the 21st Lancers had trotted out of the *zariba*, a number of Mahdist look-outs on *Jebel* Surgham had made off to inform the *Khalifa* of the advance of the British cavalry. Concerned that the lancers were attempting to prevent his retirement to the city of Omdurman, Abdullahi al-Taishi gave orders to Ibrahim al-Khalil to take 2,000 men of the Black Flag to reinforce those already in the *khor*. This movement—concealed by a spur of *Jebel* Surgham—was not seen by Martin and his men, and so the British were totally unaware of the additional warriors now streaming towards their point of intended attack. The *Khalifa*, however, knew exactly what was to come, and, mounting his white donkey, it was said that he rode to a position about 500 yards from the *khor* in order to watch the coming clash for himself. However, many historians today believe this is just one of a number of myths that quickly grew around the battle; he was in fact still with the main body of the Black Flag behind *Jebel* Surgham, debating his next move.

Osman Digna's plan was to tempt his enemy into a trap, and the *khor* provided what seemed a suitable place in which to do it. He instructed all his riflemen to take up positions outside of the *khor* on its northern bank in order for them to be easily seen by the British cavalrymen. Those armed with spears and swords were then told to sit down and remain close to the ground in the depression so they were concealed from the enemy. Although there was an initial low murmur of quiet voices between the warriors, noise discipline was soon enforced and the men waited in complete silence for the expected attack. This silence, however, would later be broken by the arrival of the reinforcements, much to the delight of Osman Digna, increasing the number of available riflemen from thirty to about 150, not to mention many additional spear and swordsmen. Some 2,000 Mahdist warriors were now packed into *Khor* Abu Sunt, and the trap was set.

At about the same time as Abdullahi al-Taishi was prevaricating about what to do next, the 21st Lancers had begun to descend from the ridge of *Jebel* Surgham, a movement that was accompanied by a cessation of fire from the Mahdist marksmen, who now began to disappear altogether. The cavalrymen advanced at walking pace for about 300 yards, during which time they could only see a line of about 100 to 150 dark blue, motionless men a quarter of a mile to their left-front. It was now thought by Martin and some of his officers that the body of warriors in the *khor* had shrunk to around 250 to 300, although it was assumed the remainder of the previously estimated 700 to 1,000 were just out of view behind a small nearby ridge. An order was then given for the regiment to form a line of squadron columns, after which they continued to advance at the walk until they were within 300 yards of the distant men.

The squadrons next began to wheel slowly to the left before advancing in columns of troops at the trot towards the *khor*. Moments later, the dark blue line of men ahead of them suddenly appeared to drop down onto their knees as if to take aim and fire at the advancing cavalrymen; this being exactly what they were doing. A volley of rifle fire—the Mahdist riflemen were under the direct command of Ibrahim Said—then spewed forth, and, despite the fire being initially ill-aimed, a few of their bullets eventually began to find their mark, with a number of men and horses crashing violently to the ground. Martin, who had been pondering whether to attempt to out-flank his enemy rather than mount a charge directly at them, now ordered the trumpeter to sound 'Right wheel into line'. With each troop being made up of twenty-five men if at full-strength, the sixteen troops of the regiment immediately swung round, and, according to Churchill, '… locked up into a long galloping line, and the 21st Lancers were committed to their first charge in war.'

In the *khor* itself, Osman Digna shouted out orders to his men concealed in the depression. Their primary objective was to knock the British cavalrymen off the backs of their mounts and get them down on the ground, where it would be easier to kill them. The secondary objective was to kill the horses, even if that meant exposing themselves to the enemy and risking death. Osman Digna then wished his men luck, after which he left the *khor* and headed off to join the *Khalifa*, hoping the superior numbers of his warriors would ensure victory in *Khor* Abu Sunt.

In a letter to his wife written days after the battle, Major Harry Finn, who commanded 'A' Squadron of the regiment, described the order and formation the lancers now took:

> 'A' was the rear squadron of the column so was on the right when the Regt. wheeled into line & galloped to the attack. The 4 Squadrons were thus in line: (1) 'A', (2) the made up one under [Captain F. H.] Eaden; (3) 'B' under [Major J.] Fowle; (4) 'C' under [Captain W. M.] Doyne. The Colonel led in front of 'B' …

As the lancers charged at speed over the short distance to the *Ansar* line, many of the cavalrymen were said to have 'bowed their helmets forward, like the Cuirassiers at Waterloo'. When they reached the half-way point, it started to become clear that the supposedly shallow *khor* was in fact about twenty feet wide and four to six feet deep, which not only offered the Mahdists better protection than first thought but also posed a lethal danger to the mass of horses now galloping towards it, and into which they must soon jump.

The focus of the cavalrymen, however, soon shifted when they saw a new group of Mahdists and a number of banners suddenly and unexpectedly rise up from the ground. To the shock and horror of Martin and his men, the enemy force now before them was far larger than previously believed, having risen—depending on the estimates given by various period sources—to between 1,500 and 3,000 warriors, although around 2,000 is the most likely figure. It was clear the *Khalifa* had set them a trap, but it was now too late to abandon the charge, since the men and horses were already fully committed.

Some of the *Ansar* warriors began moving forward, as if to meet the lancers head-on, while many more behind simply stood their ground waiting to meet the coming onslaught; the pressure of the forward movement of the spear and swordsmen had in fact forced the riflemen in front of them to unintentionally move forward also. In places it seemed as though the greatly reinforced mass of warriors lined the edge of the *khor* in ranks as many as twenty deep. This sight, however, did not deter the officers and men of the 21st, who now quickened their pace further, since they knew they must get up as much speed as possible in the hope of literally smashing their way through.

Churchill, who was leading a troop on the right of the line of the charging cavalry, took a quick look over his shoulder to see what effects the Mahdist fire was having on his men. Satisfied that few had been hit, he re-sheathed his sword then drew his Mauser pistol and cocked it, believing the pistol more useful at close-quarters than his sword. At that moment, he noticed that his troop was beginning to overlap with that to the right of him under the command of Lieutenant Frederick William Wormald, and so he shouted to him 'to shoulder'. It was, however, only moments later that both troops finally hit the enemy line after unintentionally forming a crescent formation, a result of Churchill's command

The Battle of Omdurman: Charge of the 21st Lancers

to his fellow officer. Fortunately for both officers and their men, the two troops struck the *khor* diagonally, allowing them to gallop through the dry water feature rather than have to jump down into it; this also allowed the two troops to hit their enemy at a faster pace while keeping their formation, something the centre troops were unable to achieve. It is said that at the moment the lancers hit the Mahdist line the cavalrymen let out a loud roar while the warriors shouted 'Allahu Akbar!'

Now in the middle of a mass of warriors, Churchill recalled:

> Straight before me a man threw himself on the ground.... My first idea therefore was that the man was terrified. But simultaneously I saw the gleam of his curved sword as he drew it back for a ham-stringing cut. I had room and time enough to turn my pony out of his reach, and leaning over on the off side I fired two shots into him at about three yards. As I straightened myself in the saddle, I saw before me another figure with uplifted sword. I raised my pistol and fired. So close were we that the pistol itself actually struck him. Man and sword disappeared below and behind me. On my left, ten yards away, was an Arab horseman in a bright-coloured tunic and steel helmet, with chain-mail hangings. I fired at him. He turned aside.

Churchill's troop smashed its way through a line of men four-deep, knocking many of them 'A. O. T.' (arse over tip). However, one of the lieutenant's troopers was knocked—or otherwise fell—from his horse, at which moment a group of warriors immediately set about stabbing him to death with their spears and swords as he lay helpless on the ground. A number of horses were also wounded—most likely by the hooked knives carried by some of the warriors, which were designed to hamstring and bring down the animals and their riders—but most of the troop managed to find its way through unscathed. Yet, if they thought they were lucky to survive the initial contact with their enemy, any sense of relief was shorted lived, for they now found themselves in among scattered groups of warriors and individual, fierce combats quickly erupted between the two opposing forces.

Pulling up his horse, Churchill looked around him to see Mahdist warriors in almost every direction, so he rode for those nearest and began shooting at them directly into their faces at point-blank range. Having accounted for at least three of his enemy killed, the lieutenant then noticed that a mass of warriors had begun forming up at only twenty yards distance. This impressive sight transfixed Churchill, who sat motionless on his grey Arab polo pony watching the fearsome spectacle. This fixation, however, was quickly broken when two *Ansar* riflemen got down on their knees and levelled their weapons at him in an attempt to shoot him. Finally, realising the imminent danger he was now in, Churchill yanked on the reigns of his horse to turn and canter away, the cracking of the Mahdist rifles sounding behind him as he made off. The lieutenant then rode back over to the men of his troop, having fired all ten rounds from the magazine of his pistol. He had somehow remained unharmed throughout.

Corporal Wade Rix, an NCO in Major Finn's squadron, hit a Mahdist warrior in the left-eye with his lance. However, the shock of the impact was so forceful, at the moment the corporal's horse jumped down into the *khor*, that his lance shattered, the pieces dropping to the ground in all directions. Rix then desperately drew his sword as he watched a nearby warrior raise and aim what appeared to be a flintlock musket or rifle, somehow managing to strike him with the tip of his blade before the man could fire his shot. The Mahdist, now smothered in his own blood, was no longer a threat, and so the NCO pushed his horse on into the frenzied fight in the *khor*.

Meanwhile, in the centre of the line of the 21st Lancers, it was a rather different story. As the centre troops hit the front ranks of the *Ansar*, many of them were forced to jump onto the hedges of spears now in front and below them in the *khor*. It was noted by one unnamed officer that the Mahdists did not break nor showed any fear of the cavalry, but rather they 'bunched' together and bravely stood their ground. The warriors slashed at the horses with their swords or impaled them in the side with their spears. A number of Mahdist riflemen even placed the muzzles of their weapons point-blank on the necks of the British horses, pulling their triggers and brining the poor animals and their riders violently down to the ground. Perhaps unsurprisingly, many of the horses who managed to miss the waiting spears and bullets hit the ground so hard that they came crashing down on their knees and lost their riders. As the now dismounted cavalrymen hit the ground, they were immediately pounced upon by dozens of Mahdist warriors, who frenziedly stabbed their fallen enemies to death.

The centre troop that suffered the most at this moment of the charge was No. 2 troop under the command of Lieutenant Grenfell. Having jumped into the *khor* and frantically charged their way through, the men of the troop came to a high bank made of boulders, which the horses struggled to climb their way up and over in order to escape the mass of surging warriors behind them. It was also during this desperate scramble for safety that Grenfell was killed, having been struck in the wrist with a blade before a sword was thrust through his back. After the battle, his helmet would be found with almost a dozen holes made by the points of spears. Of the twenty men of the troop, only one sergeant and three enlisted men survived.

Another troop in the centre was that of Lieutenant the Honourable Raymond de Montmorency, who had managed to force his way through the *khor* unharmed. Having got through to the other side, he turned around in order to find his troop sergeant, Lance-Sergeant Edward Carter, but noticed Lieutenant Grenfell had been wounded and knocked from his horse. Seeing the man on the ground, the lieutenant immediately rode back in an attempt to save the officer. Dismounting once he reached him, he realised that Grenfell was dead; nevertheless, he lifted the body onto the back of his own horse, but the surrounding din of battle must have frightened the animal, since it bolted and galloped away before the officer could remount. Watching helplessly as his horse made off at speed, the lieutenant realised he was now surrounded by dozens of Mahdist warriors, and death appeared certain. A short distance away was Captain Paul Aloysius Kenna, who, seeing the desperate situation Montmorency was now in, sharply turned his horse and cantered towards the lieutenant in the hope of helping him, fighting his way through and past many warriors as he did so. Corporal Fred Swarbrick was also present; he managed to catch Montmorency's frightened horse and lead it back to the lieutenant for him to remount. Now almost surrounded, the three men began to attempt to hack their way out. Eventually, they managed to reach a place of relative safety. For their actions, both Montmorency and Kenna would be awarded the Victoria Cross, while Swarbrick would receive the Distinguished Conduct Medal.

Lieutenant-Colonel Martin had suffered a near-disaster when his horse fell while jumping into the *khor*. Scrambling to get to his feet, he saw many warriors around him, seemingly everywhere, cutting and slashing at the British cavalry. Knowing he would be killed if he remained on foot, he quickly turned to his charger—which was still struggling on its side on the ground—and frantically managed to get it back on its feet. Once up, he remounted, and, with only a stick in his hand, he rode on and pushed his way through to the other side of the *khor*, somehow getting all the way through without sustaining even the slightest of injuries.

Major W. G. Crole Wyndham, who was second-in-command of the regiment, also managed to ride unscathed most of the way to the other side of the *khor*; but as he attempted to clear it, his horse simply dropped down dead, having being shot during the initial impact on the *Ansar*'s line. Now on foot, the major drew his pistol with one hand and tightly gripped his sword with the other, as a group of warriors suddenly surged towards him. Seeing him in danger, Kenna dashed over and put the major on his horse, then, remounting behind him, spurred the animal on and escaped the immediate *mêlée* as the two men fired their pistols wildly at the Mahdists. Unfortunately, their horse—likely wounded—gave way and the two men became separated in the confusion.

Elsewhere, Lieutenant the Honourable R. F. Molyneux of the Blues and Royals, who was attached to the 21st Lancers, was similarly pushing his way across the *khor* when a bullet struck his horse; both animal and rider came crashing to the ground. Clambering to his feet, the officer drew his pistol and aimed it at a nearby warrior, but as he pulled the trigger, he was hit in the wrist by the blade of a sword, violently knocking the pistol out of his hand and deeply cutting him. Like Montmorency, Molyneux now found himself virtually surrounded by frenzied warriors, but he then spotted a mounted lancer who was not far away and called out to him for help. This cavalryman was Private Thomas Byrne of 'B' Squadron, who had already been wounded by a bullet in his arm during the charge to the *khor*. Despite his painful wound, the private immediately fought his way through to assist Molyneux, being narrowly missed by a spear that had been thrown at him as he did so, although he would, moments later, suffer a stab wound to his chest from another spearman. The arrival of Byrne was enough for the Mahdists to take their attention off Molyneux, who promptly took the opportunity to run away. Byrne was then able to escort the lieutenant to safety, after which he was told to seek medical attention, but the private refused in order to make his way back towards the fighting. Eventually, he would faint from loss of blood, but would mercifully survive the action.

Another officer taking part in the charge was Lieutenant Smyth, who, in a letter to his sister written shortly following the action, recalled the moment he and his horse reached the *khor*:

> Every side a compact mass of white robed men, apparently countless, still firing and waving swords. Find myself at nullah [*khor*]. … Am met by swordsman on foot. Cuts at my right front. I guard it with sword. Next, man with fat face, all in white having fired, missed me, throws up both hands. I cut him across face. He drops. Large bearded man in blue, with two edged sword and two hands cuts at me. Think this time I must be done for but pace tells and my guard carries it off. Duck my head to spear thrown which just misses me. Another cut at my horse, miss guard, but luckily cut is too far away and only cuts through my breastplate and gives my horse a small flesh wound on neck and shoulder. Then I remember no more till I find myself outside with four or five of my troop.

Lieutenant C. S. Nesham, having ridden most of the way through the *khor*, suddenly found the bridle of his horse being grabbed by a Mahdist. The officer immediately struck the man with his sword, but the warrior succeeded in cutting one of the reins, which resulted in Nesham's arm suddenly flying out to the side. Another Mahdist then attempted to strike the lieutenant's arm with his sword, cutting and almost severing it from the rest of the officer's body. Both warriors continued cutting at him frenziedly, one strike wounding him in the leg while another split his helmet and struck him in the head. A third sword strike hit him in the shoulder, a wound which resulted in his right-arm becoming virtually paralysed. Nesham's horse also suffered, receiving several stabs through the saddle into its back. The warriors, seeing their target was now almost certainly a dead man, grabbed at his legs and attempted to pull him off his mount in order to finish him off on the ground. But luck was, at last, on the officer's side, for his wounded horse suddenly bolted and cantered off, taking its rider with him. Badly wounded, Nesham found himself back among other members of the 21st Lancers, after which he was carried off to receive much-needed medical attention.

The charge of the 21st Lancers had been an almost disaster; one officer and twenty men had been killed and a further four officers and forty-six men wounded. In addition, some 119 of the 320 horses had been either killed or wounded. Mahdist casualties were twenty-three killed during the charge with an unknown number wounded. The whole affair had lasted less than two minutes, and many afterwards struggled to exactly remember what had happened during the brief but sharp and furious combat. Corporal Rix would not be the only lancer to see his lance disintegrate in his hand upon impact with its target, and many of the cavalrymen had to draw their swords instead, the latter of which also quickly broke as they came into contact with the heavier broadswords used by the Mahdists.

For Osman Digna, however, his carefully planned trap had seen a degree of success, although perhaps not as successful as he might have hoped. He had managed to avoid the advantage of long-range fire enjoyed by his enemy, instead drawing them into close-quarter combat where his superior numbers would play to his own advantage. The element of tactical surprise was also achieved, a factor of immense importance in warfare of any type and of any period. As we have seen, the men of the 21st Lancers had been fooled into thinking their enemy were much weaker than anticipated, exactly what Osman Digna had intended.

Not everything, however, had gone according to plan for the Hadendowa chief. The riflemen, who were the bait for the trap, were supposed to be the only warriors outside of the *khor*, but as the British cavalry began its charge many of the sword and spearmen in the depression moved forward against orders to meet the charge head-on; this resulted in sections of the *khor* being more lightly defended than intended, thus inflicting fewer casualties on the lancers than might have otherwise been the case. Also, once the British cavalrymen hit the warriors in *Khor* Abu Sunt, they were too slow in recovering from the shock of the impact, losing valuable seconds in what was always going to be an incredibly fast-paced action. Despite this, it is still perhaps fair to say that Osman Digna had once again proved his position as one of the ablest of all military commanders of the *Ansar*.

With his regiment now in poor shape, Lieutenant-Colonel Martin decided against reforming to mount a second charge, instead issuing orders for the remaining men to advance towards the enemy's flank, where, from a distance of 300 yards, he ordered two squadrons to dismount and open a fire with their carbines. The time was now 9.30 a.m. As the fire swept across the *khor*, the warriors attempted to advance on the cavalrymen, but due to the intense carbine fire they finally gave up and began to make off back behind *Jebel* Surgham in order to re-join the Black Flag. It was during the carbine fire on the Mahdists that the remaining dismounted lancers were finally able to escape the *khor*—Privates William Brown and Andrew Rowlett of 'B' Squadron were the last two to emerge; both were wounded. Brown had previously managed to get out of the *khor* but had gone back in to rescue Private John Varney by dragging him out, after which he went back in a second time to get Rowlett. With the Mahdists now gone, some of the men of the 21st Lancers rode back to the *khor* to find the body of Lieutenant Grenfell, who, as with a number of others, was hastily buried in a shallow grave.

Many military people at the time—and indeed many historians since—believed the decision to charge was a mistake, which, considering the greater number of casualties inflicted on the Mahdists by the carbines than by the charge itself, may hold some truth. However, the men of the 21st Lancers were almost certainly spoiling for a fight, since, until that fateful day on 2 September 1898, they had so far not been able to play any significant part in the campaign. As if to add insult to injury, they had also been left to watch the Egyptian cavalry fight more than its fair share of the action. Thus, the officers and men of the regiment were absolutely determined to enter the fray before the campaign was over, and they knew it was now almost at an end. At the time, it was considered a heroic action by the British public reading their newspapers back home, and the charge has gone down as one of the most epic military actions of the late-Victorian period, as reflected in the award of three Victoria Crosses. Many have also claimed that the charge of the 21st Lancers at the Battle of Omdurman was the last full-scale British cavalry charge in history; this claim is much debated today, with the charge of the 20th Hussars against Turkish infantry in 1920 during the Chanak Crisis being a strong contender for the distinction.

While the men of the 21st Lancers now attempted to recover from their ordeal, the Battle of Omdurman was entering its next phase.

12

The Battle of Omdurman: MacDonald's Saving Action

While the 21st Lancers had been grappling with the Mahdists in *Khor* Abu Sunt, Kitchener had made the decision to evacuate his camp at Egeiga and make an advance towards the city of Omdurman. The order to move out was given at 8.30 a.m.; the Anglo-Egyptian army advanced in rank of brigades beginning from the left of the line of the *zariba*, with Collinson's 4th Egyptian Brigade acting as reserve and offering protection to the rear of the transport column. Also covering the left- and right-rear was the Egyptian cavalry and the Camel Corps. Thus, the two British brigades advanced towards the ridge situated between *Jebel* Surgham and the Nile, while the 2nd and 3rd Egyptian Brigades advanced towards the mountain itself. 1st Egyptian Brigade advanced further out to the west, although the latter was instructed to stay within supporting distance of the remainder of the army. By 9.30 a.m., the infantry had reached the sand ridge that ran from the western end of *Jebel* Surgham to the river, where the order was given to halt so the brigades could form up for the final advance on the city.

It is said that when Abdullahi al-Taishi returned to his Black Flag four warriors came to him carrying the body of a dead man. When he asked who the man was the warriors informed him it was Ibrahim al-Khalil; in response, the *Khalifa*, who was visibly upset, raised his hands above his head and began to recite the *fatiha* (the opening chapter of the Qur'an), upon which those around him joined him in the recital. Shortly afterwards, news also came to him that the Anglo-Egyptian force was on the move in the direction of Omdurman. Abdullahi al-Taishi now went into deep thought about what to do next; questioning whether he should commit the Black Flag to an all-out attack of Kitchener's army or attempt to get his warriors back to Omdurman before the enemy could reach it in hope of defending the city.

It was during the halt, while the British and Egyptian brigades manoeuvred into their allocated positions, that information came to Kitchener that Abdullahi al-Taishi and a large number of his warriors were not heading for Omdurman as originally thought, but were in fact currently located on the eastern slopes of *Jebel*

Surgham. What was more, a party of *Ansar* marksmen, under the command of an *amir* by the name of Khayr al-Sayyid, unexpectedly appeared on the summit of the mountain and began shooting down at the troops of the *Sirdar*'s army below. It was now clear that the *Khalifa* was intending to mount an attack on the flank of the Anglo-Egyptian army as it advanced towards the city.

Kitchener responded by ordering the three leading brigades to change front half right, while instructions were also sent to Maxwell's 2nd Egyptian Brigade to deploy two companies to storm the heights of the mountain and drive off the Mahdist riflemen, a task which they completed successfully. As the brigades manoeuvred, the sound of heavy firing could be heard from the direction of MacDonald's 1st Egyptian Brigade, which now appeared to be heavily engaged against thousands of the Kahlifa's warriors. The next phase—sometimes referred to as the second phase or phase two—of the Battle of Omdurman had begun.

During the reorganising of the brigades, MacDonald's brigade was required to exchange places with Lewis' 3rd Egyptian Brigade in order to allow the former to take up position on the right of the echeloned line. As this movement was carried out, MacDonald's brigade became separated from the main body of the Anglo-Egyptian army by about a mile, and was marching around the western side of *Jebel* Surgham when the brigadier-general suddenly found himself faced with a large force of Mahdist warriors, who had advanced from *Jebel* Surgham towards the west. Seeing this mass of enemy coming towards him, MacDonald gave instructions for his brigade to halt and form into line in order to meet the coming attack.

Abdullahi al-Taishi's force now opposing MacDonald numbered around 20,000 men. As we have seen, the Mahdist leader had held his Black Flag in reserve during the first attack of the battle, keeping it in the hope of delivering the final knockout blow to Kitchener's army. With the first attack a total failure, he realised that the entire future of the *Mahdi*'s legacy was on the verge of total destruction. He also realised that he now had to commit what forces he had left in order to make one final all-out effort to save his state, although it was highly unlikely that it would succeed. Seeing MacDonald's brigade separated from the main body of the *Sirdar*'s army, the *Khalifa* sensed an opportunity to inflict some sort of significant defeat on his enemy. Indeed, he heavily outnumbered the 1st Egyptian Brigade, since MacDonald had only about 3,000 infantrymen.

Yet the decision to attack had not been made by Abdullahi al-Taishi himself, since he was still prevaricating whether to actually order the assault or abandon the idea altogether and fall back to Omdurman. It was, in fact, Ya'qub who gave the order. The body of the *Ansar* that eventually attacked MacDonald had been lined up over a 4,000-yard front in twenty-three lines, and it is said that Ya'qub, angered by the loss of Ibrahim al-Khalil, had jumped onto his horse, armed only with a spear and galloped up and down the line, shouting words of encouragement to inspire his men for the renewed assault. The Mahdist warriors responded by enthusiastically raising and waving their weapons above their heads.

From about 9 a.m., Ya'qub had began reorganising his men for his intended attack. The Black Flag—which had been reinforced by survivors from the earlier fighting—was divided into fifty-one standards, each numbering anywhere between twenty-five to 1,500 warriors. Its senior commanders included Osman al-Dikaym, Muhammad al-*Mahdi* (the oldest surviving son of the *Mahdi*), Muhammad Wad el-Bishara, and Muhammad al-Zaki. Unfortunately for the *Khalifa*, the warriors of the Black Flag were overwhelmingly armed with swords and spears, only around 1,000 men possessing firearms, many of which were old relics and long obsolete; the Remingtons had been largely taken by the *muluazimayya*.

The advance of the Black Flag finally begun when Muhammad al-*Mahdi*—who was visibly irritated at having to wait for the order to attack while watching the Anglo-Egyptian troops advance towards Omdurman—was said to have cried out 'How long do we wait till they grasp our hands?', at which moment he rode on ahead alone. Seeing and hearing this, Osman al-Dikaym and Muhammad Wad el-Bishara spurred their horses forward after him; behind them, the warriors of the Black flag followed. Both men, however, would be gunned down within moments of commencing their advance.

Seeing the oncoming *Ansar* warriors, MacDonald sent a messenger to Lewis asking to be sent reinforcements and give protection to his rear. However, Lewis refused, citing that he had orders from Kitchener to close the gap that had formed between his and Maxwell's brigades. While it is nothing more than speculation, it is possible that the colonel was acting out of a form of snobbery, since MacDonald had been raised from the ranks, a relatively rare occurrence during the Victorian period which many officers of social standing looked down upon. That said, Lewis was known for not being prepared to challenge orders, and few dared to challenge Kitchener. Nevertheless, the former ranker remained calm and was determined to meet the threat head-on without Lewis' assistance. It perhaps should be noted that MacDonald was suffering physically after being kicked by a horse, an incident that had resulted in a broken foot; but he was not going to let his injury get in the way of his duty.

Meanwhile, the two companies of Maxwell's brigade that had been sent up *Jebel* Surgham to drive off the Mahdist marksmen had begun a long range fire from the summit down on Ya'qub's advancing warriors below. It would not take long for MacDonald to become aware of this support he was now receiving from the mountain. As the fire from these two companies began to have an effect on the warriors, the brigadier-general took the opportunity to order out his artillery. This included some eighteen field guns and eight Maxims, which were set up in a matter of moments, after which they awaited the order to fire.

It would be some 300 to 400 Baggara horsemen, galloping ahead of the warriors on foot, who first clashed with 1st Egyptian Brigade. It was assumed at the time that these mounted Mahdists were attempting to smash a hole in MacDonald's line, through which the warriors following on foot would then pour through and engage the Egyptian and Sudanese troops at close-quarters. As the men awaited the Mahdist horsemen, some of the Sudanese troops opened fire prematurely without orders, a result of letting their nerves and feelings of excitement get the better of them. A substantial number of the Sudanese troops were also said to be too eager to charge at the oncoming Mahdists, but the officers—who knew they would be slaughtered if they did so—managed to keep them back and in line. As at Abu Hamed, an angry MacDonald dealt with these troops by riding down the line in front of the men and knocking up their rifles as he passed. After two minutes of being put back in their place, the Sudanese troops became calm and steady once again.

There is a story that has become entwined with the Battle of Omdurman legend which suggests MacDonald had taken a serious personal risk by riding along the line formed by his Sudanese troops to instil discipline in them. Only a few days before the battle, a Sudanese soldier had threatened to kill the brigadier-general, and, unperturbed by the threat, MacDonald had calmly walked up to the private in question and ordered him to load his rifle. Once this was done, he turned his back on his would-be killer and waited, but the man simply fell down on his knees and begged the brigadier-general for mercy. After that, there was apparently no further threats or acts of discontent in the brigade.

George Warrington Steevens, the war correspondent of the *Daily Mail*, recalled the moment he realised the battle had resumed:

It was now twenty minutes to ten. The British had crested a low ridge between Gebel Surgham and the Nile; Maxwell's brigade was just ascending it, Lewis's just coming up under the hill. Men who could go where they liked were up with the British, staring hungrily at Omdurman. Suddenly from rearward broke out a heavy crackle of fire. We thought perhaps a dozen men or so had been shamming dead; we went on staring at Omdurman. But next instant we had to turn and gallop hot-heeled back again. For the crackle became a crashing, and the crashing waxed to a roar. Dervishes were firing at us from the top of Gebel Surgham, dervishes were firing behind and to the right of it. The 13th Sudanese were bounding up the hill; Lewis's brigade had hastily faced to its right westward, and was volleying for life; Macdonald's *bey*ond, still facing northward, was a sheet of flashes and a roll of smoke. What was it? Had they come to life again? No time to ask; reinforcements or ghosts, they were on us, and the battle was begun all again.

Unfortunately for the Baggara, they were met by the fire of the artillery and Maxims at around 1,100 yards range; this tore through the ranks of the horsemen, gunning them down before they could reach MacDonald's line. Despite the failure of the Baggara, the thousands of foot warriors charged on regardless. MacDonald now

The Battle of Omdurman: MacDonald's Saving Action 169

brought his infantry forward into line with the artillery, from where the soldiers delivered volley after volley of rifle fire into the leadings ranks of their attackers, while the Maxims swept their fire up and down the *Ansar* lines and the field guns continued to pound them. Few of the warriors in the front ranks survived unscathed, many of them crashing into the sandy and dusty ground, after which those behind scrambled over their now dead or wounded comrades to continue the assault; none of the *Khalifa*'s men, however, were able to get within 300 yards of MacDonald's brigade. Those carrying banners thrust the shafts into the ground in an attempt to act as rallying points before again renewing the attack, but the Maxim and rifle fire of the Egyptian and Sudanese troops again cut them down in their droves. Within the matter of minutes, the ground in front of 1st Brigade was literally littered with the mutilated bodies of many dead and dying Mahdists.

At the moment MacDonald was bearing the brunt of the attack of the Black Flag, Kitchener was watching through his field-glasses from the position occupied by Maxwell's 2nd Egyptian Brigade. The *Sirdar* had finally found the *Khalifa*'s main force and he was determined to engage it. Orders were quickly issued to Wauchope's 1st British and Lewis' Brigades to form up in line, while Major Tudway's Camel Corps trotted off to support MacDonald on his right. Instructions were also issued to Lyttelton's 2nd British and Maxwell's Brigades to push forwards over the slopes of *Jebel* Surgham towards the west. It would also not be long before the 32nd Field Battery of the Royal Artillery was in action, relentlessly shelling the right-flank of Ya'qub's line. Moments later, additional Maxim guns opened fire, including two that had been painfully dragged up to the summit of the mountain—thanks to the efforts of Lieutenant Robert Byron Drury Blakeney—which were now spraying a murderous fire down on their adversaries below. This heavy fire soon began to tell on Ya'qub's surging mass of warriors, the right-flank of which now started to show signs of buckling. Eventually, the right-flank indeed broke, and large numbers of Mahdists could be seen fleeing for their lives in the direction of Omdurman. Behind them, they left countless dead and wounded laying on the field.

Nevertheless, the warriors who had attacked MacDonald's brigade were still very much in the fight and were continuing to press their assault. The Egyptian and Sudanese troops of the 1st Egyptian Brigade, however, stood their ground as they fired relentless volleys and rapid independent fire at their attackers. MacDonald's artillery also fired shell after shell of shrapnel, which, combined with the effects of the rifle fire of the infantry, again tore its way through the ranks of the *Ansar*. Yet on the Mahdists came, pushing ever closer to their enemy despite their horrific and devastating suffering.

The advance of the other brigades, however, had forced Ya'qub to redirect a large number of his warriors away from the attack on MacDonald. This somewhat helped reduce the pressure on the 1st Egyptian Brigade, but thousands of Mahdists still continued to attempt to rush MacDonald's lines. There was also an uneasy moment for Kitchener, when the men of the 7th Egyptian Battalion, which was positioned on the right of Lewis' brigade, began to lose their nerve and started to slowly retire. In an attempt to shore up this weak point in his line, the *Sirdar* ordered the 15th Egyptians to fix bayonets and take up positions behind the 7th. The movement worked, and the line once again became steady as the advance continued.

It would be during the assault on MacDonald's brigade that Ya'qub himself was hit by Maxim gun fire (although some accounts say it was artillery fire). He was shot from his horse and fell to the ground dead, while still clutching his spear, some 600 yards from MacDonald's front line; it has been claimed that Ya'qub's death was witnessed by the *Khalifa* himself, who was a few hundred yards away on a small knoll. Seeing their commander go down, two mounted Baggara warriors attempted to recover his body, but both also quickly became victims of the Maxims. Others, too, tried to carry Ya'qub's body from the field, only to share the same fate as their beloved leader. Some of the warriors, however, lost their nerve and began to falter under the sheer weight of their enemy's fire, while others, no doubt spurred on with anger following the loss of Ya'qub and close comrades, fanatically rushed forward in desperate attempts to get to the Egyptian and Sudanese troops; all were gunned down.

Babikr Bedri recalled the fear he felt during the latter stages of the Battle of Omdurman:

> I ask you to believe, reader, that I who had risked my life against the steamers, I who had never feared to meet the enemy, I who started out to take Ḥalfā with only eight companions—today I rubbed my face into the sand trying to bury my head in it, thoughtless of suffocation, so distracted was I by the fear of death, which in dangers no less acute than this I had sought so eagerly.

Another warrior by the name of Bābikr Muṣṭafā, who had been standing next to Bedri, was hit by a bullet in the hand. Seeing this, Bedri remembered the pact that he had made with some of his comrades earlier that day regarding the pretence of being wounded. He, therefore, immediately took off his turban and smeared it with the blood of Muṣṭafā, after which he bound it around his left-arm so as to appear wounded himself. Turning to his unwounded comrades he then said 'Now two of us are wounded!', at which point four of his companions jumped up from cover and carried both Bedri and Muṣṭafā away to safety, following which the four men who had carried them simply ran off and fled the battlefield altogether.

Bedri, however, remained with the wounded man along with another warrior called Mukhtār Muḥammad. Both men held Muṣṭafā and attempted to carry him further away from the fighting by heading towards the west, running as fast as they could to get to some 'low land and safety'. Despite their best efforts, the trio did not seem to be able to get out of the danger zone, and so the wounded

Muṣṭafā asked his companions to 'Let go my hand!' as his wound was hurting so much due to being carried. As Bedri and Mukhtār Muḥammad let him go, he sprang to his feet and ran off faster than either of his unwounded comrades could run themselves, both being unable to catch Muṣṭafā up when they chased after him. Thus, the fire of the Anglo-Egyptian troops was so intense that some, once courageous, men of the *Ansar* did what they could to escape the action and what they must have felt was surely a certain and meaningless death.

Other Mahdists who had begun to retreat actually had a change of heart and started to rally around their banners in a last act of defiance. However, the Maxims of MacDonald's brigade soon made short-work of these easy targets, mowing them down within seconds of them reaching their banners. Then, to the delight of Kitchener who had just made his way down the slopes of *Jebel* Surgham, the Black Flag of the *Khalifa*, which was by now riddled with bullet holes, was seized by one of his men. Moments later, the captured banner was taken to Kitchener as a prize, but this almost proved a disaster, since the sailors aboard the steamers—who could make out the flag but not those carrying it or near it—thought it marked the enemy and began firing at it. Thankfully for the *Sirdar* and his staff, Slatin had already spotted the danger and immediately got those carrying the standard to bring it down to the ground.

The joyous moment of the capture of the Black Flag standard was, however, over as quickly as it had come when a messenger came galloping up to the *Sirdar* to inform him that, in Lieutenant Blakeney's opinion, an estimated 10,000 Mahdist warriors under Osman al-Din's Green Flag were now about to hit MacDonald's brigade from the north. Decisive and always one to remain calm, Kitchener immediately ordered the 1st Lincolns to break away from their position with Wauchope's brigade and march at the double to the assistance of MacDonald.

The warriors of the Green Flag had just arrived on the battlefield from their earlier pursuit of Broadwood's cavalry into the desert. The colonel's ploy at drawing them off had worked, but they were now ready to enter the battle against MacDonald's brigade. Blakeney's estimate of 10,000 was, in fact, too low, since there were actually between 15,000 and 20,000 additional warriors now streaming towards the brigadier-general's position. The news of this new imminent attack was delivered to MacDonald by Captain St. G. C. Henry of the Camel Corps, who had galloped down the slopes of *Jebel* Surgham to 1st Egyptian Brigade. It was perhaps a timely arrival, since the brigadier-general was about to order a counter-attack of Ya'qub's warriors, a plan he was now forced to abandon. The final phase—usually referred to as the third phase or phase three—of the battle was now about to begin.

The men of 1st Egyptian Brigade suddenly felt themselves coming under an enfilading fire directed at them from their right. MacDonald now became very concerned, for he had formed up his men in line to repel Ya'qub's Black Flag attack to his front, but now he was about to be assaulted in his rear. He did, however, still have the 9th Sudanese in reserve, which he ordered to redeploy from column into line on his right-flank, so as to face the new threat. He also instructed the 11th Sudanese and a battery of his artillery to similarly redeploy to the left to be ready to receive the Green Flag attackers, while his remaining infantry battalions and guns continued to keep up their fire on the faltering attack of the Black Flag.

As the warriors of the Green Flag closed in, they opened a furious fire on the Sudanese troops which inflicted a high number of casualties. However, it was obvious that the two infantry battalions and a single battery of artillery had little hope of repelling the mass of Mahdists now surging towards them at speed. The brigadier-general, though, was merely biding his time, for he knew the Black Flag attack was virtually out of momentum, and, believing it now safe to do so, he gathered together his battalion commanders and drew in the sand his plan to deal with the Green Flag attack. Orders were given to the 10th Sudanese and a second artillery battery to come about and face the oncoming attackers. In addition, instructions were also given to the 2nd Egyptians to manoeuvre to their right at an angle to the rest of the brigade in line, thus also facing Osman al-Din's warriors. With the repositioning complete, MacDonald, at last, seemed ready to meet his newly arrived opponents head on.

Facing the oncoming attack, the Egyptian and Sudanese troops nervously awaited the order to fire, but they did not have to stand idle for long. The firing of the troops, however, evidently reflected their nerves, for it was poorly aimed and performed too quickly; the officers are said to have addressed their men individually to increase accuracy, even snatching their rifles to readjust the sights to meet the new ranges of the enemy before handing the weapons back. It would not be long before the Mahdists were within a mere forty yards of the Sudanese troops, some of the latter still firing high and missing their intended targets. So furious was the firing that the troops quickly began to run out of ammunition, with many of the men finding themselves down to less than a dozen cartridges. The officers and NCOs had to work their way up and down the line dishing out extra ammunition, although it was seemingly expended faster than could be replenished. The Maxims and field guns, of course, added their weight to the fire and again cut swathes through the oncoming *Ansar*.

Again, the Mahdists simply came on, taking much punishment but appearing not to falter in their initial charge. Soon, they were within only ten yards of McDonald's line, and the spearmen finally got their chance to throw their spears at the Egyptian and Sudanese soldiers, who, again almost out of ammunition, began to make ready for hand-to-hand combat. Outnumbered ten to one, it was perhaps obvious to many that the Mahdists were on the verge of inflicting nothing short of annihilation on 1st Egyptian Brigade; all now appeared virtually lost. Thankfully for MacDonald's troops, however, the Lincolns arrived just in the nick of time. Among the British infantrymen was Private George Teigh:

Our Regiment was ordered to the right to reinforce the Soudanese and here we had to double across the Dervishes' firing line, which caused us to have a lot of casualties. We formed up on the right of the Soudanese and formed into line, when volley firing was again given. It was between five and ten hundred yards we were firing. We fixed bayonets and fired about 30 volleys and then we advanced again across the battlefield and [suffered] several wounded.

The fire of the Lincolns, which initially began as independent fire, was highly accurate and quickly inflicted a substantial number of casualties on the Mahdists. Once all of the battalion's companies were in place, the order was given to switch from independent fire to company volleys, the effects of which caused even greater devastation among the ranks of the Green Flag. Volley after volley rippled from the Lincolns, while the fire from the Sudanese once again became intense. Facing a combination of Lee-Metfords, Martini-Henrys, Maxims, and field artillery, the Green Flag warriors gradually began to lose momentum, and their attack then completely stalled. A barrage of artillery shells from other batteries, located behind the left-wing of Kitchener's line, suddenly began bursting through the Mahdists, leaving countless numbers of them dead and wounded on the now heavily blood-soaked ground. However, in a last-ditch but suicidal attempt to reach MacDonald's brigade, a group of around 400 to 500 Baggara horsemen made a dash towards their enemy, but their fate was inevitable; all were shot down without a single one reaching the Sudanese infantry—the nearest warrior getting to just within twenty yards.

Perhaps the final blow to the Mahdist attack, however, came when the three remaining battalions of the 1st British Brigade arrived, including the Camerons, Seaforths and Warwicks. Some 3,000 British infantrymen were now bearing down on the *Ansar* warriors, the latter of who simply broke and abandoned their assault. The attacks of both the Black and Green Flags had been totally defeated, and the battle was all but over. MacDonald now ordered his men to advance, chasing the fleeing *Ansar* back towards the Kerreri Hills.

While watching the surviving warriors make off towards Omdurman, a quietly pleased Kitchener turned to his staff and said 'I think we've given them a good dusting, gentlemen!' after which he issued further orders; this time, five brigades were to advance towards the city in line over a broad two-mile front. The firing at last began to greatly slacken and eventually the order to 'cease fire' was given. It was now 11.30 a.m., and Kitchener had decisively won the Battle of Omdurman and broken the *Khalifa*'s army.

Steevens, who had watched the closing moments of the battle, later recorded what he witnessed:

The avenging squadrons of the Egyptian cavalry swept over the field. The *Khalifa* and the *Sheikh*-ed-Din had galloped back to Omdurman. Ali Wad Helu was borne away on an angareb with a bullet through his thigh-bone. Yakub lay dead under his brother's banner. From the green army [Green Flag] there now came only death-enamoured desperadoes, strolling one by one towards the rifles, pausing to shake a spear, turning aside to recognise a corpse, then, caught by a sudden jet of fury, bounding forward, checking, sinking limply to the ground. Now under the black flag in a ring of bodies stood only three men, facing the three thousand of the Third Brigade. They folded their arms about the staff and gazed steadily forward. Two fell. The last dervish stood up and filled his chest; he shouted the name of his God and hurled his spear. Then he stood quite still, waiting. It took him full; he quivered, gave at the knees, and toppled with his head on his arms and his face towards the legions of his conquerors.

Lieutenant Pritchard described the scene now in front of his own eyes:

> The *Khalifa*'s body-guard had died to a man round his black flag, the last man standing by it continuing to fire on our battalions till he fell. The ground for yards round the flag was piled with corpses, and the flag was guarded only by dead men when our men reached it. Major Hickman, commanding the Fifteenth Battalion, pulled it up, and sent it to the *Sirdar*. Slatin *Pasha* rode up and inquired from a wounded Dervish near the flag whether the *Khalifa* was killed. The man replied that the *Khalifa* had been protected by a hole being dug for him in the ground, and he had only been gone ten minutes before, having mounted on a fast camel.

The death toll for the Battle of Omdurman amounted to two British officers and twenty-three men killed, and ten officers and 133 men wounded. It would be the 21st Lancers who suffered the most in terms of the British regiments, with one officer and twenty men killed, and four officers and forty-six men wounded. Of the infantry, the Cameron Highlanders suffered the most, losing two men killed, and two officers and twenty-seven men wounded. The Egyptian and Sudanese regiments lost two officers and eighteen men killed, with a further eight officers and 273 men wounded. In total, Kitchener's losses amounted to four officers and forty-one men killed, with a further eighteen officers and 406 men wounded.

Casualties among the soldiers were not the only British losses of 2 September, with a number of war correspondents also being killed. These included: The Honourable Hubert Howard of *The Times* and *The New York Herald*, who was killed near the gate to the *Mahdi*'s tomb (see next chapter); Colonel Frank Rhodes, also of *The Times* was wounded by a bullet that tore through the flesh of his right-shoulder during the early part of the battle; Mr Williams of the *Daily Chronicle* received a minor wound to his cheek from either a spent bullet or a chip of stone that was the result of a ricochet; and finally, although not as a direct result of the battle, Mr Cross of *The Manchester Guardian* contracted enteric fever at Abeidieh and died shortly after Kitchener's victory.

Mahdist casualties were estimated to have included 10,800 killed (this figure was based on a body count conducted the day after the battle) and 15,000 wounded, while a further 5,000 were taken prisoner. Total *Ansar* casualties, thus, amounted to a staggering 38,800. These figures, however, need to be treated with a degree of caution, since the estimate for the wounded would have been a particularly difficult one for the British to determine, with many of the wounded warriors having made off from the battlefield during their retreat to Omdurman. Whatever the true figure, it would almost certainly have run into the tens of thousands. Also, of those wounded it is without doubt that many more later died of their injuries in the hours, days and weeks following the battle; the total number of which can never be known for sure. The difference in casualty numbers between the two armies is a stark one, although perhaps not unexpected due to the differences in levels of firepower (A further breakdown of the casualty statistics can be seen in Appendix C).

A total of 444,000 Lee-Metford and Martin-Henry rifle rounds had been expended by the Anglo-Egyptian force, with a further 67,000 rounds fired by the Maxims. The artillery also fired around 3,500 shells during the course of the battle. The total amount of ammunition fired by the Mahdist riflemen, of course, remains unknown.

Captain Haig was critical of Kitchener's tactics following the order to advance from the *zariba*. The future field marshal argued that the *Sirdar*'s only plan was to defeat the Mahdists by engaging them from the *zariba*, and once the force moved out of camp he seemed to have 'no plan, or tactical idea, for beating the enemy'. Haig also argued that Kitchener should have thrown his left-flank forward to *Jebel* Surgham, while drawing in his right-flank in order to gradually extend his left southwards, which, he believed, would have cut off the *Ansar* and prevented the warriors retiring towards Omdurman. To the captain, it appeared that Kitchener had recklessly exposed one of his brigades to the enemy, while the remaining five were in no position to properly support it. To him, it also seemed fortunate that 'the flower of the dervish army exhausted itself first in an attack and pursuit of the cavalry'. Haig, of course, was writing sometime after the event, but he may have had a point, although, as it turned out, Kitchener was ultimately victorious. However, it should be remembered that MacDonald was supposed to stay within supporting distance of the other brigades, but, due to the terrain, the brigades drifted off course and the gap increased. The lack of training of the non-British brigades has also been cited as a factor in the increasing distance, since the Egyptian and Sudanese troops were not as well drilled as their British counterparts.

There was also a problem of rivalry and competition between the two British brigades, a result of 2nd Brigade having been given orders to lead the advance, something the officers and men of 1st Brigade did not like at all. Both wanted to be in Omdurman first, so both began what can only be described as a race between them. It is, perhaps obviously, no wonder the advance of the British brigades then failed to be conducted in the orderly manner in which they ought to have done.

The real problem, however, was that the 2nd and 3rd Egyptian Brigades struggled to keep up with the British, which in turn resulted in MacDonald's brigade becoming increasingly isolated out to the west. Nevertheless, the Anglo-Egyptian army had advanced with such enthusiasm and jubilation to finally arrive at the city that many officers failed to understand the potentially disastrous situation that MacDonald would have to deal with later.

In his book *Karari*, Sudanese historian 'Ismat Hasan Zulfo makes the following comment regarding the *Ansar*'s failure at the Battle of Omdurman:

> The nub of the problem was generalship. All the outstanding commanders of the *Mahdiy*a were absent from the field on 2 September. Wad al Nujumi had been killed on a suicidal mission. Abu 'Anja was dead, as was Al Zaki. Al Nur Anqara was far away in al Qadarif. The commanders of 2 September were quite different. Ibrahim al Khalil, for all his intelligence and maturity on strategic matters, had not had the experience of facing Hicks or Graham or Gordon.

It is certainly true that the leadership of the Mahdist army was not what is once was. The *Khalifa* simply did not have the qualities of his predecessor, the *Mahdi*. Despite their superior numbers, it is hard to see how the *Ansar* could have inflicted a major defeat on Kitchener's Anglo-Egyptian army, which was well-trained, highly-disciplined, and supported by machine guns and artillery as well as a flotilla of gunboats—a far-cry from the forces commanded by Hicks or Gordon. As mentioned in earlier chapters, the Egyptian troops were of a far higher quality than those previously sent to face the Mahdists during the previous decade prior to the Battle of Omdurman. Even the Sudanese troops, who Wingate described as 'almost savages' and observed that they 'require greater control', more than proved their worth in action. The British troops, of course, could always be relied upon to remain steady in battle. It is, therefore, hard to see how the ultimate outcome could have been any different, even if the *Mahdi* himself had still been alive to command the *Ansar* on the day of the battle.

A major error on the part of the commanders of the *Ansar* in the final phases of the battle had been the gap between the attack of the Black Flag and that of the Green Flag. Indeed, both were meant to have been conducted simultaneously, but there was a thirty-minute delay between the commencement of the two. This, of course, allowed the Black Flag to be defeated before attention was turned to confronting the Green Flag. What should have been a single attack in the form of a pincer movement actually became two completely separate attacks, thus giving MacDonald the opportunity to defeat each in turn. Had the plan been executed as intended, MacDonald's brigade may not have been able to withstand the assault; while this would not have won the battle for the *Khalifa*, it would have inflicted terrible losses on Kitchener's army.

The weaponry of the *Ansar* was also a major factor in its defeat, since the vast majority of it was old and obsolete. Putting aside the obvious mismatch between the modern firearms of the Anglo-Egyptian army and the swords and spears of the Mahdists, the thousands of Remington rifles in the possession of the latter were also very much outdated by the 1890s. Never during the *Khalifa*'s reign did he attempt to acquire new, more modern firearms to replace those taken off the bodies of dead Egyptian troops years earlier. Similarly, no attempt was made to modernise the artillery arm of the *Ansar*, the majority of guns of which never made it to the battlefield anyway. If Abdullahi al-Taishi's warriors had been in possession of better rifles and received training in their proper use, the Mahdists would undoubtedly have inflicted far more casualties on Kitchener's army than they did, which may have changed the course of the battle. However, it should be recognised that even if the *Khalifa* had tried to update his armouries, it is highly unlikely he would have been able to obtain modern weapons in any substantial numbers, since the Mahdist state of Sudan was somewhat remote and cut off from much of the outside world. Either way, with the weapons the warriors had at their disposal there was little hope of holding up to the devastating firepower of the British and Egyptian troops.

Other criticisms that have been levelled at Abdullahi al-Taishi include his choice of tactics. Long before he faced Kitchener at Egeiga, he had shown little of the military skills of his predecessor. In particular, his victories in Abyssinia had only been achieved at an incredibly high cost in the lives of his men, while the decision to invade Egypt in 1889 was almost certainly doomed to failure before it even began; the latter seeing the loss of Abd ar Rahman an Nujumi, who had been an able senior Mahdist commander. He also failed to make any attempt to attack Kitchener's lines of communication and supply, leaving the *Sirdar* free to supply his advancing army without any interference. Finally, Abdullahi al-Taishi's decision to conduct a frontal assault of the Anglo-Egyptian army entrenched within a *zariba* in broad daylight must have been seen as a major mistake by many of his senior commanders, since it played into Kitchener's hands and offered the latter an advantage over the former due to the disparity of the weaponry used by the two opposing sides. It could be argued that the *Khalifa* would have been better to have drawn his enemy further into Sudan and attacked him on more advantageous ground, a tactic the *Mahdi* would no doubt of employed. Whether Abdullahi al-Taishi could have achieved victory in such a way is still probably unlikely, but he may have at least greatly reduced the number of casualties suffered by his army, while at the same time increasing those inflicted upon his enemy. Of course, such an analysis as the above is made with the benefit of hindsight, and it is easy to criticise from the safe distance of over a century.

Although Kitchener could now claim victory over the main Mahdist army on the field, the city of Omdurman still needed to be taken, and the *Khalifa* had not yet been apprehended or killed. There was still much dangerous work to be done.

13

The Fall of Omdurman

Abdullahi al-Taishi had lost the Battle of Omdurman; the *Ansar* was broken, and its surviving warriors were fleeing from the field in their thousands, leaving behind thousands more of their dead and dying comrades. Most headed for the city in the hope of finding refuge, including the *Khalifa*, who, upon reaching it, immediately set about making preparations for its defence. However, he ensured an escape route was planned in the likely event of the loss of the city. For the men of the Anglo-Egyptian army, who were now advancing to seize their ultimate prize and put the final touches to their avenging of the death of Gordon, the fighting did not seem quite over yet, a fact welcomed by many of its officers who still sought glory before the day was out.

Unfortunately for the *Khalifa*, many of his warriors had little interest in continuing any resistance against the *Sirdar* and his army. Indeed, while the latter phases of the battle had raged, the remaining men of the 21st Lancers, including Lieutenant Churchill, had advanced in the direction of the city, encountering what seemed to be endless streams of Mahdists who had been wounded—many were in fact only pretending to be wounded—and now seeking the safety of Omdurman. The British cavalrymen grew increasingly near to these straggling warriors, but, before any thoughts of engaging them could be had, they watched in bemusement as many of the Mahdists simply threw their weapons down onto the ground in what appeared to be a desperate attempt to show their adversaries that they no longer wished to fight. Others threw up their hands as a gesture of surrender, while others still pleaded for mercy and for their lives to be spared. It would not take long for the men of the 21st to realise that they had, perhaps, already played their part in the day's fighting. The warriors were surrendering in large numbers; as these were accepted, the number of Mahdists offering themselves as prisoners increased at an ever growing pace.

Not all, of course, wished to become prisoners, and another uninterrupted stream of warriors could be seen giving the cavalrymen a wide berth in a bid to escape capture before continuing their flight to wherever they were going.

The men of the 21st were inevitably delayed as they disarmed the surrendering warriors, greatly slowing their advance to the city. The capacity for the lancers to take prisoners, of course, was small and many thousands of Mahdists in fact escaped capture whether they intended to or not; the presence of the mounted British troops did prevent many of the *Khalifa*'s men from reaching the city, since they effectively blocked the route. As a result, far fewer warriors arrived back at Omdurman than Abdullahi al-Taishi had hoped; thousands had simply ignored his orders to return to the city for its defence, most making off to the south and deeper into Sudan.

The men of the 21st did, however, make an attempt to attack the stream of warriors who were trying to avoid them by opening fire with their carbines. This fire was kept up for some time, but it did not appear to do much to discourage the relentless lines of Mahdists scurrying off in the distance. Unfortunately for Martin, he simply did not have enough men to stop them, especially following the almost disastrous charge earlier that had seen so many lancers and their horses either killed or wounded. Well-aimed carbine fire was now all that could be offered to harass the enemy. Churchill later estimated that 20,000 Mahdists escaped; although there is no way to verify this figure today, it is almost certain the number was indeed in the thousands.

Meanwhile, the attacks of the Black and Green Flags on MacDonald's brigade had by this time been defeated, and Kitchener had given orders for his army to reform and resume its advance on the city. The lancers soon saw their comrades come marching over the hills of sand near *Jebel* Surgham and begin pouring onto the plains that lay between the mountain and the city. Above the brigade in the centre, the *Khalifa*'s Black Flag could be seen proudly displayed aloft as a trophy by the men who had captured it. For the battle weary men of the 21st, it was quite a sight to behold.

At midday, orders were sent to the cavalrymen to rejoin with the main body of the army. The order to cease fire was also given, and the men remounted to ride the three miles that separated them from the infantry. The day was now approaching its hottest hour, and the men were exhausted from their ordeal of combat and the march to the city. Both men and animal alike were in great need of food and water, it was time for some respite; a halt, therefore, was ordered at *Khor* Shambat so the men could get some rest. Within a short time of this pause being ordered, thousands of khaki-clad British troops could be seen drinking water from the Nile and refilling their canteens, while thousands more sat resting on the surrounding hot sands. The Egyptian and Sudanese troops did the same, while the horses and other animals were led down to the river to quench their thirst also. To Churchill, the 'scene was striking'.

Elsewhere, Broadwood's Egyptian cavalry had advanced in pursuit of the fleeing *Ansar*. During the attacks on MacDonald's brigade, they had watched from the southern slopes of the Kerreri Hills; after it became obvious the *Khalifa*'s final attacks had failed, the lieutenant-colonel ordered his cavalrymen to form two lines—the first of four squadrons and the second of five squadrons—to make ready to give chase. The subsequent pursuit had taken them towards the west for two miles before changing course towards the south-west for a further three miles, reaching a place known as Round-top Hill. During this time, the Egyptian cavalry had also begun disarming and taking an increasing number of warriors prisoner. These then had to be escorted back towards the main Anglo-Egyptian force near the river to be guarded by the infantry.

Unlike the 21st Lancers, however, the Egyptian cavalry would encounter small, isolated pockets of resistance, some of it determined and particularly deadly. As after the attack on the *zariba*, a number of Mahdists lay on the ground pretending to be dead, springing up with spear in hand as an Egyptian cavalryman rode by unsuspectingly. Other warriors simply charged head-on at the mounted soldiers, in what can only be described as a suicidal and futile gesture of defiance. Others still used what available cover there was in order to avoid being lanced, hiding in bushes out of reach and firing wildly at Broadwood's men. Little groups of warriors also formed spontaneously in an attempt to make a final stand, possibly believing that certain death merely awaited them anyway if they surrendered.

These acts of resistance, however suicidal they might have been for the Mahdists, also inflicted a number of casualties on the Egyptian cavalry. The further the cavalry advanced in pursuit, the further the number of wounded increased until such a point that it was deemed wise to abandon the chase. Major Philip Walter Jules Le Gallais, however, decided he would make one last attempt at cutting off a group of retreating warriors before withdrawing. Leading three squadrons towards the Nile and in parallel to *Khor* Shambat, the cavalrymen broke into a gallop and conducted a charge at the tail end of a stream of fleeing Mahdists. These warriors, seeing the cavalrymen bearing down on them at high speed, bravely held their ground and opened a fire on the Egyptians, killing and wounding a number of the cavalrymen and their horses. The fire of the Mahdists was so devastating that Le Gallais almost immediately ordered his men to break off the attack and retire back towards *Jebel* Surgham. It had been a fruitless charge that had only resulted in the meaningless loss of life among the Egyptian troops. Broadwood again issued orders for his men to re-join the Anglo-Egyptian army resting near the river, and all attempts at pursuing or harassing the retreating *Ansar* were finally abandoned.

The cavalry now rested and watered their horses until, at 4 p.m., they received instructions to ride around the outskirts of the city of Omdurman in order to prevent anyone from attempting to leave it. Once in position, the British and Egyptian cavalry were able to complete a full-encirclement of the city, while keeping at least a mile distance between them and the nearest houses or buildings of Omdurman's suburbs. Other orders to the infantry had been given earlier, at about 2.30 p.m.; these infantrymen included those of Maxwell's 2nd Egyptian

Brigade, which was formed into line of company columns and marched out of *Khor* Shambat. The brigades's formation included: the 14th and 12th Sudanese on the left, the Maxim guns and 8th Egyptians in the centre, and the 32nd Field Battery and the 13th Sudanese on the right.

As the infantry slowly advanced into the city, Kitchener and his staff rode forward in front of the 14th Sudanese, while the band of the 11th Sudanese followed behind with the captured Black Flag. Despite the numerous mud-built houses and other buildings of the city, Maxwell's brigade was able to keep in formation along a broad front, while the remainder of the Anglo-Egyptian army followed on behind. Soon, the streets of Omdurman's suburbs were crammed full with British, Egyptian, and Sudanese troops, all steadily pushing forwards to the old city walls, where they expected to finally come face-to-face once again with the warriors of the *Ansar* now defending Omdurman.

After advancing towards the middle of the city for about two miles, Kitchener and his staff came to the great wall that protected its centre. Moments later, a number of shots suddenly rang out from the wall in front of them, where an estimated 200 Mahdists warriors could be seen making a somewhat half-hearted attempt at a defence. However, their fire was poorly aimed and proved totally ineffective in its intention. The Maxim guns were ordered into action; after only fifteen minutes, the defenders were driven off and all resistance came to end. Several guns of the 32nd Field Battery were then instructed to move forward to prevent the return of the warriors on the wall, while the *Sirdar*, in company with the remaining guns of the battery and the 14th Sudanese, rode around the wall to the east in hope of finding a suitable entrance into the centre of the city.

Although a breach in the wall had been made previously by the gunboats, it was found to have been barricaded; somewhat incredibly, the main gate was seen to be wide-open and undefended. Kitchener, along with his escort, entered through this gate; what awaited them were terrible scenes of suffering and destruction. Men, women, and children alike were seen strewn across the city: many dead; others horrendously injured; with most of it the result of the earlier bombardment of the gunboats. Numerous warriors of the *Ansar* were encountered, again most already dead or near death, and those that had already perished were fast decomposing in the heat, further adding to the horrors now before the eyes of the *Sirdar* and his men. Nor was it just humans who had suffered; large numbers of animals of various descriptions were likewise encountered lying dead or wounded on the ground, with rotting corpses seemingly everywhere. According to Churchill, the air was filled with a 'sickening smell' that few would ever forget.

In an attempt to win the trust of the ordinary people of Omdurman, Kitchener had sent forward a number of men acting as interpreters, who reassured the residents that the *Sirdar* and his army had come as liberators, and that mercy would be shown to all who laid down their weapons and offered no resistance. As these interpreters tentatively made their way around the city, increasing numbers of local armed men appeared and began throwing down their weapons, and soon mass piles of arms of all descriptions littered the ground. Not all, however, would surrender so easily, and the Egyptian and Sudanese troops frequently had to use force to disarm resistant warriors, or even open fire on them using Maxim guns; many were shot or bayonetted, but most, however, eventually agreed to surrender when faced with such overwhelming force. The disarming operation would continue for some time, and, while this process went on, the *Sirdar* pushed on deeper into the city on his way to find the tomb of Muhammad Ahmed. While *en route*, an attempt was made against Kitchener by several warriors who had refused to surrender, but both were gunned down by the escorting Sudanese soldiers or bayonetted. The Mahdists did, however, manage to kill or wound several of the *Sirdar*'s escort, reminding all that the number of casualties of the campaign had the potential to increase further still.

The first building of interest that Kitchener came to was Abdullahi al-Taishi's house, a structure surrounded by a defensive wall and a number of other smaller buildings of various functions. The *Sirdar* and his staff pulled up their horses in front of the main doorway: to their right, they could see some sheds with corrugated iron roofs and what appeared to be a praying square directly in front of them. Behind the house was the unmistakable image of the *Mahdi*'s tomb, with its dome towering above. Other buildings occupied by the authorities of the Mahdist state were close by; the *Khalifa* had chosen his residence well, being near almost everything of importance. After taking in the scene before them for a few moments, both Maxwell and Slatin dismounted and entered the house in the hope of finding Abdullahi al-Taishi. Their search of the house proved a fruitless one, for the *Khalifa* had already quietly made his escape through a rear exit, taking his personal treasures and servants with him.

By now, the light had begun to fade, and a near disaster almost struck the party of officers and war correspondents gathered around the *Khalifa*'s house. Hubert Howard, reporting on the campaign for both *The Times* and the *New York Herald*, attempted to take a photograph of the building, but as he set up his camera, there was a sudden and horrendous explosion that was accompanied by the clatter of pieces of shrapnel hitting the iron roofs and walls of the buildings. Miraculously, no one appeared hurt, but it was obvious to the British officers, if not the correspondents, that the fire had come from one of their own guns and not the *Ansar*. Fearing a second shell would land at any moment, several gallopers were immediately despatched to find the officer in charge of the guns of the 32nd Battery—several of which had been positioned on the west side of the wall to cover the main thoroughfare through the city—and order him to cease firing at once.

Similar orders to ceasefire on the *Khalifa*'s house were transmitted to the gunboats. A second shell, however, had whistled overhead, again seemingly fired at the residence, but it later became known that it was likely aimed at a group of Mahdist warriors who had been seen by members of Kitchener's escort gathering near Abdullahi al-Taishi's compound to the south-west. Maxim fire was also heard, which was being directed at another group of warriors who, it was later learned, were covering the retreat of the *Khalifa* as he slipped out of the city. Despite the mass surrenders of Mahdist warriors, Omdurman was still a very dangerous place to be.

Kitchener and his staff now moved on, riding back towards the main thoroughfare. Several more shells whistled overhead, then, as if from out of nowhere, Howard was struck in the head by what was either a bullet or other shell fragment and instantly killed. Soldiers from Maxwell's brigade were ordered to cover his body; he would not be the last casualty that day. Attention now turned to apprehending the *Khalifa*; a pursuit was immediately ordered since it was believed he had not long begun his flight from the city and would still likely be found nearby. Slatin galloped out of Omdurman to deliver the news to the waiting army outside, and almost at once, Broadwood's Egyptian cavalrymen poured out of camp in hope of quickly finding their prey. As it would turn out, Abdullahi al-Taishi would not be caught up with for over a year to come, and it would not be the *Sirdar* who dealt the final blow.

The *Mahdi*'s tomb was examined next. The building was found to be about thirty-six square feet and attached to a mosque. Inside lay a wooden sarcophagus within which the remains of Muhammad Ahmed had been laid to rest. Above the building was an impressive dome that reached up about seventy feet high. The whole building, however, was found to be greatly damaged by the lyddite shells that had rained down on it earlier from the gunboats and other shells from the howitzer batteries; what was once an impressive building was now nothing more than an impressive mess.

Eventually, Kitchener and his escort reached the prison of Omdurman, where over thirty prisoners were set free. Among them was Charles Neufeld, a German merchant who had been taken prisoner by the Mahdists some twelve years earlier while transporting a consignment of rifles to the friendly Kabbabish tribe on behalf of the Egyptian authorities. For much of this period, he had remained in prison in a similar fashion to Slatin and Ohrwalder, but without the luxury of escape. Bennet Burleigh, now present in the city with Kitchener and his escort, recalled the plight of the prisoners:

> All of them wore heavy leg chains, and a few were handcuffed besides. The principal jail deliveries were by disease and the gallows; the latter were in almost daily use. Three rough sets of them stood together near the great wall. Limbs of trees stuck into the ground, with a cross-piece overhead, which was how the gallows were fashioned. A last victim of the *Khalifa* was cut down shortly after the troops entered Omdurman.
>
> Neufeld was found under a mat-covered lean-to built against the mud-wall. There was no other protection for the prisoners from the sunshine or rain than

coarse worn matting spread upon sticks and laid against the walls. The enclosure was without any sanitary arrangements whatever. A well had been dug near the middle of the yard and from there the prisoners drew all the water they used.

Neufeld, in his book *A Prisoner of the Khaleefa: Twelve Years Captivity at Omdurman*, also recalled the moment he was freed:

> Idris [Neufeld's jailer], in his anxiety to secure his prisoners, had us all chained in gangs earlier than usual, and this linking of my gang to the common chain had only just been completed when Idris came, frightened out of his life, as one could tell by his voice, to tell me that the 'place was filled with my English brothers,' that a big, tall man, who, he was told, was the dreaded *Sirdar*, had asked for me, and that I was to come at once.
>
> It seemed an age while the chain was being slipped from my shackles, and then, led by Idris, I made my way to the gate of the Saier. I was crying dry eyed; I could see a blurred group, and then I was startled out of my senses by hearing English spoken—the only words of a European language I had heard for seven long years. From that blurred group, and through the gloom, came a voice, 'Are you Neufeld? Are you well?' And then a tall figure stepped towards me, and gave my hand a hearty shake. It was the *Sirdar*. I believed I babbled something as I received the handshake from one, and a slap on the shoulder from another, but I do not know what I said. Looking down at my shackles, the *Sirdar* asked, 'Can these be taken off now?—I am going on.'

By this time, Idris had long disappeared and attempts to find him in order to have Neufeld's chains removed failed. Darkness was now beginning to fall, and so the liberated merchant was put on the back of an officer's horse and ridden out of the city to the camp now occupied by the bulk of the Anglo-Egyptian army outside Omdurman to the north. The shackles still attached to Neufeld consisted of three sets of leg irons, which were fastened around his ankles. Attached to these was an iron bar, said to be around fourteen pounds in weight, and several thick chains. Further attempts to remove the restraints again proved futile, and so the next day he was sent aboard the gunboat *Sheik*, where a vice and chisel were used to finally remove them.

Other prisoners freed from their years of captivity included a number of Europeans, such as Joseph Ragnotti, Sister Teresa Grigolini and thirty Greek citizens; all no doubt feeling extremely relieved to finally regain their freedom. Sister Grigolini, an Italian missionary, had been taken prisoner in 1883 at El Obeid, where she had been the lady superior at the local convent. While a prisoner at Omdurman, she had married a Greek gentleman by the name of Dimitri Cocorempas, the couple later having a son called Joseph while still in captivity.

The city's main arsenal was also located, in which large stocks of locally-made rifle ammunition and thousands of weapons of varying descriptions were found, including: spears, swords, rifles, and flint-lock muskets, as well as banners, flags, drums, riding equipment for camels, and a whole host of other military related items and supplies. Incredibly, some sixty cannons were also discovered, showing that that *Ansar* did have a considerable artillery arm. Curiously, these had not been used at the Battle of Omdurman, although, perhaps, their numerous and obsolete types may have made them difficult to bring into action. Much of these weapons and supplies were instantly recognised as being once owned by the Egyptian Army, having being seized as war booty years before.

While Kitchener and his staff investigated the city, Abdullahi al-Taishi was continuing his flight on the back of his little donkey, in company with his favourite wife, a number of personal servants and a Greek nun, the latter of who was being held as a hostage. Before leaving the city—according to an account left by an Abyssinian servant boy, which must be treated with a degree of caution—the *Khalifa* had calmly eaten some food before visiting the *Mahdi*'s tomb in order to make prayers one last time. It was, according to this account, at about 4 p.m. when news first reached him that Kitchener had entered the city, after which he quickly made his preparations to leave and began his journey southwards, deeper into Sudan.

His initial flight was said to have been a leisurely one, and when the *Khalifa* had travelled a distance of some eight miles, he was met by a group of camels. Mounting these faster animals, the Mahdist leader soon caught up with what was left of his defeated army, who, despite the fact Abdullahi al-Taishi had led them to disaster, bid him a warm welcome and escorted him in his continued retreat. Among these fugitives were Osman Digna and Osman al-Din (in Churchill's account, he also lists Ibrahim al-Khalil as one of the fugitives, but he had in fact been killed during the Battle of Omdurman). How many of the *Khalifa*'s men now accompanied him is not clear; Churchill puts the figure at around 30,000, which, given the number of casualties and the fact many fled the battlefield in various directions, seems somewhat high. Whatever the true number, it was almost certainly in the thousands and still presented a formidable, albeit greatly demoralised, force.

Broadwood and his Egyptian cavalry were following the *Khalifa*, but both the men and horses were now almost exhausted after their considerable exertions during the battle. This fact may help explain why they were unable to catch up with the *Khalifa* on his slow-moving donkey prior to reaching the waiting camels; however, the time they set off in pursuit may have been the overriding factor in their failure to capture their prey. Another issue facing Broadwood was that he did not know the terrain that lay ahead, a problem exacerbated by the fact the pursuit was taking place in the dark. Indeed, the ground was found to be swampy in many places, greatly slowing the advance when horses got stuck in the wet sand, following which an impassable *khor* was encountered, where a number of horses fell and injured their riders. At 10 p.m., the colonel decided it was too difficult and dangerous to continue the pursuit, and ordered his men to rest for the night. During the night, the sound of cracking rifle fire and the occasional artillery shell could be heard in the distance, betraying the fact that the city of Omdurman was still not yet fully under the *Sirdar*'s control. A steamer had been ordered up the Nile to take supplies to Broadwood, which he was to rendezvous with the following day.

The pursuit was resumed at 3 a.m. on the 3rd, the bright moon now lighting the way ahead; at 7 a.m., the cavalrymen reached the agreed location to meet with the steamer. As Broadwood's men approached, they could see the vessel had arrived before them, but it soon became apparent, to the horror of the Egyptians, that a 300-yard-wide swamp lay between them and the steamer, making it impossible to receive the much-needed supplies. There was no other choice but to continue the pursuit along the river, with the steamer sailing along in the hope of finding a better place to unload. After advancing a further seven miles it was becoming obvious to all that the impassable gulf between the cavalry and the vessel was showing no signs of giving way, and without food the pursuit could simply not be continued. Reluctantly, the colonel ordered his men to halt and rest during the hottest part of the day, after which they remounted and began to make their way back to the main Anglo-Egyptian force. The capture of the *Khalifa* would have to wait for another day.

The Egyptian cavalry, however, were not the only ones attempting to find and apprehend the Mahdist leader. A force of 750 friendly tribesmen under the command of Abdel-Azim had also set off in pursuit, and had managed to cover a much greater distance than Broadwood. The tribesmen, of course, knew the lay of the land and they were less encumbered than their Egyptian counterparts, rendering them faster while avoiding impassable obstacles. On the 7th, Abdel-Azim reached a place called Shegeig, located about 100 miles south of Khartoum, where he came by information that the *Khalifa* was heading for El Obeid, protected by a powerful bodyguard, and well-supplied for his journey. El Obeid was still garrisoned by a Mahdist force of over 3,000, and Abdullahi al-Taishi was obviously hoping to seek sanctuary at the town. Faced with such overwhelming numbers, Abdel-Azim now abandoned his own pursuit and started back for Omdurman in order to deliver this information to the *Sirdar*.

In the immediate aftermath of the Battle of Omdurman and the subsequent capture of the city, Kitchener was accused of brutality and even war crimes. Such charges lay in the fact that he allegedly ordered all wounded Mahdist warriors laying on the ground to be put to death at the point of the bayonet. This, of course, likely refers to the numerous incidents where warriors would act as if dead only to suddenly spring up and attack an unsuspecting soldier who was passing by. However, further allegations were also made that some Egyptian and Sudanese troops went on a looting rampage after the fall of the city, during which unarmed men, women, and children were attacked and similarly put to death in cold blood without interference from their officers. Even the gunboats were accused of killing fleeing fugitives by the use of Maxims and artillery as they sailed down the Nile.

Such claims first appeared in Ernest Bennett's article *After Omdurman*, published in *The Contemporary Review* in January 1899. The article itself goes into depth regarding the Geneva Convention, and in particular Article VI of the convention which states: 'Wounded or sick soldiers shall be brought in and cared for to whatever nation they belong'. In regards to this, Bennett, who was present with Kitchener's force during the reconquest of Sudan, makes the following observations and points in his article:

> Immediately after the repulse of the first Dervish attack at Omdurman our troops advanced in echelon towards Omdurman, and as I marched with Colonel Lewis' Native Brigade on the right we soon came across dead and wounded Dervishes. On our left along the lower slopes of Gebel Surgham a large number of camp-followers and native servants were already busy amongst the white-clad figures which lay stretched in little groups as our shell fire or the long-range volleys of the Lee-Metfords had struck them down. These looters had armed themselves somehow or other with rifles, spears, and even clubs, and made short work of any wounded man they came across. Poor wretches who in their agony had crawled under the scanty shade of a rock or shrub were clubbed to death or riddled with bullets by the irresponsible brutality of these native servants, who were in wholesome dread of a Dervish, even when prostrate, that they frequently fired several shots into bodies already dead before they advanced to strip the corpse of its *gibbeh* or arms ... It is simply scandalous that unauthorised camp-followers should have thus allowed to loot and massacre under the very eyes of a British general.

Bennett also observed that similar acts were carried out by the fighting men:

> This wholesale slaughter was not confined to Arab servants. It was stated that orders had been given to kill the wounded. Whether this was so or not I do not know, but certainly no protest was made when Soudanese despatched scores of wounded men who lay in their path. The Dervishes who were stretched on the sand within a few yards were bayoneted, or, in some instances, stabbed with their own spears.

Even the British soldiers came under criticism from Bennett:

> At one place, on the western slopes of Surgham, I noticed a fine old Dervish with a grey beard, who, disabled by a wound in his leg, lay prostrate beside a small bush. He had apparently attempted to escape towards Omdurman with the rest of the *Khalifa*'s forces who survived, but his wound had prevented this, and the fugitive had sunk down on the ground about eight yards behind his son, a boy of

seventeen, whose right leg had also been lacerated by a bullet. Neither the father nor the son *had any weapons at all* [Bennett's italics], yet a Highlander stepped out of the ranks and drove his bayonet through the old man's chest. The victim of this needless brutality begged in vain for mercy, and clutched the soldier's bayonet, reddening his hands with his own blood in a futile attempt to prevent a second thrust. No effort was made by any comrade or officer to prevent this gratuitous bit of butchery, nor, of course, could any officer have interfered very well, if the soldier—as was said to be the case—was only acting in accordance with the wishes of the general in command.

There are few, if any, wars in history where excesses and atrocities are not committed by either side during the conflict, but it is worth questioning whether the *Sirdar* was guilty of ordering such actions. Kitchener, naturally, strenuously denied giving any such orders, and a later inquiry found the claims to be 'grossly exaggerated'. Bennett's article caused a storm and provoked much anger from many quarters. Indeed, Captain Adolf von Tiedemann, a member of the Royal Prussian General Staff who was with the *Sirdar* throughout the battle and subsequent capture of the city, wrote the following in reply to the claims at the time:

> As regards the conduct of Lord Kitchener, I rode on the day of the battle from the beginning to end—i.e., from 3.30 a.m. till 9 p.m.—with very short interruptions, in his immediate vicinity, and heard and saw everything ordered or done by him. It would be an insult to Lord Kitchener if I attempted to contradict the insinuations made against him personally; such evident calumnies would never be given credence to for a moment in the mind of any intelligent man possessed of common sense. If the *Sirdar* had been so bloodthirsty as the writer of the article [*After Omdurman* by Ernest Bennett] in question wishes us to believe, he would have found opportunities enough at every step during his entry into Omdurman to gratify his desires, for, after the *Khalifa* had fled from the town, crowds of unarmed Dervishes rushed towards him, and it would have been easy enough for his escort to have cut them down. Lord Kitchener received them with kindness, and, as everyone on his staff can testify, he did all in his power to put a stop to the street fighting which broke out here and there in the town.

Tiedeman went on to defend the decision to kill wounded Mahdist warriors on the battlefield:

> As regards the killing of the wounded on the battlefield, that was a necessary measure which was as regrettable as it was indispensable. After the first attack of the Dervishes had been repulsed, and when the Anglo-Egyptian army was moving off by brigades to its left towards Omdurman, I myself left the staff and rode over a great part of the battlefield, but I registered a mental vow never to do

so again. A wounded and apparently defenceless Dervish laying on the ground is much more dangerous than his fellow with a whole skin and arms in his hand rushing against one. One knows perfectly what to expect from the latter, while the apparent helplessness of the former makes one forget the necessary caution and also the fact that a bullet fired by a wounded man makes quite a big hole as one fired by an unhurt person. During my ride over the battlefield I several times saw Dervishes who had been lying on the ground suddenly rise and fire off their rifles into the ranks of the troops marching near them or who had already passed by them, and for these latter is was simply demanded, as a measure of self-preservation, that they should secure themselves against such attacks by a chain of scouts pushed to the front.

Concluding his defence of Kitchener and the Anglo-Egyptian army, Tiedeman noted the following:

One heard of a large number of cases in which not only British, but also black, soldiers received and treated their wounded enemies with great kindness, although at times they had poor reward for it. I myself saw a man of the 32nd Field Battery giving a wounded Dervish a drink out of his water-bottle, holding up his head the while with his hand, and then leaving him a piece of bread, which he took out of his own haversack, on the ground beside him.

It is without doubt that Egyptian, Sudanese, and British soldiers alike very quickly learned of the dangers of coming close to wounded Mahdists warriors or those seemingly dead. It is, therefore, perhaps understandable that Kitchener's troops were unwilling to risk their lives unneccessarily by leaving the wounded untouched, as disagreeable as such an act might now seem today. It should also be remembered that Bennett was a war correspondent, and everyone knew of Kitchener's outright, public dislike of the newspapermen; he had kept them at arms length prior to the 1898 campaign to retake Khartoum, only agreeing to them being close to the action relatively late in the war. On the eve of the Battle of Omdurman, Kitchener was allegedly heard telling a group of correspondents to 'Get out of my way, you drunken swabs'. One might question if Bennett was trying to get back at the *Sirdar* in some way.

That said, it would be extremely naïve to think Kitchener's men did not commit any acts that were in direct violation of the Geneva Convention, and it is highly likely that some officers and NCOs simply ignored the actions of their men. Many had seen what the Mahdist warriors could and would do to their enemies, and feelings of anger and bitterness towards the *Ansar* must have been present among the *Sirdar*'s troops, especially after seeing much-loved friends and comrades killed and wounded. However, Bennett admits he did not directly hear the alledged order to kill given by Kitchener—he only admits to hearing it from a third-party—while Tiedemann is adament that no such order was given.

Other claims have been made that Kitchener gave orders to his men to plunder the grain found in the *Khalifa*'s house, but that the looting got out of hand and extended to much of the city. Again, it would be naïve of us to think no such widespread plundering went on, and it is hard to believe that no civilians were killed while attempting to protect their property from the invaders. However, it is questionable that the *Sirdar* encouraged wholesale looting of Omdurman, rather it is highly likely that a number of soldiers—in an overexcited state—got out of control and acted *bey*ond their orders.

Whatever the truth, this more than a century old debate continues among historians today, especially since Kitchener was such a cold and authoritarian fugure; his later treatment of the Boers and the controversial issue of concentration camps in South Africa are usually also thrown into the mix. The moral debate aside, the *Sirdar* had achieved his goal of defeating the *Ansar* in battle and capturing Omdurman, an achievement for which he was greatly loved by an adoring British public back home, and one that made him a household name to the present time.

On the 4th, Kitchener issued orders for the tomb of Muhammad Ahmad to be destroyed, with the *Mahdi*'s remains disinterred and dumped into the Nile like pieces of unwanted rubbish; this act was probably inspired by the throwing of Gordon's body into the river some sixteen years earlier, and was performed by none other than the deceased general's nephew. Muhammad Ahmed's skull, however, remained in the *Sirdar*'s possession a little longer; it was said that Kitchener considered keeping it as an ashtray, although eventually it was sent to the Royal College of Surgeons in London. This caused a bit of a stir within official circles—even Queen Victoria was said to have objected to the lack of respect shown to the remains of a foreign ruler—and Lord Comer decided the right thing to do was to bury it; the skull was returned and laid to rest in a little unmarked grave in an Islamic cemetery near to Omdurman.

The major-general next visited what remained of Gordon's old residence in Khartoum. It was found to be little more than a ruin, as was the rest of the once prosperous city. It was decided to hold a memorial service for Gordon on the 5th, the ceremony taking place in the ruined residence. Attending were representatives from every battalion and unit comprising the force that had fought at Omdurman, with the soldiers formed up on the bank of the river. During the ceremony, a Union Jack was hoisted above the roof of Gordon's old palace, while the gunboat *Melik* fired a salute and the troops presented arms. Next came the band of the Grenadier Guards, who played the British and Egyptian national anthems, after which the troops gave three cheers for Queen Victoria, then another three for the *Khedive* of Egypt, Abbas Hilmi *Pasha*. One eyewitness recalled seeing Kitchener looking emotional during the service, a rare sight that was unlikely to be seen in public again.

Abdullahi al-Taishi and the *Ansar* had been defeated, and the cities of Khartoum and Omdurman retaken. General Gordon had been avenged, and the reconquest of Sudan was deemed a complete success. The *Khalifa*, of course, still had to be apprehended, but for Kitchener there was now a more pressing matter to be resolved first, in what became known as the Fashoda Incident.

14

The Fashoda Incident

On 7 September 1898, a mere five days after the Battle of Omdurman, unexpected news came into the city from a surprising source. One of Abdullahi al-Taishi's steamers, the *Tewfikeyeh*, which had been in the employ of General Gordon over a decade earlier, appeared on the Nile, seemingly unaware of recent events. As soon as it docked in the city, Kitchener's men boarded the vessel and took the crew prisoner. The captain of the steamer was then interrogated, during which he claimed he had been sent up river to the White Nile by the *Khalifa*, but had to abandon his journey and return to Omdurman after being fired on by what he described as well-armed black men commanded by white officers. As evidence of this claim, the captain then produced a number of bullets that had supposedly been fired at the steamer; they were of a small calibre, nickel plated, and clearly of European, not local, manufacture. Further examination of the vessel showed it was riddled with many more of these well-made bullets. This information was immediately transmitted to Kitchener, who at once realised that other Europeans—most likely members of an expedition of some sort—were now at the town of Fashoda in southern Sudan, itself an old Egyptian military outpost. But who were they and what were they up to?

Gossip among the British officers and men was rife, some believing these Europeans were Belgians from the Congo, while others felt they were Italians, or possibly even French. A few argued they may in fact be British, maybe members of another official or private expedition of some description. Further questions were asked of the crew of the *Tewfikeyeh*, but to the Mahdists, all Europeans looked the same and they were unable to shed any light on the actual nationality of those who had fired on them, much to the annoyance of the intrigued British officers. There were, of course, some who knew exactly who these mysterious Europeans were and why they were at Fashoda, but they were not in a position to say just yet.

The *Sirdar* pondered what to do next, and, in a perhaps unsurprising move, he issued orders for all newspaper war correspondents to leave the city and embark on their return journey to Cairo; if something was afoot in southern

Sudan, Kitchener did not want these journalists knowing about it. With the newspapermen out of the way, he left the city on the 10th aboard the mail steamer *Dal*, with the steamers *Fateh*, *Nasr*, *Sultan*, and *Tewfikeyeh* following behind, each towing a barge carrying supplies and men; the *Abu Klea* was to follow later. Aboard these vessels was an Egyptian field battery, a company of the Cameron Highlanders, and the 11th and 13th Sudanese Battalions. The *Sirdar*'s intention, of course, was to ascertain for himself exactly who these mysterious Europeans were, or rather confirm his own suspicions.

After sailing 310 miles south from Khartoum, the little flotilla of steamers came to a place called Renkh, where they found the steamer *Safieh*—another vessel from the time of Gordon's siege in 1885—along with a number of other smaller boats. A force of an estimated 500 Mahdist warriors on the east-bank was also present; upon seeing Kitchener's troops, they almost immediately opened fire. For a short while, there was an exchange of fire between the two sides, during which a shell, fired on the orders of Commander Keppel, hit the *Safieh* in her boiler; this rendered the steamer useless, much to the disgust of the *Sirdar* who had hoped to add her to his fleet. Eventually, however, the Mahdists gave up the fight and the men of the 11th Sudanese were landed, who then quickly took a number of prisoners. It was soon discovered that these warriors had recently conducted offensive operations against the Europeans at Fashoda, but had broken off their attack, in face of superior firepower, in order to wait for reinforcements from Omdurman.

With the dispersal of the small Mahdist force, the *Sirdar*'s little fleet resumed its journey down the Nile. On the 18th, the steamers reached a point just ten miles short of Fashoda, where orders were given for the men to rest for the night. Kitchener then penned a letter addressed to the person in charge at the village, informing him that a small fleet of steamers would appear on the river in the direction of the settlement the next day. The purpose of this letter—which was delivered by two Sudanese soldiers, much to the astonishment of the recipients— was so Kitchener could avoid any accidental clash of arms.

Setting off in the morning, the *Sirdar* and his flotilla came to within five miles of the town, when a rowing boat came into view flying what was the unmistakable French flag; any question of who the Europeans were now being laid to rest. After meeting in the river, one of the occupants of the little boat, which consisted of one Senegalese sergeant and two privates, handed a letter to the British officers; this note informed Kitchener that Fashoda was now in possession of a French expedition of exploration, and that it had been since 10 July. What was more, the letter was signed by Captain Jean-Baptiste Marchand, who congratulated the *Sirdar* on his great victory over the *Khalifa* and the *Ansar*. News in Sudan, it seemed, travelled fast.

Nevertheless, the *Sirdar*'s steamers continued their journey to the village regardless, and, as the settlement came into view, another French *Tricolore* could be seen flying above its buildings. When the vessels finally came alongside the riverside village to berth, Marchand could be seen in front of what appeared to be eight French officers and about 120 Senegalese soldiers, the latter of which were armed with modern repeating rifles, as well as a number of local warriors armed with spears. The French expedition, however, possessed no artillery or machine guns. Once the *Dal* was made secure, the French captain climbed aboard, at which point he was promptly taken to see Kitchener in private. It is said that the *Sirdar* congratulated the captain for what he had accomplished, but the latter replied by saying 'it is not I but these soldiers who have done it.' Following this remark, Kitchener later claimed 'then I knew he was a gentleman.' The two would talk in private for the next forty-five minutes.

Marchand had been born on 22 November 1863 at Thoissey in Ain, France. He had studied at l'Ecole militaire de Saint-Maixent before enlisting in the French army in 1883, being commissioned as a sub-lieutenant following four years in the ranks. In 1889, he was sent to Senegal, where he saw active service during which he was wounded twice. He was, however, made a Chevalier of the Legion of Honour for he services in the French colony as a reward. In 1890 he was promoted to lieutenant, followed by captain two years later. It would be in this latter rank that he led the expedition to Fashoda, for which he is best remembered today. In later life, he would serve in both the Boxer Rebellion in China, fighting in a coalition alongside the British, and the First World War on the western front, finally retiring from military service in 1919.

Despite what both the British and French officers knew would become a difficult confrontation, the latter, it should be noted, appeared relieved to see the former on the steamers as they approached. This was due to the fact that the small French expedition had, of course, very recently fended off an attack from the *Khalifa*'s warriors, a skirmish that had left them with little in the way of available ammunition, while they also had only enough rations for the next three months. Seeing fellow Europeans, therefore, was a warmly welcomed sight, albeit not under the best of circumstances. Conversely, it was said that the British officers held much admiration for their French counterparts, who, despite losing twenty percent of their number, had held firm at Fashoda and accomplished their mission, itself a not inconsiderable task.

During their meeting, Kitchener made it clear to Marchand that he considered the presence of armed French troops at Fashoda as an infringement on territory that came under control of the Egyptian Government in Cairo; and by extension, this also meant an infringement on the British Government in London. The Frenchman replied by informing the *Sirdar* that he and his men were in Fashoda on instructions of his own government in Paris, and that without receiving orders to withdraw, he was not going to agree to leave. However, as a compromise, he agreed to the erection of the Egyptian flag in the town, a concession no doubt made in the face of several battalions of Sudanese infantry backed by artillery and a company of British soldiers. Unbeknown to the British officers at this time was the fact that Marchand had, before the arrival of Kitchener's river force, sent his own steamer (the *Faidherbe*) south to bring up both supplies and additional men. The French captain, therefore, knew reinforcements would not be long arriving.

The meeting ended without agreement, and Marchand left the *Dal* and returned to his officers and men on shore. Kitchener then ordered his steamers to sail further down the river for another 300 yards, where further instructions were issued for the artillery and infantry to be landed. An Egyptian flag was then raised about 500 yards from the *Tricolore* and within the ruins of an old bastion, which was given a salute by the men and the boats. With this ceremonial task complete, the *Sirdar* ordered the 11th Sudanese and the steamer *Nasr* to remain near Fashoda, while the rest of the force re-boarded the other boats and proceeded sixty-two miles south to Sobat, this being reached on the 22nd. Another Egyptian flag was hoisted at this location, and the 13th Sudanese, along with the *Abu Klea*, were instructed to hold the position, all under the command of Colonel H. W. Jackson. With the remainder of his steamers and soldiers, Kitchener then began his journey back to Omdurman to report his findings to the Foreign Office in London via telegraph. A major diplomatic incident, in the wake of the British reconquest of Sudan, had begun.

Before examining the diplomatic row between Britain and France over possession of Fashoda, it is perhaps useful to briefly consider the journey Marchand and his men had made to get there in the first place. Marchand's original mission had been proposed by himself, which involved marching a force of around 200 men to Bahr al-Ghazal; the purpose of the expedition was to give France a degree of influence at future diplomatic talks regarding the Nile Valley, during what would later become known as the 'Scramble for Africa'. The expedition, however, would be considered a civilian one, and under no circumstances was the captain to fly the French flag in the region nor agree to any treaties with the local tribes; he was, after all, technically going to be in Egyptian territory, and confrontation with Egypt was to be strictly avoided. On 30 November 1895, the French authorities secretly approved the mission.

The mission, however, did not actually begin until the following year, when, in March 1896, the British Government was finally forced to act after receiving the plea for help from the Italians, who had suffered serious reverses against the Mahdists. With news of Kitchener's advance into Dongola being authorised by London, the French authorities, fearing the British would reach the Upper Nile Valley before them, sent orders to Marchand to get his expedition underway as quickly as possible, and what has been called the 'Race to Fashoda' commenced.

Although Marchand's mission was to secure the right to take part in possible future diplomatic talks regarding the region for France, there was, of course, another more secretive goal. This included going *bey*ond Bahr al-Ghazal and establishing himself at the village of Fashoda. Should he need to agree treaties with local chieftains along the way to achieve this, he was also secretly authorised to do so. Officially, however, no mention of Fashoda was ever made. As with any expedition of this nature, it would take time and the men would face many unknown dangers; success could not be guaranteed.

Several years later, on 4 June 1898, after spending months at Fort Desaix in the Bahr al-Ghazal region, Marchand made preparations for the final leg of the journey to Fashoda. At his disposal was a small flotilla of boats, including the *Faidherbe*, which he loaded with supplies and seventy-five locally recruited *tirailleurs* in addition to the boat crews and a handful of French officers and NCOs. One reason for the lengthy delay was the fact that the river was so low, so the boats, heavily laden with men and supplies, were unable to move, since they would run aground and get stuck in the river. However, in early June, the river was finally deemed deep enough to attempt the journey. The *Faidherbe*, being by far the largest of the boats, still could not make the move, and so Marchand had it disassembled and hauled by locally-acquired slave-labourers over 400 km of difficult terrain. It was then, with great difficulty, reassembled and launched into the river, which had slowly risen during the journey over land, thanks to the long-expected rains.

Although the first few days of the trek passed by uneventfully, the going became increasingly difficult and dangerous. Mosquitoes were a persistent problem, and the men got lost, but, on the 26th, they at last reached Bahr al-Ghazal. An advanced party had also been sent ahead earlier, with the two parties now uniting. After some rest, the expedition resumed its journey, pushing on along the river; at 5 p.m. on Sunday 10 July, Marchand and his men finally reached Fashoda. It had been an arduous and thoroughly unpleasant few weeks, but worse was yet to come.

Fashoda itself was little more than a ruin, the old fortress having being reduced to its foundations. Nevertheless, Marchand and his officers were delighted to take possession of the village; their mission had been successfully accomplished. The following morning, the French troops set about clearing an area for the establishment of a new fort, which would cover an area of thirty-five square yards. Bricks were stacked, ready for building the new defences, and the outline laid out. An official dedication ceremony was also held later in the day, but, as the order to present arms was given to the men, the flagpole snapped and the *Tricolore* came fluttering down to the ground. For some of the French officers, this appeared to be a bad omen of things to come.

On 25 August, two steamers were suddenly and unexpectedly spotted approaching the village along the river, both towing barges packed with Mahdist warriors. One of the vessels then fired a shot from one of its cannons, at which point Marchand knew he was about to face an overwhelming force of the *Khalifa*'s warriors. The French had at their disposal a total of almost 100 men, all armed with modern rifles and well-trained to use them. The Mahdists, on the other hand, had an estimated force of between 1,200 and 1,500 warriors, many armed with rifles as well the artillery, the latter of which Marchand did not have.

Fortunately for the small French force, the troops had entrenched themselves and could fire on their targets from a greater range than their adversaries. Luck then smiled on Marchand, for one of the enemy steamers broke down and became stranded, rendering it an easy target for the French troops who poured a relentless hot rifle fire into it. The Mahdists attacked nevertheless, but the superior weapons in the hands of the French soldiers proved their worth, and the warriors soon found their assault rapidly faltering. Unable to get to grips with their enemy, the *Khalifa*'s men broke off and headed off towards the north having failed in their mission to dislodge Marchand's expedition at Fashoda.

The French captain knew the Mahdists would be back. It would, however, be shortly after the repulse of this attack that the *Faidherbe* arrived, much to the relief of the French troops. The steamer could now be sent back down river for supplies and additional men, hopefully returning in time before the renewed assault by the Mahdists. The expected attack, of course, would never come, rather news arrived that the *Khalifa*'s army had been decisively defeated by an Anglo-Egyptian force under command of Major-General Kitchener at the Battle of Omdurman. Then, just over two weeks later, the *Sirdar* himself arrived aboard his own flotilla with a small but formidable army.

The presence of a French expedition at Fashoda had not come as a surprise to the British and Egyptian authorities in London and Cairo, since, early in 1898, the French had in fact made their intentions known in the form of a telegram before Marchand had even set off. To add to this, the French captain and his officers let it be known that they were determined to reach the Upper Nile before the British, in order to 'display the French flag between Khartoum and Gondokoro'. Although some in Kitchener's staff may not have been aware of the nationality of the mysterious Europeans seen by the Mahdists at Fashoda, it is certain that Kitchener did, especially since the timetable to advance on Khartoum and Omdurman was brought forward years before originally intended. The so-called Fashoda Incident, therefore, although not directly related to the reconquest of Sudan, was a direct result of it and is intertwined with its story.

Indeed, Lord Salisbury had, on 2 August 1898, sent a despatch to Lord Cromer in Cairo, within which he outlined what actions should be undertaken following the successful recapture of Khartoum from the Mahdists. In this despatch, the prime minister made it clear that he was authorising Major-General Kitchener to send an armed flotilla up the White Nile and another up the Blue Nile, the former, under the command of the *Sirdar* himself, proceeding as far as Fashoda, while the latter advanced to Rosiéres. Salisbury was keen to avoid armed conflict with France, and he instructed that Kitchener was to seek further advice should French officers and soldiers be encountered, but that in no way was the major-general to allow the French to think the British Government would recognise Paris' claims in the region. As well as the French, the prime minister was worried that the Abyssinians might be encountered; if so, his instructions for dealing with them would be the same.

In response to the *Sirdar*'s request for further instructions following his encounter with the French expedition, the government in London formally asked the French authorities to order Marchand's withdrawal from Fashoda and the Nile Valley. Unsurprisingly, the French refused, even though they knew the British, who had just reclaimed Sudan for Egypt, were unlikely to ever agree to French troops occupying part of the territory. The stand-off between the two European countries would last for several months; neither, especially Britain, were prepared to negotiate on the matter.

News of the meeting between Kitchener and Marchand reached Théophile Delcassé, the newly appointed French foreign minister, on 26 September. However, since Marchand had originally set off on his expedition some two and a half years earlier, the political landscape in Europe had by now changed significantly since it was first authorised. Firstly, relations between Britain and Germany had greatly improved, especially after the capture of Khartoum, with the Kaiser personally sending Queen Victoria a letter of congratulations on the matter. Secondly, Russia, which was still engaged with Britain in the so-called 'Great Game'—a sort of Victorian cold war between the two powers—was not showing any signs of siding with France in the ensuing diplomatic row. Thirdly, Britain, which had spent a very large sum of money on the reconquest of Sudan—not to mention the loss of British and Egyptian troops—was simply not going to back down in the Upper Nile, especially when it was deemed of such strategic importance. Fourthly, France was distracted from events in Africa by the re-opening of the Dreyfus Affair, which had begun in 1894—which would not be fully resolved until 1906—and was considered politically more important by those at home.

Delcassé, despite being known as a fervent colonialist and extremely patriotic, had little appetite in fighting the issue out with the British; he needed to find a way out that would result in no loss of political reputation for him or France. He assured Sir Edward Monson, the British ambassador to Paris, that Marchand was nothing more than an explorer, and that he did not command a proper military expedition at Fashoda, a claim that was an outright lie. Monson, who was not fooled for a moment, made it clear to Delcassé that the British Government was not prepared to move on the issue. The British message was clear, withdraw unconditionally or face potential conflict.

The stalemate continued, then, in October, Delcassé instructed Baron de Courcel—a known and respected anglophile—to go to London to meet with Salisbury in order to negotiate a political solution acceptable to both countries. Delcassé was hoping the British would agree to France keeping a token presence in the Upper Nile, specifically at Bahr al-Ghazal, in return for withdrawing Marchand and the main body of his expedition. Unfortunately for the French foreign minister, at a meeting on 5 October, the British prime minister displayed no interest in the proposal and rejected it.

Five days later, in a rare move by a British prime minister, Salisbury released a number of parliamentary papers containing information on how the negotiations between Britain and France had been going. Now public, members of parliament from all parties threw their weight behind the prime minister against France. Even the Liberal statesmen Lord Rosebery and Sir William Harcourt made speeches in support of Salisbury over the issue. The newspapers, too, backed the Government; some, such as the *Daily Mail*, went as far as to call for aggressive military action. By the last week in October, the Royal Navy was put on alert and war orders sent to the Mediterranean fleet. Britain, even if it meant going to war, was still not going to back down.

Salisbury's ploy of releasing the papers had in fact been too successful in uniting the country against France. The call for war grew increasingly stronger and attracted a number of influential backers, a dangerous position that threatened peace in Europe; two old adversaries, who had not fired a shot at each other since the final defeat of Napoleon in 1815, now seemed on the verge of renewed hostilities. Fortunately, the prime minister managed to persuade his cabinet that war, unless it was utterly unavoidable, with France was not worth the loss of British lives over such a desolate place as Fashoda. There would be no backing down or giving way to France, but nor would an ultimatum be sent to Paris that might provoke a military conflict.

Delcassé, meanwhile, also knew that France was in no position to fight the British should hostilities break out. The French navy, despite its perceived reputation at the time, simply could not hope to take on the might of the British Royal Navy. Indeed, the French admiralty knew a naval conflict between the two powers would be a short one, with the British navy likely celebrating victory within the matter of weeks. As Anglophobic as she was, Russia was not prepared to send her ships to help the French; even if she had been, her fleet was currently trapped in the Baltic ice. War for France was not an option either.

With news of British warships preparing for possible war, Delcassé finally gave way and offered to accept Salisbury's terms. To save face, the French foreign minister made it known that Marchand was in a dire situation at Fashoda, having being attacked by Mahdists and lacking enough supplies and men to hold out much longer. To help persuade Marchand to withdraw, orders were sent to Fashoda for Captain Albert Ernest Augustin Baratier, the officer next in line of command of the expedition, to return to Paris; this journey was facilitated by Kitchener's steamers. In just over two weeks, the officer was back in the French capital, where he informed Delcassé that Marchand and his expedition were in fact in good order, having received additional supplies of ammunition and food thanks to the *Faidherbe*. He even went as far as to argue that the Sudanese garrison left by the *Sirdar* was on the verge of mutiny, and that they could be easily defeated in battle if necessary. Delcassé, however, was having none of it and insisted the withdrawal would take place.

Angry that Delcassé seemed so happy to betray Marchand, Baratier left the meeting vowing to do what he could to prevent the withdrawal from Fashoda. However, before he could do anything meaningful to this effect, the officer was given orders to return to Fashoda to get him out the way. On 3 November, following intervention by Félix François Faure (the president of France), final orders were sent from Paris to Fashoda via Cairo for the expedition to retire, and the political crisis came to an end. The following day, Salisbury made a speech at the Guildhall in the City of London to the effect that the French had backed down, at which the audience broke out into cheers and loud applause.

Left with little choice but to o*bey* his masters back in Paris, Marchand reluctantly instructed his men to pack up their possessions and equipment for the journey home. Originally, the retirement was to be made aboard British steamers to Cairo, but, as a concession, the French expedition was granted permission to leave via Abyssinia and Djibouti, so as to avoid a degree of the humiliation they were now to endure. Two soldiers of the expedition, however, were too ill to make this arduous journey, and so were taken by the British to Cairo, where they were to convalesce before rejoining their comrades. The actual departure began on 12 December, although an official ceremony to mark the occasion was performed the day before, with the French troops lined up and presenting arms as the *Marseillaise* was played. As they sailed past aboard the *Faidherbe*, the French raised their hats to their British counterparts on shore. Baratier commented that he felt 'We are fleeing' from the scene, but Marchand merely remarked that one day the Sphinx would laugh.

Kitchener had long returned home before the French backed down, arriving back in England while the political row between the two countries was at its height. He received a hero's welcome by both the public and the Royal Family, as well as grant of £30,000, an expensive ceremonial sword, and a state banquet in his honour. In addition, he was made a Knight Grand Cross of the Order of the Bath (GCB) and received a number of honorary academic awards; it was at this point that he became known as 'Lord Kitchener of Khartoum'.

While the Fashoda Incident was starting to be played out in Sudan and Europe, British forces would clash with warriors under the command of *Amir* Ahmed Fedil near Gedarif, located 130 miles south-west of Kassala. The *amir*, who was said to have 5,000 fighting men at his disposal, was a supporter of Mahdism and he had belatedly marched out with 3,000 warriors on 7 September to answer the call of assistance from the *Khalifa*. Thus, he was far too late to take part in the decisive battle fought five days earlier. Lieutenant-Colonel Parsons, commanding a force of 1,400 men, was instructed to advance on Gedarif—now perceived as being weakly defended—in order to take it. The majority of the lieutenant-colonel's men were from the 16th Egyptian Battalion and the Camel Corps, but he was also reinforced by a number of locally recruited irregulars of the Arab Battalion and other levies.

Parsons' column crossed the now greatly swelled Atbara River—thanks largely to the considerable efforts of Major Henry Merrick Lawson of the Royal Engineers—and concentrated at El Fashir before marching out along the left-bank of the river on the 17th. When he came within two miles of Gedarif, the lieutenant-colonel came into contact with a sizeable force of Mahdists, estimated to be made up of 1,500 riflemen and 1,700 spearmen, at 9 a.m. on the 22nd.

The Mahdists were quick to launch an assault, the main thrust of which was aimed at Parsons' left-front, where they came up against the men of the 16th Egyptians under Captain Augustus de Segur McKerrell and the Arab Battalion under Captain E. B. Wilkinson. Quickly deploying into line, Parsons' men opened a heavy fire on their attackers, which savagely tore through the ranks of the warriors, mowing many of them down within moments of their charge commencing. In the face of such losses, the Mahdist attack quickly faltered and the warriors began to retire.

Despite their losses, the warriors launched a second attack, this time against Parsons' baggage train. The transports were under the protection of the Camel Corps and a party of levies, the former under the command of Captain Charles Christie Fleming of the Royal Army Medical Corps, who was not only the medical officer but also in charge of transportation. The defenders and attackers quickly became engaged in a desperate fight, but Fleming's men firmly stood their ground and fended off the Mahdists until the 16th Egyptians arrived to finally put the warriors to flight.

It would be during this second assault that the fifth and final Victoria Cross of the Sudanese campaign was awarded to Captain Alexander Gore Arkwright Hore-Ruthven of the 3rd Battalion of the Highland Light Infantry, who was in command of the Camel Corps detachment. Having spotted a wounded Egyptian officer lying on the ground only fifty yards in front of the oncoming Mahdists, the captain rushed forward to pick the man up with the intention of carrying him back to the line of the 16th Egyptians. When some of his pursuers got too close, Hore-Ruthven dropped the wounded man on the ground in order to give fire before picking him up again and continuing his run towards the Egyptian troops. He had to do this several times before finally brining the officer to safety, saving the wounded man from what would certainly have been a vicious and painful death.

Interestingly, Hore-Ruthven almost did not receive his medal. He had gone absent without leave from his militia battalion—which at that time was in Scotland—in order to be present for the campaign in Sudan. The captain had been trying to get a commission in the regular army, but he was under the regulation minimum height for a regular officer. This failure no doubt resulted in much frustration for Hore-Ruthven, who simply decided to take matters into his own hands and head out for Egypt. A furious debate followed the recommendation of a VC for the captain, but, thanks to royal intervention, the award was confirmed in the *London Gazette* of 3 March 1899.

With both attacks defeated, Parsons ordered his force to resume its advance to Gedarif, which was occupied at midday. The remains of the Mahdist garrison consisted of only 150 men and two obsolete guns under the command of *Amir* Mir Angara, who surrendered without offering any resistance. Parsons' losses for the action near Gedarif amounted to fifty-three killed and sixty-one wounded, while Mahdist casualties were uncertain.

Ahmed Fedil would attempt an attack on British occupied Gedarif on the 23rd, conducting his assault during the night. Unfortunately for the *amir*, his attack was easily repulsed and came to nothing. The next day, Parsons carried out a reconnaissance in force of the surrounding area, and managed to ascertain that the warriors who had attacked Gedarif were retiring to the south towards Karkoj on the Blue Nile. He was also able to capture large numbers of Mahdist deserters, who informed the lieutenant-colonel that Ahmed Fedil's force was fast breaking up. However, it would not be the last the British would see of the troublesome *amir*.

Despite these further minor victories against the Mahdists, Abdullahi al-Taishi was still at large and continued to pose a potential and serious threat to the stability of Sudan. A number of officers, including the *Sirdar* himself, would attempt to catch him, but the final blow would not be dealt by Kitchener, but by the recently promoted Lieutenant-Colonel Reginald Wingate.

15

The Pursuit and Death of the *Khalifa*

While Kitchener was dealing with Marchand at Fashoda, Abdullahi al-Taishi was continuing his flight towards Kordofan, following the course of the White Nile. He arrived at a place called Duem, from where he abandoned the river route and made off towards Lake Sherkeleh, located about 120 miles to the south-west. Later, in January 1899, intelligence was received by the British that claimed the *Khalifa* had been largely abandoned by the remnants of his army and was now only supported by a relatively small number of followers. Having pursued the Mahdist leader in the wake of the Battle of Omdurman, the Egyptian Army had arrived at Duem and established a post there. From here, instructions were passed to Colonel Frederick Walter Kitchener—the younger brother of the *Sirdar*—to take with him 900 men of the 2nd Egyptians and the 14th Sudanese, supported by a detachment of fifty men of irregular cavalry, and head towards the location where Abdullahi al-Taishi was now believed to be.

Unfortunately for the colonel, the *Khalifa* had long gone by the time he arrived. However, it was evident from the debris left behind that the area had indeed been recently used as a camp, but not by just a few hundred men as previously believed; instead, it had been a site occupied by thousands of warriors. Walter Kitchener, as he was known, ordered his men to construct a *zariba*, after which a number of scouts were sent out to conduct a reconnaissance of the surrounding area. Some of these scouts actually managed to locate Abdullahi al-Taishi, who was present with an army numbering an estimated 7,000 warriors within only three miles of the *zariba*.

This presented the colonel with a problem, since his force, which was lacking artillery, was simply not strong enough to engage the *Khalifa* and ensure his defeat. He was also low on supplies of water, and so reluctantly issued orders for his men to strike camp and make back towards the river. Mahdist scouts had also located Walter Kitchener's little force, and the *Khalifa*, in the hope of defeating it, led his warriors to the *zariba*, only to find it abandoned by the time he got there. Although he knew the British force was heading for the river, Abdullahi al-Taishi decided not to pursue any further in case he came into contact with a larger Anglo-Egyptian force. Having given up the chase, the colonel returned to Duem before journeying on to Cairo. Thus, the first major attempt to apprehend the *Khalifa* following the fall of Omdurman ended.

In June, further reports arrived that Abdullahi al-Taishi's warriors were conducting raiding operations against the tribes in and around the area of Lake Sherkeleh, pointing to the fact that the *Khalifa* himself was still likely in the area. However, the British were pleased to also learn that their prey had suffered an attack at the hands of the Tagalla tribe, the warriors of which had managed to inflict heavy casualties on the Mahdists, reducing their effective strength from the previously estimated 7,000 warriors to under 4,000. Naturally, this news encouraged the military authorities back in Cairo to order another attempt to catch their man. First, however, they had to wait for the rainy season to end, since it was rendering any attempt at operations virtually impossible.

The situation, however, appeared to change dramatically in September, when further intelligence was obtained that Abdullahi al-Taishi was now near a place called Jeb el-Gheddeer—a mountainous area located some 100 miles from Fashoda—with a much larger force, estimated to be 10,000 strong. In addition, other intelligence suggested that an *amir*, by the name of Arabi Dafalla, was seeking to join up with the *Khalifa*, thus adding his own warriors to an already considerable Mahdist army. It seemed Abdullahi al-Taishi was growing stronger by the day, and, for the British, he needed to be stopped before he could realistically pose a significant threat to the stability of Sudan.

The *Sirdar* was in Europe when he received the news that Abdullahi al-Taishi was near Jeb el-Gheddeer, and he at once headed back to Cairo. Arriving at the Egyptian capital on the 26th, he lost no time in setting off for Omdurman, where he issued orders for a new force to be assembled in the hope of confronting the *Khalifa*. Major-General Kitchener had hoped to keep the assembly of his expeditionary force a secret in order not to alert Abdullahi al-Taishi to his intentions. However, since it was to be made up of 6,000 men—including four battalions of infantry, the Camel Corps and artillery—it proved difficult to keep it away from the prying eyes of those in and around the city. The new expeditionary force was concentrated on the White Nile at Kaka, and would come under the direct command of the *Sirdar* himself.

The journey to Jeb el-Gheddeer was conducted via steamers and by marching overland. Leading was the Camel Corps and the artillery, with the infantry following on a short distance behind. On 11 October, Kitchener arrived aboard the steamer *Dal* to take command of the force. The *Sirdar* now hoped to finally engage the *Khalifa* in one last battle and put an end to him and the Mahdist movement once and for all.

Kitchener's expedition then journeyed down the Nile to Kaka, where the men disembarked and travelled overland to Fungar. Upon arriving at the latter, he learned that Abdullahi al-Taishi had already left the same place around thirty hours earlier. What was worse was the fact that the direction the *Khalifa* was heading in was to the north across an area known for having no available supplies of water. This made any pursuit by the *Sirdar*'s force impossible, since they could not carry enough water for the men and animals. A disappointed Kitchener, therefore, called off the pursuit and ordered his men back to Omdurman. With the troops back in the city, the *Sirdar* travelled once again to Cairo.

At Khartoum on the 20th, Wingate, who was in command of the city, was informed that a Mahdist force under the command of Ahmed Fedil was on the Nile near a place called Dakhila. The following day, Colonel Lewis was also told that two *rubs* of warriors had crossed the river at this point, and that more were believed to be preparing to do the same. According to Lewis:

> On the 22nd instant *Sheikh* Bakr Mustafa proceeded with my leave south, with a view to cutting off flocks, etc. from the crossing Dervishes. But on the same day I heard that no considerable force of Dervishes had crossed, but that 60 rifles had been sent (under Nur-Selah) to scout and collect food, and this was confirmed by a prisoner (a Rizigat horseman) sent in to me by Bakr [a *sheikh* commanding Arab irregulars] in the evening. Bakr returned on the 23rd instant. On the 24th news was received that Fedil's women were being taken across, covered by the 60 rifles above named, and that the crossing, which began on the 22nd instant, would still take some days. Bakr sent up 300 men on west bank to cut off women. I also heard, on fairly good authority, that Fedil had ordered the crops on the west bank opposite here to be raided, and talked of marching north towards the Kenana country in case of food being unobtainable by other routes.

The steamers *Melik* and *Dal* arrived at Khartoum on the 24th; aboard which were Major Fergusson and Captain Sir Henry Hill, along with one other officer and thirty men of the 9th Sudanese Battalion and 200 men of the 10th Sudanese Battalion. With the arrival of these reinforcements, Wingate asked Lewis to move out and attack Ahmed Fedil.

At 5 p.m. on the 25th, Lewis marched out with 653 men of the Egyptian Army, who were supported by 495 irregular troops, including 380 under the command of *Sheikh* Bakr. He also had two Maxims under the command of Captain Sir Henry Hill, the guns being operated by Sergeants Lambert and Troubridge of the Royal Marine Artillery. As the men were about to commence their march, further news came in that Bakr and Ahmed Fedil had clashed in a skirmish on the west-bank of the river, during which the latter had been wounded. Following this minor engagement, Ahmed Fedil had re-crossed back over to the east-bank.

After marching for several hours, Lewis issued orders to his men to halt and get some rest at a village called Abu Zogholi, located about a third of the distance to Dakhila. The advance then resumed at 3 a.m. on the 26th, with Lewis' force arriving at Ahmed's Fedil's position just before 9 a.m. Lewis described the scene before him:

> Just north of Dakhila the Nile bifurcate, one rapid but shallow stream flowing under east bank fairly straight, another very deep stream running in wide curve under the west bank, cutting it precipitously, the two enclosing an island a mile and a quarter long by 1,400 hundred yards wide, on which was the Dervish Dem. On the east side of the island is a bare slope of heavy shingle 1,000 yards wide, on the west side there is a line of low sand hills, covered with scrub and grass in irregular curves, and steep towards the river bank. On the reverse side of these sand hills, what eventually turned out to be three-quarters of Fedil's force were drawn up. Behind these sand hills the west bank of the Nile rose precipitously, in some places 50 feet high, and along it were lined about 300 riflemen, with such spearmen as had crossed in the hollows behind them, and also Ahmed Fedil and four of his Emirs. The force on the island was under command of Saadalla Mohamed, the fifth Emir, but a vast proportion of the men of the other four Emirs were also on the island.

The action began at 9 a.m. when Captain Hill ordered his two Maxim guns to open fire. Lining the opposite bank of the river for 100 yards were the men of the 10th Sudanese, the line being further extended by those of *Sheikh* Bakr and other irregulars. These men then opened a long-range fire on the Mahdists, but it had little effect on dislodging their enemy. Bakr's men, however, eventually managed to cross the river, under cover of a company of the 10th Sudanese, onto the island where they took up new positions about 800 yards from Ahmed Fedil's line. The 10th Sudanese then began to cross in companies at a ford to the north, the water being up to three and a half feet deep in places.

With many of his men now across, Lewis determined to attack Ahmed Fedil's left-flank. This assault was to be carried out by the men of the 10th, under the command of Lieutenant-Colonel Nason and Major Fergusson, the battalion advancing in alternate companies. The main body of the 10th advanced obliquely on the sand hills, while one company, under Fergusson, detached and took up positions on a knoll, a feature that had an excellent commanding view of the river bank where many Mahdist warriors had taken cover. Lewis described the ensuing attack:

> When the attacking infantry were about 400 yards from the sand hills, and 800 yards from the west bank, casualties became very frequent, so advance was hastened to the utmost extent, and Nason halted them on the east side of sand hills to recover wind. This incident was of good service to subsequent attack, for it induced several hundreds of the enemy to leave their cover and advance to a counter-attack. Nason took good advantage of the situation; crowning the ridge

of sand hills, a rapid fire was opened, repelling the Dervish advance, and then the Tenth, gallantly led by Colonel Nason, swept from north to south of the sand hills every fold of which held a party of the enemy.

Under this pressure, the Mahdist warriors started to buckle and increasing numbers of them began retreating towards the south. Here, however, they came under heavy fire from Bakr's men. Some of the warriors managed to cross over to the island, where they found their retreat was blocked by a rapid flowing channel of water. Some attempted to cross it, only to be drowned in the process. The action was proving a disaster for Ahmed Fedil, but it was not over yet. According to Lewis:

> A further stand was made on this island by 300 Jehadia and Arabs, and they kept two companies employed for an hour and a half before the survivors surrendered. The main position was carried by 11.30 a.m. Hill preceded the advance of infantry on the sand hills by a well-directed Maxim fire, and then did what he could to keep down the fire from West Bank while attack was being launched. In spite of that the fire from West Bank was very accurate, and to withdraw our wounded it was necessary to bring the Maxims (which Hill had crossed as attack was concluded) to 450 yards range, and then fire was not silenced till 3 p.m.

British losses for the action amounted to twenty-four NCOs and men killed, while one British officer (Major Fergusson), six Egyptian officers, and 117 men were wounded. Another soldier was also listed as missing. In addition, Bakr lost fourteen of his men killed and another seventeen wounded, while casualties among the other irregulars amounted to two killed and five wounded. The wounded men were cared for by Captain James Willes Jennings of the Royal Army Medical Corps, who had earlier been seen risking his life under fire to treat the men where they fell.

In his official report, Lewis admits to not knowing the total casualties inflicted on Ahmed Fedil's force, since he was unable to count their killed due the pressing work of caring for his own wounded. However, he did estimate that around 500 warriors were killed on the island and in the river, with further heavy loss believed to have been suffered by those positioned on the west bank from the fire of the Maxims.

As well as the casualties, Lewis recorded that Bakr captured 1,524 of Ahmed Fedil's men, while another 156 later came in to surrender. Some 576 rifles were also recovered following the action, along with a huge number of spears and other bladed weapons of varying type; the lieutenant-colonel was of the opinion that the *amir* must have lost close to 900 of his rifles as a result of his defeat. Ahmed Fedil, however, had escaped and was believed to be making towards Jabel Tabi to the south-west with 200 to 300 of his best remaining riflemen as escort.

At 4 p.m. on 21 November 1899, Lieutenant-Colonel Wingate marched out of Fachi Shoya with a force of 3,700 men. After advancing for five miles to the south-west, he gave orders for his men to halt and rest at 6 p.m., after which they resumed their march at 10 p.m. They would travel through the moonlit night towards Nefisa, some fifteen miles away. During the advance, the lieutenant-colonel had ordered his cavalry to scout out two miles ahead of the column; they came across and drove in ten Mahdist horsemen.

Information came to Wingate's attention that Ahmed Fedil was at Nefisa with a strong force and a large quantity of grain, the latter having been procured following a raid on El Alub. It was believed that the *amir* had been collecting men and supplies with the intention of joining the *Khalifa* at Gedi. Now within only a short distance of Nefisa, Wingate gave orders for his transports to be placed in a defensive position and for the main body of his force to take up fighting formations ready to assault Ahmed Fedil's camp. However, after commencing the final advance on Nefisa, the lieutenant-colonel's cavalry scouts returned with the news that the *amir* and his men had already gone.

It appears that Ahmed Fedil had learned of Wingate's approach at the last minute, since, when the latter occupied Nefisa, much of the grain was found still in storage and had not been taken away, betraying the fact that the Mahdists had left in a hurry. However, a sick warrior had also been left behind, who was taken prisoner by Wingate. Upon interrogation, the Mahdist informed the lieutenant-colonel that Ahmed Fedil had fled to Abu Aadel, which lay only five miles away. A reconnaissance by Arab irregulars, under Captain Mahmud Hussein, of Abu Aadel was then carried out, confirming what the sick warrior had told his interrogator.

Wingate, understandably, feared that Ahmed Fedil would merely move further to the south in order to join up with forces under Abdullahi al-Taishi and continually stay one step ahead of his own men. He, therefore, immediately issued orders for Lieutenant-Colonel Bryan Thomas Mahon of the 8th Hussars to take with him the Egyptian cavalry, the Camel Corps, four Maxims, two field guns, and some irregular Sudanese infantry and make for Abu Aadel at best possible speed. Once there, he was to open an attack on Ahmed Fedil's camp with the view of pinning him down until Wingate could catch up with the rest of his column.

Mahon duly arrived at Abu Aadel, and, to his delight, found that the *amir's* force was still encamped there. He immediately ordered his mounted troops to take up a commanding position about 300 yards from the Mahdist camp, after which the order to open fire was given. Moments after the firing began, the Maxims and artillery guns where wheeled into position and similarly opened fire on their enemy. A short while later, the slower-moving Sudanese irregular infantrymen arrived on foot and began to add their weight of fire to the developing action just as the Mahdists commenced an attack of their own. Ahmed Fedil's counter-attack had been directed at the Maxims and the artillery, due to the fact they had taken up positions easier for the warriors to reach. In fact, the Mahdist assault was able to get within a mere sixty yards before it was checked by the combined fire of the Maxims and the carbines of the Camel Corps.

With the counter-attack repulsed, Mahon ordered his entire line to advance towards the Mahdist camp. As they moved forward, the men had to push their way through thick bush, which was acting to partially conceal Ahmed Fedil's position, but many of the warriors had already begun to retire or flee. Due to the bush, it was hard to see the Mahdists as they fell back, but they could soon be seen in large numbers as they emerged onto a grassy plain about a mile and a half from their camp. Mahon ordered his infantry to pursue, but it would be the men of the cavalry, Camel Corps, and the Maxims that would eventually race ahead and chase Ahmed Fedil's fleeing men for a distance of five miles.

The skirmish ended in success for Mahon, although he had not been able to keep them contained as planned before Wingate arrived. Nevertheless, he had killed an estimated 400 warriors and wounded many more. Large quantities of precious food supplies had also fallen into his hands, as well as a number of weapons and even some prisoners. Mahon's losses were extremely light, including: Captain Mustapha Effendi Shahin of the Camel Corps, who was dangerously wounded, while one enlisted man was killed and another three wounded.

The astute Wingate now poured over the various intelligence reports that were coming in as regards to the whereabouts of the *Khalifa*; they proved to be somewhat conflicting and confusing. However, he determined that Abdullahi al-Taishi had been at El Homara, but that he had likely left that place three days earlier. The lieutenant-colonel also knew he had hoped to join with Ahmed Fedil at Gedid, from where he would likely advance northwards. Sure that this was the case, Wingate gave instructions for his men to begin an advance towards Gedid at midnight, which, after a somewhat trying march, was reached at 10 a.m. on the 23rd.

Again, it was found that the Mahdists had evacuated their position before the arrival of British forces. Thankfully, however, greatly needed supplies of water were located, much to the relief of Wingate who was worried that without enough water he would have to abandon his pursuit. A Mahdist deserter was also apprehended, who, without needing much persuasion, informed the lieutenant-colonel that Abdullahi al-Taishi had in fact established a new camp some seven miles to the south-east. Captain Mahmud Hussein and his Arab irregulars where once again tasked with conducting a reconnaissance of the area, where they found the Mahdist force to be at a place called Umm Diwaykarat. This news was gleefully received by Wingate, who later wrote that:

> It was now clear that our occupation of Gedid had placed the *Khalifa* in an unfavourable position, strategically: his route to the north was barred, his retreat to the south lay through waterless and densely wooded districts, and, as our seizure of grain supplies in Fedil's camp would render his advance or

retirement a matter of considerable difficulty, it seemed probable that he would stand. I therefore decided to attack him at dawn, on the 24th.

At 12.20 a.m. on the 24th, Wingate marched out of Gedid with his fighting troops, leaving instructions for his transports to follow on a few hours later. Ahead of the column the cavalry and the 'galloping Maxims' provided a screen for the advance at a distance of about half a mile, while the Camel Corps offered protection on each flank. The advance, however, was slower than hoped, since the roads were found to be wooded in places, and the pioneers had to first cut their way through for the troops to pass. Despite these delays, Wingate's force had come within three miles of the *Khalifa* and his army by 3 a.m.

Mahon next carried out a brief reconnaissance for himself, before the entire force was ordered forward under strict noise discipline. During the advance the sudden noise of beating *noggaras* and the sounding of *ombeyas* could be heard in the distance, but, by 3.40 a.m., the noise died away and near silence returned. At about the same time, Wingate's men reached some high ground overlooking the Mahdist camp, and to their delight it was covered in tall grass which provided excellent cover to help conceal their final approach. Orders were then issued for the entire force to halt and for the cavalry to be brought in, after which they were replaced by infantry *picquets*. It was time to lay down and rest, and to make ready for the intended attack at dawn.

Unfortunately for Wingate, he was not to achieve the surprise as he had wished. At 5.10 a.m., the infantry *picquets* were being driven in by Mahdist warriors, who could be just made out in the distance in the poor light. Instructions were quickly given for the entire force to fall in and make ready for action, the Maxim and artillery guns being brought into action within only five minutes. As the guns roared, the infantrymen began firing volleys at the approaching warriors. Due to the dim light, it was not immediately clear where the main thrust of the Mahdist attack was to come, but, with the fire becoming particularly heavy to the left, Wingate and his officers soon realised their enemy was trying to turn their left-flank. In response, the lieutenant-colonel pushed forward his right-flank to enable the men making up that part of the line to direct their fire in support of those on the left, while the left portion of the line was extended.

Eventually, the daylight improved and the Mahdist warriors could be clearly seen. Volley after volley was directed at them, as were the fire of the Maxims and the guns; all ripping through the ranks of their enemy just like they had in all the previous actions. Again, it was hopeless for the warriors to achieve victory over the superior firepower of Wingate's troops, who stood firm and continued to deliver their disciplined fire uninterrupted. Soon the attack began to falter, and warriors could be seen making off in various directions. At 6.25 a.m., a ceasefire was ordered, then the entire line was instructed to move forwards towards the *Khalifa*'s camp, which lay little more than a mile away.

The Pursuit and Death of the Khalifa

As Wingate's troops advanced, dozens of Mahdists offered to surrender and threw down their weapons. Once the camp was reached, it was found to be full of thousands of women and children, who, fortunately, had escaped the intense fire of the Egyptian Army and their irregular counterparts. Warriors, who had previously made off, slowly began to return to their camp, where they abandoned their weapons and asked to be taken prisoner. Meanwhile, the cavalry had begun a pursuit of other fleeing warriors, but it soon became apparent that the vast majority had surrendered and only a handful continued their desperate bid to escape. A few shots, however, persisted to be exchanged with a small number of Mahdists under the personal command of *Amir* Khatim Musa, but when he surrendered himself so did his warriors. The Action of Umm Diwaykarat, the last clash of any consequence of the Sudan campaign, had come to an end.

At that moment, no one knew that Abdullahi al-Taishi, the *Khalifa* and successor of the *Mahdi* of Sudan, had himself been killed during the fighting. Wingate later recorded:

> Immediately in front of the line of advance of the 9th Sudanese, and only a few hundred yards from our original position on the rising ground, a large number of the enemy were seen lying dead, huddled together in a comparatively small space; on examination, these proved to be the bodies of the *Khalifa* Abdulla et Taaishi, the *Khalifa* Ali Wad Helu, Ahmed-el-Fedil, the *Khalifa*'s two brothers, Senuousi Ahmed and Hamed Mohammed, the *Mahdi*'s son, Es-Sadek, and a number of other well-known leaders.

Wingate also later ascertained the circumstances of the *Khalifa*'s death:

> At a short distance behind them lay their dead horses, and, from the few men still alive—amongst whom was the Emir Yunis Eddekein—we learnt that the *Khalifa*, having failed in his attempt to reach the rising ground where we had forestalled him, had then endeavoured to make a turning movement, which had been crushed by our fire. Seeing his followers retiring, he made an ineffectual attempt to rally them, but recognising that the day was lost, he had called on his Emirs to dismount from their horses, and seating himself on his 'furwa' or sheepskin—as is the custom of Arab chiefs, who disdain surrender—he had placed *Khalifa* Ali Wad Helu on his right and Ahmed Fedil on his left, whilst the remaining Emirs seated themselves round him, with their body-guard in line some twenty paces to their front, and in this position they had unflinchingly met their death.

With his prey now dead, Wingate allowed the surviving warriors to bury their beloved leader and other senior commanders according to their beliefs and customs, although the ceremonies were carried out under strict supervision.

News of Abdullahi al-Taishi's death sparked wholescale surrenders of the remaining Mahdist warriors in the area, and by late afternoon some 8,000 men in all had been taken prisoner. In addition, over 6,000 women and children were placed under Wingate's protection, while large quantities of rifles, spears, and supplies were rounded up. Among the prisoners was Osman al-Din, the *Khalifa's* eldest son and intended successor. One senior Mahdist, however, had escaped following being wounded early in the fighting; this *amir* was none other than Osman Digna.

Casualties for the action included three killed and twenty-three wounded for Wingate's force. The Mahdists were said to have lost, during the previous two days, over 1,000 killed and wounded, while a total of 9,400 men, women and children were taken into custody. The reconquest of Sudan, begun in 1896, but with its roots in the early 1880s, was finally over. British involvement in Sudan, however, would continue for some time yet.

16

Aftermath and Legacy

In terms of its objectives, Kitchener's reconquest of Sudan was a complete success. He had put the *Ansar* to flight in a major battle—after which it never recovered—and recaptured the cities of Omdurman and Khartoum. Perhaps most importantly for the British public back home, he also avenged the death of General Gordon and virtually, but not entirely, destroyed Mahdism. Although he did not personally deliver the final death-blow to the *Khalifa*, his successor as *Sirdar*, Francis Reginald Wingate, was able to do so just over a year after the decisive action of the campaign.

In addition to the military success, the cost of the war had been less than originally envisaged by both London and Cairo. On 26 February 1899, Lord Cromer submitted a report that stated the operations from spring 1896 to the end of major operations in late 1898 had cost a total of 2,354,354 Egyptian pounds (£E). The largest single expense had been the construction of the 760 miles of railway, which totalled £E1,181,372. Some 2,000 miles of telegraph cables had also been laid, at a cost of £E21,825; the construction of six gunboats had amounted to £E154,934. Actual military expenditure was a mere £E996,223.

It is probably fair to say that the three men who played the most significant roles in the campaign in Sudan were Major-General Kitchener, Lord Cromer and Lieutenant-Colonel Wingate. Kitchener, of course, prosecuted the military campaign with a combination of his forceful personality and incredible attention to detail, while Cromer not only dealt with the political aspects but also offered the *Sirdar* his support from beginning to end. Wingate, in addition to the killing of the *Khalifa*, was instrumental in galvanising British public opinion against Mahdism and creating support for the mounting of the campaign.

Although the British had re-conquered Sudan with a view to restoring the territory to Egypt, the ensuing governance of the country would be a joint Anglo-Egyptian one under the Anglo-Egyptian Condominium Agreement. This arrangement was put on an official footing from 1899, with Sudan itself being administered by a governor-general, who was appointed by Cairo only following the required blessing from London. In effect, Sudan became part of the British Empire, a fact that Abbas II, the then *Khedive* of Egypt, did not like but had little choice but to accept.

War had broken out with the Boers in October 1899, and Kitchener would vacate his position as *Sirdar* of the Egyptian Army in order to join Lord Roberts and the British reinforcements *en route* to South Africa. The position was then passed to Wingate in December, a role he would keep until 1916. During this time, he would also act as governor-general of Sudan, again succeeding Kitchener, who also briefly held the post from January to December 1899.

During his time as *Sirdar* and governor-general, Wingate would authorise a number of military operations in Sudan. One such minor expedition was that mounted against the Nyam Nyam tribe in the south of Bahr al-Ghazal province in mid-1905. The cause of friction between the Anglo-Egyptian authorities and the tribe can be traced back several years earlier, when, in the autumn of 1903, a small military escort was despatched with gifts intended for *Sultan* Yambio, the paramount chief of the Nyam Nyam. The purpose was to enter into friendly negotiations with the tribal leader to bring the territory he presided over in Sudan, located near the Congo Free State border, under the administrative control of the Sudanese authorities at Khartoum.

Commanding the little force—which at the time was described as more of an 'embassy' than a 'force'—was Captain Armstrong of the Lancashire Fusiliers. During the journey, Armstrong was accidentally killed by an elephant, and so command passed to the senior non-commissioned officer, Colour-Sergeant Boardman of the Liverpool Regiment. More misfortune befell the little party when it finally arrived in Nyam Nyam territory, where the local tribesmen unexpectedly turned out to be hostile towards the British. Faced with overwhelming odds, Boardman wisely abandoned the mission.

In February 1904, another small expedition, consisting of 100 men and two guns under the command of Captain Wood of the Royal Irish Fusiliers, made a further attempt to open talks with Yambio, only to also find themselves attacked by Nyam Nyam warriors under the command of Rikhta, the *Sultan*'s son. British losses included three men killed and another eight wounded.

Following the failure of these two missions, it was determined that a larger expeditionary force would be needed to forcefully place Nyam Nyam territory under Anglo-Egyptian administration. As such, a force was assembled under the command of Major W. A. Boulnois of the Royal Artillery, who was also the commandant and governor of Bahr al-Ghazal province. This force was split into two columns, known as the Eastern column and the Western column. Combined, they were to exert military force to ensure Yambio's submission. A third column would be added later.

During its advance in January 1906, the Eastern column, under the command of Captain A. Sutherland of the Argyll and Sutherland Highlanders, came into contact with troops of the Congo Free State at Iré, who, it was quickly ascertained, were actually part of a Belgian expedition under the command of Commandant Charles Lemaire. It turned out that the Belgian explorer had established five outposts in Sudanese territory, the issue of which was subsequently 'negotiated' between London and Brussels.

The Western column, under the command of Boulnois himself, fought a short skirmish with Nyam Nyam warriors on the 3 February, the latter having attempted to ambush the former. By the 7th, the column had occupied Yambio's village, the chief having fled before the troops arrived. He was, however, located by a third column under the command of Lieutenant Fell of the Royal Navy, who, following another brief skirmish, dispersed the remaining Nyam Nyam forces, but again the *Sultan* escaped. The three columns now united and went in pursuit of Yambio on the evening of the 8th, the chief being eventually found and killed in yet another clash of arms. Within days all resistance ended, and the Nyam Nyam tribe and their territories finally submitted to Anglo-Egyptian authority. Despite the destruction of the *Khalifa*, the need for an expedition into southern Bahr al-Ghazal highlighted that not all of Sudan was—or wanted to be—under government control.

Another example of the lack of government control in certain parts of Sudan can be seen in the strong 'patrol' sent to deal with the inhabitants of the Nyima Hills in the south of Kordofan province in October and November 1908. The inhabitants had conducted several raids against tribes friendly to the Anglo-Egyptian authorities, seizing a number of people as slaves. The object of the expedition was to free those taken in the raids and to assert government authority, something which had been persistently ignored since the reconquest of Kordofan in 1899.

The expedition was placed under the command of Major A. R. Lempriere of the West Yorkshire Regiment, and consisted of: half a squadron of cavalry, one section of mountain guns, one section of Maxims, four squadrons of the Camel Corps, seven companies of infantry, and about 500 locally recruited 'friendlies'. These forces concentrated at Dilling, the administrative centre of the province, before making for Fassu Hill on 1 November. According to Wingate in his despatch of 29 December 1908:

> This [Fassu Hill] was attacked from two sides at dawn on the 3rd and carried after seven hours hard climbing and considerable resistance. Very few captures were however made, the inhabitants hiding in caves and burrows in the rocks.

Losses amounted to one Egyptian officer and one Egyptian soldier killed, while one British officer and twenty-five Egyptian Army troops were wounded.

On the 10th, a similar assault was carried out on Funda Hill, where a number of the enemy were captured, after which numerous inhabitants of the Nyima

Hills came into the Egyptian camp with offers of submission and to pay the fines demanded of them as punishment for their earlier raids. Later, on the 18th, a similar assault was made on Katla Kurun Hill, with the cavalry and Camel Corps advancing towards it from one side while the infantry did the same on the other. The tribesmen were taken completely by surprise and offered little in the way of resistance. The local chiefs now submitted to Lempriere's demands, and operations formally came to an end on the 22nd.

Wingate, in his despatch, made the following comments in justification of the expedition:

> I desire to place on record my entire approval of the manner in which the operations were carried out under conditions rendered particularly arduous by the rocky and precipitous nature of the country. If slave-raiding was to be put an end to in Dar Nuba, a salutary lesson was absolutely necessary. Further procrastination would only have encouraged the people in the belief of their own invulnerability and the inability of the Government to enforce its commands. The trouble would undoubtedly have spread and given rise to endless misery and unrest among the whole of the inhabitants. I venture to think that this has now been effectually obviated by the results achieved by the late Patrol, and I consider that the excellent spirit, discipline and endurance shown by the Officers, non-commissioned officers and men comprising the force is deserving of high commendation.

The last major military expedition ordered by Wingate during his long tenure as *Sirdar* and governor-general was the British invasion of Darfur during the First World War. Following the virtual defeat of Mahdism in 1899, the Anglo-Egyptian authorities had reinstated Ali Dinar as the *Sultan* of Darfur. However, as the years passed by, he became increasingly distant and even actively resistant to the Sudanese authorities at Khartoum. To make matters worse, it was alleged that Ali Dinar was gravitating towards the Ottoman Empire, who the British were then at war with. The real cause, however, was possibly due to the fact the British believed the French were contemplating invading Darfur themselves, something unacceptable to both London and Cairo, even though France was now an ally.

Using Ali Dinar's supposed support of the Ottomans as a pretext, Wingate assembled an expeditionary force under the command of Lieutenant-Colonel Philip James Vandeleur Kelly of the 3rd King's Own Hussars. The expedition was a sizeable one, and consisted of: two companies of mounted infantry, five companies of the Camel Corps, three companies of the 14th Egyptians, six companies of the 13th and 14th Sudanese, a Maxim battery, two artillery batteries (including six 12½-pounders and two additional Maxims), and two companies of the Arab Battalion—the whole totaling around 2,000 men of all ranks.

Operations commenced on 16 March 1916, when leading elements of Kelly's force crossed the border into Darfur and occupied the village of Um Shanga on the

20th, meeting little resistance as it advanced. Water at the village was not found to be in plentiful supply, so the lieutenant-colonel pushed on with a flying column to *Jebel* el-Hella in the hope of finding additional supplies. However, as the little column approached the village it encountered a force of 800 Fur horsemen who attempted to envelop Kelly's men, a movement only prevented by the intense fire of the Egyptian troops. Continuing its advance, the column encountered another sizeable force of the enemy, but no clash of arms occurred. Eventually, *Jebel* el-Hella was reached and a number of nearby wells seized. However, problems of supply caused much delay, and it was not until these were overcome—which included the building of a road to allow supplies to be transported by trucks—that Kelly could resume his offensive.

In May, the advance on El Fashr was resumed, with Kelly's force being split into two columns. On the 22nd, the expedition finally clashed with the main Fur army near the village of Beringia. The Egyptian troops formed square while the artillery began shelling the Fur troops who were seen in trenches that had been dug earlier. The Egyptian artillery also opened a fire on a party of Fur horsemen, who had been spotted forming up nearby.

While Kelly's main force made preparations to launch an assault on the village, the Camel Corps under Major Huddleston of the Dorsetshire Regiment, acting on his own initiative, entered Beringia where he and his men came under fire from Fur troops, forcing him to quickly withdraw. As the major fell back, the Furs pursued, after which they were fired upon by Kelly's square. Moments later, the Fur warriors in the trenches suddenly launched an assault of the southern side of the square. This attack was met by furious fire from artillery, Maxims, and rifles from the Egyptian troops, but the Furs kept up their attack for around forty minutes before they finally faltered and drew off. Sensing victory, Kelly then ordered his infantry to conduct their own assault, which finally proved too much for the Fur army; it now broke completely under the pressure.

Kelly's casualties amounted to two killed and eighteen wounded, with a further three later dying of their wounds. Fur casualties, in contrast, were believed to be over 1,000 in total, including 231 killed and ninety-six deemed as 'seriously wounded'.

Following the action, the expedition resumed its advance to El Fashr and camped for the night a few miles away from the Darfur capital. At 3 a.m. on the 23rd, Kelly found himself coming under attack by a Fur force consisting of 300 infantrymen and 500 horsemen. The attack, however, was quickly repulsed for only a single gunner wounded; Fur casualties were unknown. Later, at 6 a.m., another mounted force of Fur troops of some hundreds was encountered, the latter quickly being driven off by artillery fire and bombs dropped by aircraft of the Royal Flying Corps. At 10 a.m., Kelly and his men finally entered El Fashr, which, save for some women, was found to be virtually deserted.

Ali Dinar had already fled, and there would be several more minor skirmishes before the *Sultan* was caught and killed on 9 November. Following the occupation of El Fashr, Darfur was incorporated into Sudan, and thus added to Britain's growing number of imperial possessions. Wingate would be appointed British high commissioner to Egypt in 1917, being replaced as *Sirdar* and governor-general of Sudan by Sir Lee Stack, while Kelly was made governor of Darfur and later promoted to brigadier-general.

Unsurprisingly, many in Sudan were unhappy that their country was ruled over by the British and Egyptians. In 1924, Ali Abd al-Latif, a Sudanese military officer, established the White Flag League, a nationalist movement that sought Sudanese independence. The league was made up of around 150 members, most being either junior government officials or junior officers of the Egyptian Army. They also advocated unity with Egypt, thus, in addition to independence, the movement dreamed of the entire Nile Valley forming a union.

In the same year, a revolt broke out against the British—an event attributed to the league—during which Stack was assassinated; after this, he was replaced by Sir Charlton Spinks. In response, Field Marshall Edmund Allenby issued orders for all Egyptian military units to be withdrawn from Sudanese territory and returned to Egypt. However, some of the Egyptian troops refused to withdraw and many of them mutinied at Khartoum. The Egyptian military authorities in Cairo, rather than the British, subsequently also issued orders for their soldiers to return to Egypt, and this time the troops agreed and duly pulled out. This left the Sudanese troops on their own, and the British eventually put an end to both the revolt and the White Flag League. The calls for an independent Sudan and the expulsion of the British, however, remained as strong as ever.

Meanwhile, in Egypt the nationalists were seeing a little more success than their Sudanese counterparts, when, in February 1922, the British declared Egypt independent and established the Kingdom of Egypt. This Unilateral Declaration of Egyptian Independence, as it was known, in reality gave Egypt only nominal independence, since the British retained control over the country's foreign policy, all military matters and full authority over Sudan. In addition, the British also ensured they retained complete control of the Suez Canal, the all-important gateway to India.

In 1936, Britain and Egypt signed the Anglo-Egyptian Treaty, which saw the withdrawal of all British forces except for a force deemed adequate to protect the Suez Canal. A small number of British military personnel would also remain in Egypt to help train the country's military. It was, however, another important step towards full Egyptian independence, although that would not come until the establishment of the Republic of Egypt following the Egyptian Revolution of 1952. Britain—with the assistance of France and Israel—would, of course, briefly invade Egypt again in 1956 during the Suez Crisis.

Despite the withdrawal of British troops from Egypt in 1936, the British continued to maintain substantial military forces in Sudan. The Egyptians repeatedly demanded an abrogation of the Anglo-Egyptian Condominium

Agreement, but London refused to recognise King Farouk as the sole and legitimate ruler of both Egypt and Sudan. The events of 1952, however, began to change this stance when Egypt agreed to give up its own claim over Sudan if the British offered to do the same. In late 1954, the two powers signed an agreement to bring about full independence for Sudan, and, on 1 January 1956, the country was recognised as an independent state. Finally, after 136 years of Egyptian rule (including fifty-six years of British occupation), Sudan was free to choose its own destiny, although it has since been an often turbulent and difficult one.

The last surviving British protagonist of the reconquest was said to be James Miles, who had served with the 2nd Battalion of the Rifle Brigade; he died in 1977, aged 97. Kitchener, as we have seen, died when the *Hampshire* hit a German mine and sank in 1916. MacDonald, who played a pivotal role at the Battle of Omdurman, went on to gain further distinction during the Anglo-Boer War, but he was disgraced in 1903 following claims of homosexuality and misconduct with young boys; he committed suicide the same year. Wauchope was killed during the Battle of Magersfontein in 1899, and Gatacre died while in Abyssinia in 1906. Lyttleton would also go on to serve in South Africa, retiring from the British Army in 1912 and dying in 1931, aged 85. Keppel would rise to the rank of vice-admiral in 1913 and full-admiral in 1917; he passed away in 1947, aged 84. The future career of Churchill, of course, is well-known.

Osman Digna, who escaped death at Umm Diwaykarat, was finally captured by the British in 1900; he died in 1926, aged 86. Babikr Bedri, having feigned being wounded at Omdurman, lived until 1954, just missing Sudanese independence; he became an activist in later life and campaigned for education for women.

The last survivors of the reconquest, however, remain to this day in Sudan itself, in the form of the gunboats *Melik* and the *Bordein*. At the time of writing, both vessels are the focus of the Melik Society, who wish to preserve and restore the vessels as well as stimulate public interest in shared Anglo-Sudanese history. Hopefully, these precious relics will one day become available to be seen by many, and act as an important reminder of the long and bloody wars in Sudan.

APPENDIX A

Anglo-Egyptian Orders of Battle

Battle of Firket, 7 June 1896

Major-General Horatio Herbert Kitchener (Sirdar)

River Column (Major-General Archibald Hunter)
1st Brigade (Colonel D. F. Lewis)
3rd Egyptians
4th Egyptians
9th Sudanese
10th Sudanese

2nd Brigade (Brigadier-General Hector MacDonald)
11th Sudanese
12th Sudanese
13th Sudanese

3rd Brigade (Colonel John Grenfell Maxwell)
2nd Egyptians
7th Egyptians
8th Egyptians

2nd Egyptian Field Battery
3rd Egyptian Field Battery
Half Battalion, North Staffordshire Regiment
Maxim Battery, Connaught Rangers

Two gunboats
Three armed steamers

Desert Column (Colonel John Francis Burn-Murdoch)
Six Companies of the Camel Corps
Eight Squadrons of Egyptian Cavalry
12th Sudanese (camel mounted)
One Battery of Horse Artillery (six 6cm Krupp guns)
Two Maxim Machine guns

Action at Abu Hamed, 7 August 1897

Major-General Archibald Hunter
3rd Egyptians
9th Sudanese
10th Sudanese
11th Sudanese
Battery of Field Artillery
Two Maxim Machine guns
Troop of Egyptian Cavalry

Battle of Atbara, 8 April 1898

Major-General Horatio Herbert Kitchener (Sirdar)

British Brigade (Major-General William Forbes Gatacre)
1st Royal Warwickshire Regiment
1st Lincolnshire Regiment
1st Seaforth Highlanders
1st Cameron Highlanders

Egyptian Division (Major-General Archibald Hunter)
1st Brigade (Brigadier-General Hector MacDonald)
2nd Egyptians
9th Sudanese
10th Sudanese
11th Sudanese

2nd Brigade (Colonel John Grenfell Maxwell)
8th Egyptians
12th Sudanese
13th Sudanese
14th Sudanese

3rd Brigade (Colonel D. F. Lewis)
3rd Egyptians
4th Egyptians
7th Egyptians

Eight Squadrons of Egyptian Cavalry
Two Maxim Machine guns
Battery of Horse Artillery (six Krupp guns)
Three Batteries of Field Artillery (six Maxim-Nordenfelt guns each)
Detachment of 24lb Rocket Tube

Battle of Omdurman, 2 September 1898

Major-General Horatio Herbert Kitchener (Sirdar)

British Infantry Division (Major-General William Forbes Gatacre)
1st Brigade (Brigadier-General Andrew Gilbert Wauchope)
1st Royal Warwickshire Regiment
1st Lincolnshire Regiment
1st Seaforth Highlanders
1st Cameron Highlanders
Six Maxim machine guns of Eastern Division, Royal Artillery
Detachment of Royal Engineers

2nd Brigade (Brigadier-General Neville Lyttelton)
1st Grenadier Guards
1st Northumberland Fusiliers
2nd Lancashire Fusiliers
2nd Rifle Brigade
Four Maxim machine guns of Royal Irish Fusiliers
Detachment of Royal Engineers

Egyptian Division (Major-General Archibald Hunter)
1st Brigade (Brigadier-General Hector MacDonald)
2nd Egyptians
9th Sudanese
10th Sudanese
11th Sudanese

2nd Brigade (Colonel John Grenfell Maxwell)
8th Egyptians

12th Sudanese
13th Sudanese
14th Sudanese

3rd Brigade (Colonel D. F. Lewis)
3rd Egyptians
4th Egyptians
7th Egyptians
15th Egyptians

4th Brigade (Lieutenant-Colonel John Collinson)
1st Egyptians
5th Egyptians
17th Sudanese
18th Sudanese

Cavalry/Mounted
Four Squadrons of 21st Lancers *(Colonel R. H. Martin)*
Nine Squadrons of Egyptian Cavalry *(Colonel R. G. Broadwood)*
Eight Companies of the Camel Corps *(Major R. J. Tudway)*

Artillery (Colonel Charles Long)
32nd Field Battery, Royal Artillery (eight guns including two 40-pounders)
37th Field Battery, Royal Artillery (six 5-in howitzers)
1st Egyptian Horse Battery (six 6cm Krupp guns/two Maxim machine guns)
2nd Egyptian Field Battery (six Maxim-Nordenfelt guns/two Maxim machine guns)
3rd Egyptian Field Battery (six Maxim-Nordenfelt guns/two Maxim machine guns)
4th Egyptian Field Battery (six Maxim-Nordenfelt guns/two Maxim machine guns)
5th Egyptian Field Battery (six Maxim-Nordenfelt guns/two Maxim machine guns)

Naval Forces (Captain Colin Keppel)
Sultan, Melik and *Sheikh*
1889-class armoured screw gunboats (each with two Nordenfelt guns, one quick-firing 12-pounder, one howitzer and two Maxim machine guns)
Fateh, Naser and *Zafir*
1896-class armoured sternwheel gunboats (each with one quick-firing 12-pounder, two 6-pounders and four Maxim machine guns)
Tamai, Hafir, Abu Klea and *Metemma*
Old-class armoured sternwheel gunboats (each with one 12-pounder and two Maxim-Nordenfelt guns)

Action at Gedarif, 22 September 1898

Lieutenant-Colonel Charles Sim Bremridge Parsons
16th Egyptians
Arab Battalion
Camel Corps
Arab Levies

Action near Dakhila (Rosaires Cataract), 26 December 1898

Lieutenant-Colonel D. F. Lewis
9th Sudanese
10th Sudanese
Two Maxim Machine guns
Arab Irregulars

Action at Umm Diwaykarat, 25 November 1899

Lieutenant-Colonel Francis Reginald Wingate
9th Sudanese
13th Sudanese
Battery of Field Artillery
Six Maxim Machine guns
One Squadron of Egyptian Cavalry
Six Companies of the Camel Corps

APPENDIX B

Ansar Orders of Battle

The following figures are based on period Egyptian Army intelligence reports. All numbers given should be treated as estimates only.

Dispositions Before the Battle of Firket, 1896

Dongola and Egyptian Frontier
4,600 Riflemen
8,000 Swordsmen/Spearmen
1,200 Cavalry
Eighteen guns

Eastern Sudan
6,900 Riflemen
1,100 Swordsmen/Spearmen
2,150 Cavalry
Four guns

Western Sudan
6,000 Riflemen
2,500 Swordsmen/Spearmen
350 Cavalry
Four guns

Southern Sudan
1,800 Riflemen
4,500 Swordsmen/Spearmen
Three guns

Dispositions After the Battle of Firket, 1896

Abu Hamed
460 Riflemen
1,500 Swordsmen/Spearmen
300 Horsemen
Two guns

Dongola
1,400 Riflemen
1,500 Swordsmen/Spearmen
300 Horsemen
Six guns

Hafir
320 Riflemen
1,100 Swordsmen/Spearmen
80 Horsemen

Kerma
250 Riflemen
100 Swordsmen/Spearmen
150 Horsemen
One Nordenfelt machine gun

Amri
30 Riflemen
(Reinforced later by 1,000 Riflemen and 1,000 Swordsmen/Spearmen)

Battle of Omdurman, 2 September 1898

Dark Green Flag (Muluazimayya) (Osman al-Din)
28,400 men (including: 12,900 riflemen and 2,900 horsemen)
One French gun
One mountain gun
One Remington machine gun

Black Flag (Al-Rayya Al-Zarqa) (Ya'qub)
14,100 men (including: 1,050 riflemen and 1,600 horsemen)
One Krupp gun
One Nordenfelt gun

Green Flag (Al-Rayya Al-Khadra) (Khalifa Ali wad Ullu)
5,400 men (including: unknown number of riflemen and 800 horsemen)

Osman Digna (No Flag)
3,400 men (including: 360 riflemen and 190 horsemen)

Red Flag (Al-Rayya Al-Hamra) (Khalifa al-Sharif)
80 men

Amir Osman Azrak
70 men

APPENDIX C

Casualty Statistics

The following casualty statistics have been compiled from the London Gazette and other period sources. Discrepancies in the sources are common, although the below is believed to be an accurate reflection of losses suffered. It is also certain that a number of the wounded later died of their wounds in the days, weeks and months following the actions.

Battle of Firket, 7 June 1896

Egyptian

	KILLED		WOUNDED	
	OFFICERS	MEN	OFFICERS	MEN
Egyptian Army	0	20	0	83

Ansar

KILLED OR WOUNDED	800 to 1,000 (estimated)
PRISONER	600 (estimated)
TOTAL	1,400 to 1,600 (estimated)

Battle of Abu Hamed, 7 August 1897

Egyptian

	KILLED		WOUNDED	
	OFFICERS	MEN	OFFICERS	MEN
Egyptian Army	2	21	3	61

Ansar

KILLED	250 to 450 (estimated)

Following the Battle of Abu Hamed, it is said General Hunter ordered the bodies of his enemy thrown into the river, in an attempt to let Kitchener know the battle had been won after the corpses floated downstream.

Battle of Atbara, 8 April 1898

Anglo-Egyptian

	KILLED OFFICERS	KILLED MEN	WOUNDED OFFICERS	WOUNDED MEN
British Brigade	3	22	10	32
Egyptian Army	0	57	21	365
TOTAL	3	79	31	447

Ansar

KILLED	3,000 (estimated)

During the Battle of Atbara, the Anglo-Egyptian forces also captured a large number of prisoners, quantities of banners, war drums, rifles, and ten guns.

Battle of Omdurman, 2 September 1898

Anglo-Egyptian

	KILLED OFFICERS	KILLED MEN	WOUNDED OFFICERS	WOUNDED MEN
21st Lancers	1	20	4	46
1/Grenadier Guards	0	0	1	4
1/Northumberland Fusiliers	0	0	0	2
1/Royal Warwicks	1	1	1	6
1/Lincolns	0	0	1	17
2/Lancashire Fusiliers	0	0	0	6
1/Seaforth Highlanders	0	0	1	17
1/Cameron Highlanders	0	2	2	27
2/Rifle Brigade	0	0	0	8
Egyptian Army	2	18	8	273
TOTAL	4	41	18	406

Ansar

KILLED	10,800 (body count on 3 Sept.)
WOUNDED	15,000 (estimated)
PRISONER	5,000 (estimated)
TOTAL	**30,800**

In addition to the casualties, it was estimated that the Anglo-Egyptian Army expended 444,000 rifle rounds, 67,000 Maxim rounds, and 3,500 artillery rounds.

Action near Gedarif, 22 September 1898

Egyptian

KILLED	53
WOUNDED	61

Ahmed Fedil's casualties for this action remain uncertain.

Action near Dakhila (Rosaires Cataract), 26 December 1898

Egyptian

KILLED	24
WOUNDED	124
MISSING	1

Arab Irregulars

KILLED	16
WOUNDED	22

Ahmed Fedil

KILLED	500+ (estimated)
WOUNDED	Unknown
PRISONER	1,680

Action at Umm Diwaykarat, 25 November 1899

Egyptian

KILLED	3
WOUNDED	23

Ansar

KILLED OR WOUNDED	1,000 (estimated)
PRISONER	9,400 (including men, women and children)

Included in the number killed is Abdullahi al-Taishi, while Osman al-Din, the *Khalifa*'s eldest son, was taken prisoner.

APPENDIX D

Victoria Cross Citations

Battle of Omdurman, 2 September 1898

The following citations for the award of the Victoria Cross appeared in the London Gazette of 15 November 1898.

> The Queen has been graciously pleased to signify Her intention to confer the decoration of the Victoria Cross on the under-mentioned Officers and Private Soldier, whose claims have been submitted for Her Majesty's approval, for their conspicuous bravery during the recent operations in the Soudan, as recorded against their names:

Captain Paul Aloysius Kenna, 21st Lancers

> At the Battle of Khartum on the 2nd September 1898, Captain. P. A. Kenna assisted Major Crole Wyndham, of the same Regiment, by taking him on his horse, behind the saddle (Major Wyndham's horse having been killed in the charge), thus enabling him to reach a place of safety; and, after the charge of the 21st Lancers, Captain Kenna returned to assist Lieutenant de Montmorency, who was endeavouring to recover the body of Second Lieutenant R. G. Grenfell.

Lieutenant the Honourable Raymond Harvey Lodge Joseph de Montmorency, 21st Lancers

> At the Battle of Khartum on the 2nd September 1898, Lieutenant de Montmorency, after the charge of the 21st Lancers, returned to assist Second Lieutenant R. G, Grenfell, who was lying surrounded by a large body of Dervishes. Lieutenant de Montmorency drove the Dervishes off, and, finding

Lieutenant Grenfell dead, put the body on his horse, which then broke away. Captain Kenna and Corporal Swarbrick then came to his assistance, and enabled him to rejoin the Regiment, which had began to open a heavy fire- on the enemy.

Private Thomas Byrne, 21st Lancers

At the Battle of Khartum on the 2nd September 1898, Private Byrne turned back in the middle of the charge of the 21st Lancers and went to the assistance of Lieutenant the Honourable R. P. Molyneux, Royal Horse Guards, who was wounded, dismounted, disarmed, and being attacked by several Dervishes. Private Byrne, already severely wounded, attacked these Dervishes, received a second severe wound, and, by his gallant conduct, enabled
Lieutenant Molyneux to escape.

Captain Nevill Mas-Kelyne Smyth, 2nd Dragoon Guards

At the Battle of Khartum on the 2nd September 1898, Captain Smyth galloped forward and attacked an Arab who had run amok among some Camp Followers. Captain Smyth received the Arab's charge and killed him, being wounded with a spear in the arm in so doing. He thus saved the life of one at least of the Camp Followers!

Gedarif, 22 September 1898

The following citation for the award of the Victoria Cross appeared in the London Gazette of 3 March 1899.

Captain Alexander Gore Arkwright Hore-Ruthven, 3rd Highland Light Infantry

On the 22nd September 1898, during the action of Gedarif, Captain Hore-Ruthveu, seeing an Egyptian officer lying, wounded within 50 yards of the advancing Dervishes, who were firing and charging, picked him up and carried him towards the 16th Egyptian Battalion. He dropped the wounded officer two or three times, and fired upon the Dervishes, who were following, to check their advance. Had the officer been left where he first dropped, he must have been killed.

Bibliography

Official Publications

Army Intelligence Branch, Army HQ India, *Frontier and Overseas Expeditions from India, Volume VI: Overseas Expeditions*, Calcutta, Superintendent Government Printing, India, 1911.
London Gazette editions: 3 Apr 1884; 25 Mar 1884; 20 Feb 1885; 10 Apr 1885; 25 Aug 1885; 3 Sept 1889; 3 Nov 1896; 25 Jan 1898; 30 Sept 1898; 15 Nov 1898; 9 Dec 1898; 30 Jan 1899; 5 May 1899; 18 May 1906; 27 Sept 1910; and 24 Oct 1916.

Books

Alford, H. S. L. and Sword, W. D., *The Egyptian Sudan: Its Loss and Recovery*, London, Macmillan and Co., 1898.
Anglesey, Marquess of, *A History of the British Cavalry, 1816-1919 (Vol III)*, London, Leo Cooper, 1982.
Arthur, Sir G., *Life of Lord Kitchener (Vol I)*, London, Macmillan and Co., 1920.
Asher, M., *Khartoum: The Ultimate Imperial Adventure*, London, Penguin, 2006.
Atteridge, A. H., *Towards Khartoum: The Story of the Soudan War of 1896*, London, A. D. Innes and Co., 1897.
Baird, W., *General Wauchope*, Edinburgh and London, Oliphant Anderson and Ferrier, 1900.
Barthorp, M., *Blood-Red Desert Sand: The British Invasions of Egypt and the Sudan, 1882-1898*, London, Cassell and Co., 2002.
Bedri, B., *The Memoirs of Babikr Bedri*, London, Oxford University Press, 1969.
Bennett, Sir E. N., *After Omdurman: The Contemporary Review (No. 397)*, London, Isbister and Co., 1899.
Bennett, Sir E. N., *The Downfall of the Dervishes: Being a Sketch of the Final Sudan Campaign of 1898*, London, Methuen and Co., 1898.
Burleigh, B., *Khartoum Campaign, 1898, or the Re-conquest of the Soudan*, London, Chapman and Hall, 1898.
Burleigh, B., *Sirdar and Khalifa, or the Re-conquest of the Sudan*, London, Chapman and Hall, 1898.
Butler, W. F. *The Campaign of the Cataracts: Being a Personal Narrative of the Great Nile Expedition of 1884-5*, London, Sampson Low, Marston, Searle, and Rivington, 1887.
Chaillé Long, Col. C., *The Three Prophets: Chinese Gordon, Mohammed-Ahmed (El Maahdi), Arabi Pasha*, New York, D. Appleton and Co., 1884.
Churchill, W., *A Roving Commission: My Early Life*, New York, Charles Scribner's Sons, 1930.

Bibliography

Churchill, W., *The River War: An Historical Account of the Reconquest of the Soudan*, London, Longman, Green, and Co., 1902.

Corvi, S. J. and Beckett, I. F. W., *Victoria's Generals*, Barnsley, Pen and Sword, 2009.

Cromer, The Earl of, *Modern Egypt (Vols I and II)*, London, Macmillan and Co., 1908.

Darmesteter, Prof. J., *The Mahdi: Past and Present*, London, T. Fisher Unwin, 1885.

Ellens, J. H., *Winning Revolutions: The Psychological Dynamics of Revolts for Freedom, Fairness, and Rights*, Santa Barbara, ABC-CLIO, LLC, 2014.

Fadlalla, Dr. M. H., *Short History of Sudan*, Lincoln, iUniverse, 2004.

Featherstone, D. F., *Khartoum, 1885: General Gordon's Last Stand*, Oxford, Osprey Publishing, 1993.

Featherstone, D. F., *Omdurman, 1898: Kitchener's Victory in the Sudan*, Oxford, Osprey Publishing, 1994.

Featherstone, D. F., *Tel El-Kebir, 1882: Wolseley's Conquest of Egypt*, Oxford, Osprey Publishing, 1993.

Gatacre, B., *General Gatacre: The Story of the Life and Services of Sir William Forbes Gatacre, K.C.B., D.S.O., 1843-1906*, London, John Murray, 1910.

Gleichen, Count, *With the Camel Corps Up the Nile*, 1888.

Green, D., *Armies of God: Islam and Empire on the Nile, 1869-1899*, London, Arrow Books, 2008.

Harrington, P., *Omdurman, 1898: The Eyewitnesses Speak—The British Conquest of the Sudan as Described by Participants in Letters, Diaries, Photos and Drawings*, Greenhill Books, 1998.

Haythornthwaite, P. J., *The Colonial Wars Source Book*, London, BCA, 1995.

Headly, J. T. and Johnson, W. F., *Stanley's Adventures in the Wilds of Africa*, Philadelphia, Edgewood Publishing and Co., 1890.

Jackson, H. C., *Osman Digna*, London, Methuen and Co., 1926.

Jeal, T., *Explorers of the Nile: The Triumph and Tragedy of a Great Victorian Adventure*, London, Faber and Faber, 2012.

Knight, E. F., *Letters from the Sudan: By Special Correspondent of 'The Times'*, London, Macmillan and Co., 1897.

Knight, I., *Go To Your God Like A Soldier: The British Soldier Fighting for Empire*, London, Greenhill Books, 1996.

Lipschutz, M. R. & Rasmussen, R. K., *Dictionary of African Historical Biography*, Berkeley and Los Angeles, University of California Press, 1989.

Massie, R. K., *Dreadnought: Britain, Germany and the Coming of the Great War*, London, Vintage, 2007.

McGregor, A., *A Military History of Modern Egypt: From the Ottoman Conquest to the Ramadan War*, Westport, Praeger, 2006.

Meredith, J., *Omdurman Diaries: Eyewitness Accounts of the Legendary Campaign*, Barnsley, Pen and Sword, 1998.

Milner, Sir A., *England in Egypt*, London, Edward Arnold, 1902.

Nash N. S., *Chitral Charlie: The Rise and Fall of Major General Charles Townshend*, Barnsley, Pen and Sword, 2010.

Neufeld, C., *A Prisoner of the Khaleefa: Twelve Years' Captivity at Omdurman*, London, Chapman and Hall, 1899.

Nicoll, F., *The Mahdi of Sudan and the Death of General Gordon*, Stroud, Sutton Publishing, 2005.

Pakenham, T., *The Scramble for Africa*, London, Abacus, 1992.

Pritchard, Lt H., *Sudan Campaign, 1896-1899*, London, Chapman and Hall, 1899.

Raugh, H. E. Jr., *The Victorians at War, 1814-1915: An Encyclopedia of British Military History*, Santa Barbara, ABC-CLIO, 2004.

Royale, C., *The Egyptian Campaigns, 1882 to 1885: New and Revised Edition Continued to December 1899*, London, Hurst and Blackett, 1900

Russell, H., *The Ruin of the Soudan, Cause, Effect and Remedy: A Resume of Events, 1881-1891*, London, Sampson Low, Martson and Co., 1892.

Slatin, R., *Fire and Sword in the Sudan*, London, Edward Arnold, 1896.
Snook, Col. M., *Beyond the Reach of Empire: Wolseley's Failed Campaign to Save Gordon and Khartoum*, Barnsley, Frontline Books, 2013.
Spiers, E. M. (editor), *Sudan: The Reconquest Reappraised*, Abingdon, Frank Cass Publishers, 1998.
Steevens, G. W., *With Kitchener to Khartum*, New York, Dodd, Mead and Co., 1898.
Traill, H. D., *Lord Cromer: A Biography*, London, Bliss, Sands and Co., 1897.
Warner, P., *Dervish: The Rise and Fall of an African Empire*, Barnsley, Pen and Sword Military, 2010.
Wilkinson-Latham, R., *The Sudan Campaign, 1881-98*, Oxford, Osprey Publishing, 1992.
Williams, Dr. J., *Life in the Soudan: Adventures Amongst the Tribes, and Travels in Egypt, in 1881 and 1882*, London, Remington and Co., 1884.
Wilson, Sir C. W., *from Koti to Khartum: A Journal of the Desert March From Korti to Gubat, and of the Ascent of the Nile in General Gordon's Steamers*, Edinburgh and London, William Blackwood and Sons, 1886.
Wingate, Maj. F., *Mahdism and the Egyptian Sudan: Being An Account of the Rise and Progress of Mahdism, and of Subsequent Events in the Sudan to the Present Time*, London, Macmillan and Co., 1891.
Wingate, Maj. F., *Ten Years' Captivity in the Mahdi's Camp, 1882-1892: From the Original Manuscripts of Father Joseph Ohrwalder*, London, Sampson Low, Marston and Co., 1892.
Wright, W., *Omdurman 1898*, Stroud, The History Press, 2012.
Ziegler, P., *Omdurman*, Barnsley, Pen and Sword Military Classics, 2003.
Zulfo, 'I. H., *Karari: The Sudanese Account of the Battle of Omdurman*, London, Frederick Warne, 1980.

Unpublished Sources

Finn, Maj. H., *Letters to his Wife*, Jean S. & Frederic A. Sharf Collection.
Smyth, Lt R. N., *Letters to his Sister*, Jean S. & Frederic A. Sharf Collection.

Index

Aba, Island of 22, 84
Ababda (tribe) 79, 95, 111, 114, 118
Abadar 120-121
Abbas (steamer) 30, 47
Abbas II 214
Abdel-Azim 114, 186
Abu Deleh 114-115
Abu Hamed 43, 47, 51, 95, 110, 112-114, 116, 118, 124, 134, 168
Abu Klea 43-45, 48
Abu Klea (gunboat) 105, 107, 193, 195
Abu Kru 45-46
Abyssinia 28-29, 34, 62, 65-66, 85, 177, 200, 219
Adam, Abd Allah 145
Adwa, Battle of 66-68
Agordat, Battle of 62
Ahmed, Mahmud 115-122, 125, 131-132, 142
Ahmed, Mirza Ghulam 24
Ahmed, Muhammad (the *Mahdi*) 17-19, 21-32, 34-37, 39-41, 43, 47-50, 56, 58-59, 63-65, 67, 83-86, 182-183
Ahmediyya 24
Akasha 93, 95-96, 98-99
Akasha (steamer) 105
Akasha, Skirmish near 96
Al-Daim, Muhammad al-Sharif Nur 26
Al-Dikaym, Osman 167
Al-Din, Osman 17, 88, 90-91, 140-141, 143, 152, 171, 185, 212
Al-Din Abu-al-Sadiq, Sharaf 22
Al-Habashi, Mahbub 22
Al-Kermin, Muhammad ibn Abd 48
Al-Khalil, Ibrahim 90-91, 140-141, 143, 145-146, 148, 156, 165-166, 185

Al-Latif, Abd 145
Al-*Mahdi*, Muhammad 167
Al-Mubarak, *Sheikh* Mahmud 22
Al-Qadir, Abd (see Slatin, Col. R. C. von)
Al-Rabi, Arifi 152-154
Al-Sahib, Ismail 145
Al-Sayyid, Khayr 166
Al-Shallali, Yusuf Hassan 30
Al-Taishi, Abdullahi (the Khalifa) 17, 23, 59, 63, 83-86, 90, 111, 115, 140-143, 146, 156-157, 165-166, 177-178, 182-183, 185-186, 191, 202-205, 209, 211-212
Al-Taishi, Muhammad Ishaq 145, 148
Al-Urdi (see Dongola)
Al-Zaki, Muhammad 167
Alexandria 33, 42, 69, 92, 134
Ali, Muhammad 21-22
Ali, Tahir 152
Angara, Mir 202
Anglo-Egyptian Condominium Agreement 213
Arabi *Pasha*, Ahmed 33-34, 42, 50, 92
Armstrong, Capt. 214
Artaghasi, Island of 106
Assouan 94, 103
Atbara, Battle of 79, 92, 122, 131, 133, 139-140
Atbara Fort 119, 131-134
Atbara River 95, 114, 120-121, 123, 201
Atteridge, A. H. 94-95, 101-102
Ayman, Rashid 28
Azrak, Osman 17, 90, 92, 99, 102-103, 106, 140-141, 143, 145-146, 149
Baggara (tribe/tribesmen) 23, 29,

84, 87, 91, 96, 100, 107-108, 115, 118, 120-122, 126, 132, 141-143, 167-168, 170, 173
Bahr al-Ghazal 26, 83, 195-196, 198, 214-215
Baillie, Capt. A. C. D. 129
Baker, Maj.-Gen. V. 53
Bakr, *Sheikh* 205-207
Baratier, Capt. A. E. A. 199-200
Baratieri, Gen. O. 66, 117
Baring, E. (Lord Cromer) 17, 34, 37-38, 67-68, 74, 109-110, 121, 197, 213
Barrow, Lt-Col. P. 44
Bayuda Desert 43, 114, 135
Beatty, Lt D. 107, 113, 125
Bedri, Babikr 19, 149, 170-171, 219
Bennett, E. 18, 187-189
Berber 43-44, 56, 95, 104, 113-114, 116-121, 132-133
Beresford, Capt. Lord C. 51
Betraki, Col. B. 49
Bishhara, Fadl 152
Black Flag 17, 29, 88, 91, 136, 140-141, 146, 154, 156, 163, 165-167, 169, 171-172, 174, 176, 179, 181
Blakeney, Lt R. B. D. 169, 171
Boardman, CSgt. 214
Bordein (steamer) 51, 219
Boulnois, Maj. W. A. 214-215
Broadwood, Lt-Col. R. G. 119-120, 122, 139, 143, 152-154, 171, 179, 180, 183, 185-186
Brown, Pte. W. 163
Buller, Maj.-Gen. R. 53, 55
Burleigh, B. 77, 118, 138, 150-151, 183
Burn-Murdoch, Maj. J. 95-96, 98, 100, 103
Burri 46, 49

Byrne, Pte. T. 161-162

Carter, L/Sgt. E. 160
Cator, Lt E. 111
Churchill, Lt W. S. 17-18, 80, 142-144, 157-159, 178-179, 181, 185, 219
Coldecott, Capt. G. 147
Collinson, Maj. J. 120, 134, 139, 165
Colville, Cdr. S. 105-107
Courcel, Baron de 198
Cox, Lt S. F. 127
Cromer, Lord (see Baring, E.)
Cross, Pte. 128, 131

Dafalla, Arabi 204
Dakhila 205-206
Dal (steamer) 105, 193-195, 204-205
Darfur 26, 39, 64, 83-84, 87, 216-218
David, Col. B. F. 104, 107
Davidson, Pte. A. 147
Davis, Maj.-Gen. J. 53, 55
Delcassé, T. 198-200
Dhillbat Hill 57
Dighaim (tribe) 29, 88
Digna, Osman (Hadenowa Chief) 17, 19, 36, 54, 56, 62, 85, 90, 92, 96, 114-115, 117-118, 132, 140, 156-157, 163, 185, 212, 219
Dillion, Pte. P. 147
Dongola 21-22, 68, 79, 81, 92-94, 99, 103-104, 106-109, 111, 113, 118, 195
Dongola Expeditionary Force 94, 98, 102
Doran, Capt. 132
Dreyfus Affair 198
Duem 203-204
Dufferin, Lord 34, 72

Earle, Capt. F. A. 145
Earle, Maj.-Gen. W. 43-44, 51
Ed Damer 114, 118
Egeiga 20, 136-140, 143, 145-146, 152, 155, 165, 177
Egerton, Col. C. C. 98
Egyptian Revolution 218
El-Bishara, Muhammad Wad 103-106, 167
El Fashir 117, 201
El Obeid 30-32, 35, 39, 48, 63-64, 91-92, 184, 186
El Teb, First Battle of 53-54
El Teb, Second Battle of 54, 56
Emin *Pasha* 59-62, 64-65
Emin *Pasha* Relief Expedition 59
Equatoria 25, 38-39, 60-62
Eritrea 66

Et-Tahira (steamer) 105-106
Et-Teb (gunboat) 105
Ewart, Maj.-Gen. Sir H. 56

Fahl, Abdullah 21-22
Faidherbe (steamer) 195-197, 199-200
Farag *Pasha* 48
Fashoda 28, 30, 192-200, 203-204
Fashoda Incident 191, 200
Fawzi *Pasha*, Ibrahim 39, 60
Fedil, Ahmed 200, 202, 205-209, 211
Fenwick, Capt. M. A. C. 97
Fergusson, Maj. 205-207
Feteh (gunboat) 113
Fincastle, Lord (see Murray, Lt A.)
Findlay, Capt. C. 128
Finn, Maj. H. 158, 160
Firket, Action of 17, 92, 95, 100, 103-104
Fitton, Capt. H. G. 96
Fitzclarence, Lt E. 113
Fleming, Capt. C. C. 201
Fort Desaix 196
Franks, Capt. 132
Fremantle, Maj.-Gen. L. 56

Gakdul 43-44
Gatacre, Maj.-Gen. Sir W. F. 80-81, 118, 127-128, 131, 133, 219
Gedarif 200-202
Gedid 209-210
Gemaizah, Battle of 62, 92
Geneva Convention 187, 189
Gibraltar 42, 82, 134
Giegler, C. 27, 29-30
Girouard, É. P. C. 17, 79-80, 94-95, 111
Gladstone, W. E. 33, 37-38, 42
Gordon, Gen. C. G. 17-18, 25-26, 36-43, 46-48, 50-51, 56, 58, 60-61, 63-65, 67-68, 70, 80, 94, 110, 112, 135, 176, 178, 190-193, 213
Gordon, Maj. S. 135, 154
Gore, Lt P. A. 129
Graham, Lt-Gen. G. 53-56, 58, 63, 65, 176
Granville, Lord 38
Grenfell, Lt R. S. 156, 160, 163
Grenfell, Maj.-Gen. Sir F. 62, 68, 70, 72, 74, 117
Grigolini, Sister T. 184

Hafir, Battle of 92, 105-106
Haig, Capt. D. 155, 175
Halfaya 41-42, 46
Handoub 56, 70

Harcourt, Sir W. 199
Hartington, Lord 42
Hasan, Khalil 145
Hasheen, Battle of 57
Hassan, Mohammed Zain 113
Henry, Capt. St. G. C. 171
Hewitt, Adm. Sir W. 53
Hickman, Maj. T. E. 120, 174
Hicks, Col. W. 34-35, 37, 39, 53, 63-65, 176
Hicks-Beach, Sir M. 110
Hill, Capt. Sir H. 205-207
Hilmi, Abd-al-Qadir 29-30, 32, 34
Hopkinson, Lt H. 153
Hore-Ruthven, Capt. A. G. A. 201
Howard, The Hon. H. 143, 174, 182-183
Hubbard, Capt. A. E. 144, 147
Huddleston, Maj. 217
Hudi 119-120
Hudson, Brig.-Gen. J. 56
Hunter, Maj.-Gen. A. 80-81, 93, 95, 98, 111-114, 116, 119, 121, 130, 132, 134
Hunter, Capt. M. P. 121
Hussein, Capt. Mahmud 208-209
Hussein, Col. Muhammad Ali 46
Hutton, J. F. 60

Ibrahim, Muhammad 49
Idris, Hammuda 92, 99, 102
Ismail, Adam 152-153
Ismail *Pasha* (Khedive of Egypt) 26, 38
Ismailia 27-28, 40, 48

Jaalin (tribe) 100, 137
Jabir, Ibrahim 145, 150
Jackson, Maj. G. W. 96, 130
Jackson, Col. H. W. 195
Jazira Aba 26-28
Jebel Abu *Zariba* 152-153
Jebel Daham 152-153
Jebel Gadír (see Jebel Massa)
Jeb el-Gheddeer 204
Jebel Massa 28
Jebel Royan 135
Jebel Surgham 20, 136-138, 141-146, 155-157, 163, 165-167, 169, 171, 175, 179-180
Jennings, Capt. J. W. 207
Jubara, Ahmed 29

Kassala 66, 93, 116-117, 200
Katla Kurun Hill, Assault on 216
Kelly, Lt-Col. P. J. V. 216-218
Kenna, Capt. P. A. 161
Keppel, Cdr. C. 75, 81-82, 115-116, 118, 120, 137, 193, 219
Kerma 79, 104-106

Index

Kerreri Hills 139, 143, 146, 152, 154, 173, 179
Khalifa, Ahmed Bey 114
Khartoum, Siege of 18, 37-52
Khor Abu Sunt 141, 156-157, 163
Khor Shambat 179-181
Khor Wintri 97-98, 113
Kidden 102-103
Kincaid, Maj. W. F. H. S. 121
Kirbekan, Battle of 51, 81, 112
Kitchener, Col. F. W. 203
Kitchener, Maj.-Gen. H. H. (*Sirdar*) 17, 68-71, 73, 78-79, 81-82, 93-94, 98-111, 113-125, 127, 132-133, 135-136, 140-141, 144-150, 155, 165-166, 169, 171, 173, 175, 179, 181-183, 186, 188-195, 197-198, 200, 202, 204-205, 213-214, 219
Kordofan 28, 31, 35, 60, 203, 215
Korti 43-44, 51

Lambert, Sgt. 205
Lawrie, Maj. C. E. 121, 139
Lawson, Major H. M. 201
Le Gallais, Maj. P. W. J. 122, 180
Legge, Capt. N. 102
Lemaire, Comdt. C. 215
Lempriere, Maj. A. R. 215-216
Lewis, Col. D. F. 100, 134, 167, 205-207
Lloyd, Maj. G. E. 97-98
Lutfi, Ali Bey 32
Lyttelton, Brig.-Gen. N. 80-81, 133

MacDonald, Brig.-Gen. H. 81-82, 100-101, 104, 112-113, 127, 134, 166-169, 171-173, 176, 219
Mackay, Sgt.-Maj. 129
Mackinnon, W. 60
Mahdism 18, 38, 84, 200, 213, 216
Mahdiyya 25, 58, 62, 83-84
Mahon, Maj. B. T. 154, 208-210
Mahon, Capt. D. 103
Malik, Ibrahim 152
Malta 42, 118, 134
Marchand, Capt. J. 110, 193-200, 203
Martin, Lt-Col. R. H. 134, 143-144, 155-158, 161, 163, 179
Massa, Battle of 30
Massowah 93, 116-117
Maxwell, Col. J. G. 100-101, 127, 134, 182
McKenzie, LCpl. T. 147
McKerrell, Capt. A. de S. 201
McNeill, Maj.-Gen. Sir J. 56-57
Meiklejohn, Lt R. F. 128, 130, 145

Melik (gunboat) 154, 190, 205, 219
Menilek II 65-66
Merowi 47, 111-114, 116, 134
Messalamieh Gate, The 49
Metammeh 43, 45-46, 115-116, 118, 135
Metemma (gunboat) 105-106, 113
Metemma, Battle of 62
Molyneux, Lt the Hon. R. F. 161-162
Montagu-Stuart-Wortley, Maj. E. J. 137
Money, Lt-Col. G. L. C. 127
Monson, Sir E. 198
Montmorency, Lt the Hon. R. de 160-161
Muhammad, Prophet 21, 24, 28-29, 142
Muluazimayya 17, 88, 91, 140, 152, 154, 167
Murray, Lt A. 96
Murray, Lt-Col. R. H. 129
Musa, Khatim 211
Musa, Mahsud 55

Nakhila 119, 121
Napier, Maj. R. F. L. 129
Nason, Lt-Col. 206-207
Nasr (gunboat) 113, 115, 137, 193, 195
Nasri Island 134-135
Nesham, Lt C. S. 162
Neufeld, C. 183-184
Nuba Mountains 28-30, 40, 91
Nujumi, Abd ar Rahman an 62, 70, 176-177
Nyam Nyam (tribe) 214-215
Nyima Hills 215

Omdurman, Battle of 17-19, 67, 74, 77, 82, 85, 91, 132, 138-178, 185-186, 189, 192, 197, 203, 219
Om Waragat, Battle of 64
Ohrwalder, Father J. 19, 25, 31, 39, 58-59, 63-65, 85-86, 183
Osman, Zaki 114

Paragreen, Pte. G. E. 145
Parsons, Lt-Col. C. S. B. 105, 117, 200, 202
Persse, Capt. W. H. 96, 122
Peyton, Capt. W. E. 127
Pirie, Lt A. M. 156
Power, F. 47
Pritchard, Lt H. L. 101, 105, 107, 112, 124, 130, 148, 174

Rauf *Pasha*, Muhammad 25
Rawlinson, Capt. Sir H. 147-148

Regiments:
2nd Egyptians 126, 139, 172, 203
5th Egyptians 134
5th Lancers 57
8th Egyptians 126, 181
9th Bengal Cavalry 57
9th Sudanese 73, 95, 97, 112, 126, 172, 205, 211
10th Hussars 54
10th Sudanese 74, 97-98, 112-113, 131, 172, 205-206
11th Sudanese 74, 96, 112, 114, 130, 172, 181, 193, 195
12th Egyptians 146
12th Sudanese 74, 126, 181
13th Sudanese 74, 126, 168, 181, 193, 195, 216
14th Egyptians 216
14th Sudanese 126, 181, 203, 216
15th Egyptians 170
15th Sikhs 58
16th Egyptians 117, 201
17th Sudanese 134
18th Sudanese 134
19th Hussars 44-45, 51, 74
21st Lancers 17, 78, 134, 139, 141-142, 151, 155-157, 160-165, 174, 178, 180
28th Bombay Infantry 58
Argyll and Sutherland Highlanders 214
Army Service Corps 127, 134
Black Watch 51-52, 54-56, 81
Camel Corps 74-75, 78, 96-98, 102-103, 107, 114, 123, 134-135, 139, 143, 152-154, 165, 169, 171, 200-201, 204, 208-210, 215-217
Cameron Highlanders 118, 126-130, 139, 147-148, 150, 173-174, 193
Coldstream Guards 57, 147
Connaught Rangers 78, 94, 98
Egyptian Horse Artillery 74, 77, 98, 107, 121, 124, 134, 139, 152-153, 155
Grenadier Guards 57, 133, 139, 145, 190
Lancashire Fusiliers 133, 139, 147, 214
Lincolnshire Regiment 118, 126-129, 139, 145, 147-148, 171-173
Liverpool Regiment 214
Naval Brigade 55-56
North Staffordshire Regiment 78, 93-94, 98, 104-105, 107-108
Northumberland Fusiliers 133, 139, 147

Rifle Brigade 82, 133-134, 139, 147, 219
Royal Army Medical Corps 134, 147, 201, 207
Royal Artillery 134, 137, 148, 169
Royal Berkshire Regiment 57-58
Royal Engineers 44, 79, 133
Royal Flying Corps 217
Royal Irish Fusiliers 133, 214
Royal Sussex Regiment 45, 51
Royal Marines 54-55, 57-58, 115
Royal Warwickshire Regiment 118, 126, 128-130, 139, 145, 147-148, 173
Scots Guards 57
Seaforth Highlanders 118-119, 126, 128-129, 139, 147, 150, 173
South Staffordshire Regiment 51-52
West Yorkshire Regiment 215
York and Lancaster Regiment 54-56
Rhodes, C. 111
Rhodes, Col. F. 174
Richardson, Armourer-Sergeant 105
Rix, Cpl. W. 160, 163
Roberts, Lord 214
Rosebery, Lord 199
Round-top Hill 180
Rowlett, Pte. A. 163

Sabun, Hamid 145
Sad, Muhammad Abu 145
Safieh (steamer) 51, 193
Said, Muhammad 28, 31-32
Salisbury, Lord 17, 65-68, 109-110, 197-200
Saq, Abd al-Majid Abu 145
Schnitzer, E. (see Emin *Pasha*)
Serobeti, Battle of 62
Seudamore, Mr 129
Shahin, Capt. Mustapha 209
Sharif, Muhammad 84-85
Sheik (gunboat) 184
Shendi 114, 118-120
Shilaykhat, Jabir Abu 152
Shirazi, Siyyid Ali Muhammad 24
Shukool Pass 52
Shukria (tribe) 30
Sidney, Maj. H. M. 97-98, 113

Sinkat 53, 55, 56
Slatin, Col. R. C. von 19, 35, 50, 64-65, 84-86, 94, 98, 102, 140-141, 171, 174, 182-183
Smyth, Capt. N. M. 151
Smyth, Lt R. 143, 162
Spinks, Sir C. 218
Stack, Sir L. 218
Stanford, B. (filmmaker) 150
Stanley, Sir H. M. 60-62
Steevens, G. W. (war correspondent) 18, 123, 125-126, 129, 131, 168, 173
Stewart, Brig.-Gen. Sir H. 43-45, 53-54
Stewart, Col. D. 34-35, 39, 47
Suakin, Port City of 53-58, 63, 65, 70, 74, 92, 95, 96-98, 134
Suarda 99, 102, 104
Sudan Military Railway (SMR) 17, 79-80, 94, 111
Suez Canal 25, 33, 218
Suez Crisis 218
Sultan (steamer) 193
Summaniya Dervish 22-23
Sutherland, Capt. A. 214
Suud, Muhammad Abu 26
Swarbrick, Cpl. F. 161

Taha, *Sheikh* al-Sharif Ahmed 30
Tamai (gunboat) 105-106, 113, 137
Tamai, Battle of 55-56
Taylor, Cpl. H. H. E. 147
Tewfikeyeh (steamer) 192-193
Teigh, Pte. G. 172
Telahwiya (steamer) 51
Tel el-Kebir, Battle of 34, 51, 82
Teori Wells 97
Tewfik *Pasha* (Khedive of Egypt) 26, 29, 33-34, 37-38
Thomas Cook 43, 94
Tiedemann, Capt. A. von 188, 190
Tita, Omar 96-98
Tofrek 57-58
Tokar 53-54, 56, 82, 92, 97-98
Toski, Battle of 62, 70, 74, 82
Townshend, Lt-Col. C. V. F. 146-147
Trinkatat 53-54
Tudway, Maj. R. J. 152, 169

Turshain, Ya'qub Muhammad 17, 88, 90-91, 140-141, 146, 166-167, 169-170
Tuti Island 49, 137

Ulama, The 24-26
Ullu, Khalifa Ali wad 140-141
Umm Diwaykarat, Battle of 210-211
Unilateral Declaration of Egyptian Independence 218
Urdi al-Manfukh (fortress) 21
Urquart, Maj. B. C. 129

Verner, Lt-Col. T. E. 129
Victoria, Queen 42, 68, 109, 190, 198

Wad Hamid 134-135
Wadi Halfa 43, 93-95, 103-104, 110, 112, 116, 118, 134
Wauchope, Brig.-Gen. A. G. 80-81, 133-134, 219
Whitla, Capt. V. G. 96
White Flag League 218
Wichale, Treaty of 66
Wilkinson, Capt. E. B. 201
Williams, Maj. W. H. 139, 148
Wilson, Col. Sir C. 44-46, 50-51
Wingate, Maj. F. R. 17, 19, 63-65, 73-74, 86, 94, 98, 102, 140-141, 176, 202, 205, 208-211, 213-216, 218
Wolseley, Lt-Gen. Sir G. 18, 33, 42-43, 47, 51, 58, 110
Wood, Maj.-Gen. Sir E. 34, 70, 72
Wormald, Lt F. W. 158
Wyeth, S/Sgt 127, 131
Wyndham, Maj. W. G. C. 161

Yambio, *Sultan* 214-215
Ya'qub (see Turshain, Ya'qub Muhammad)
Young, Maj. N. E. 121

Zafir (gunboat) 103, 107, 113, 115
Zanzibar 60-61
Zubair *Pasha* 83
Zulfo, 'Ismat Hasan (historian) 19, 86, 176